Destruction and human remains

Manchester University Press

HUMAN REMAINS AND VIOLENCE

Human remains and violence aims to question the social legacy of mass violence by studying how different societies have coped with the dead bodies resulting from war, genocide and state-sponsored brutality. However, rather paradoxically, given the large volume of work devoted to the body on the one hand, and to mass violence on the other, the question of the body in the context of mass violence remains a largely unexplored area and even an academic blind spot. Interdisciplinary in nature, *Human remains and violence* intends to show how various social and cultural treatments of the dead body simultaneously challenge common representations, legal practices and morality. This series aims to provide proper intellectual and theoretical tools for a better understanding of mass violence's aftermaths.

Series editors

Jean-Marc Dreyfus & Élisabeth Anstett

Destruction and human remains

Disposal and concealment in genocide and mass violence

Edited by
Élisabeth Anstett & Jean-Marc Dreyfus

Manchester University Press

Copyright © Manchester University Press 2014

While copyright in the volume as a whole is vested in Manchester University Press, copyright in individual chapters belongs to their respective authors, and no chapter may be reproduced wholly or in part without the express permission in writing of both author and publisher.

Published by Manchester University Press
Altrincham Street, Manchester M1 7JA, UK
www.manchesteruniversitypress.co.uk

British Library Cataloguing-in-Publication Data is available

ISBN 978 1 5261 1673 4 *paperback*
ISBN 978 0 7190 9602 0 *hardback*

First published by Manchester University Press in hardback 2014

This edition first published 2017

The publisher has no responsibility for the persistence or accuracy of URLs for any external or third-party internet websites referred to in this book, and does not guarantee that any content on such websites is, or will remain, accurate or appropriate.

Printed by Lightning Source

Contents

List of contributors	page vii
Acknowledgements	xii
Introduction: the tales destruction tells *Élisabeth Anstett & Jean-Marc Dreyfus*	1

Part I: Actors

1 'As if nothing ever happened': massacres, missing corpses, and silence in a Bosnian community *Max Bergholz*	15
2 A specialist: the daily work of Erich Muhsfeldt, chief of the crematorium at Majdanek concentration and extermination camp, 1942–44 *Elissa Mailänder*	46
3 Lands of *Unkultur*: mass violence, corpses, and the Nazi imagination of the East *Michael McConnell*	69

Part II: Practices

4 Earth, fire, water: or how to make the Armenian corpses disappear *Raymond H. Kévorkian*	89

5 *Sinnreich erdacht*: machines of mass incineration in fact, fiction, and forensics 117
   Robert Jan van Pelt

6 When death is not the end: towards a typology of the treatment of corpses of 'disappeared detainees' in Argentina from 1975 to 1983 146
   Mario Ranalletti
   (with the collaboration of Esteban Pontoriero)

Part III: Logics

7 State violence and death politics in post-revolutionary Iran 183
   Chowra Makaremi

8 Death and dismemberment: the body and counter-revolutionary warfare in apartheid South Africa 204
   Nicky Rousseau

9 The Tutsi body in the 1994 genocide: ideology, physical destruction, and memory 226
   Rémi Korman

Index 243

Contributors

Élisabeth Anstett has been a social anthropologist and tenured research scholar at the Centre National de la Recherche Scientifique (CNRS) in Paris since October 2009, and is a member of IRIS (Interdisciplinary Research Institute on Social issues). Her area of expertise covers Europe and the post-socialist world, on which she has published extensively. Her recent works focus on the way post-Soviet societies are dealing with the traces left by the Soviet concentration camp system, among which are mass graves, and more broadly on the legacies of mass violence in Eastern Europe, especially in Russia and Belarus. She has published, among other works, *Une Atlantide russe: anthropologie de la mémoire en Russie postsoviétique* (Paris: La Découverte, 2007) and co-edited with Luba Jurgenson *Le Goulag en héritage, pour une anthropologie de la trace* (Paris: Pétra, 2009).

Max Bergholz is the James M. Stanford Professor in Genocide and Human Rights Studies at Concordia University in Montreal, Canada. Trained as a historian, he is an expert on the Balkans and Eastern Europe, with a special focus on the history of the countries of the former Yugoslavia. His research interests include the micro dynamics of communal peace and discord, mass violence, and post-conflict remembrance. He has conducted extensive fieldwork in Bosnia-Herzegovina, Croatia, and Serbia, where he researched in central and provincial archives and conducted oral history interviews in small towns and villages. His research has been funded by grants and fellowships from Fulbright, the International Research and Exchanges Board (IREX), and the American Council of Learned Societies (ACLS), among others. He is currently working on a book entitled *None of Us Dared Say Anything: Mass Killing in a Bosnian Community During World War II and the Postwar Culture of Silence*. Based in Concordia University's Department of History, he is the Associate Director of the Montreal Institute for Genocide and Human Rights Studies.

Jean Marc Dreyfus is Reader in Holocaust Studies within the Department of History at the University of Manchester. His research interests include: Holocaust studies; genocide studies and the anthropology of genocide; the history of the Jews in Europe in the nineteenth and twentieth centuries, especially in France; the economic history of France and Germany; Holocaust memory and the politics of memory; the modern history of Alsace; and the rebuilding of post-war societies. He is the author of four monographs, including *Pillages sur ordonnances: La confiscation des banques juives en France et leur restitution, 1940–1953* (Paris: Fayard, 2003), with Sarah Gensburger, *Nazi Labor Camps in Paris* (New York: Berghahn Books, 2012) and *Il m'appelait Pikolo: un compagnon de Primo Levi raconte* (*He Called Me Pikolo: A Companion of Primo Levi Tells His Story*) (Paris: Robert Laffont, 2007). He is the co-editor of the *Dictionnaire de la Shoah* (*Dictionary of the Holocaust*) (Paris: Larousse, 2009).

Raymond H. Kévorkian is a director of research emeritus at the University of Paris 8-Saint-Denis. Of Armenian origin, he has written extensively on both the medieval and the modern history of Armenia, and is the author of eighteen books. He is a foreign member of the National Academy of Sciences of Armenia and a board member of the International Association of Armenian Studies. He is also the curator emeritus of the Nubarian Library in Paris. Raymond Kévorkian is one of the leading specialists on the Armenian genocide and his book on the subject has been published both in French and in English: *Le Génocide des Arméniens* (Paris: Odile Jacob, 2006); *The Armenian Genocide: A Complete History* (London: I. B. Tauris, 2011). He has also published *Les Yeux brûlants – mémoire des Arméniens*, with Antoine Agoudjian (Arles: Actes Sud, 2006).

List of contributors ix

Rémi Korman is a doctoral candidate in history at École des Hautes Études en Sciences Sociales, Paris. His PhD focuses on the politics of memory of the Tutsi genocide in Rwanda and more particularly on memorial processes. Through working on his PhD he has also developed a strong interest in preserving the archives of the genocide, and accordingly has recently established the website www.rwanda.hypotheses.org. He is currently working for the 'Reseau Memorha' in Lyon, an organization focused on museums and memory issues, and has recently published 'La politique de mémoire du génocide des Tutsi au Rwanda: enjeux et évolutions' in *Droit et Cultures: Revue Internationale Interdisciplinaire* (2014).

Elissa Mailänder is Associate Professor in Contemporary History at the Centre d'Histoire de Sciences Po, Paris. She gained her PhD at the École des Hautes Études en Sciences Sociales and the University of Erfurt in 2007. Her research and teaching interests are in the history and theory of violence, gender, and sexuality, material culture, and the history and theory of the everyday. An English edition of her book *Gewalt im Dienstalltag: Die SS-Aufseherinnen des Konzentrations- und Vernichtungslagers Majdanek 1942–1944* (Hamburg: Hamburger Edition, 2009) is forthcoming (*Workday Violence: Female Guards at Lublin-Majdanek, 1942–1944*). She has published several articles on the history of Nazi perpetrators and the structures, mechanisms, and dynamics of violence in German concentration and extermination camps.

Chowra Makaremi is a social anthropologist and tenured research scholar at the Centre National de la Recherche Scientifique in Paris. She has been a visiting scholar in Princeton, McGill, and Columbia Universities and has completed ethnographic fieldwork and published on issues of migration, asylum, racism, and youth delinquency. Since 2010 she has worked on memories of violence and the post-revolution era in Iran, publishing *Le Cahier d'Aziz: au coeur de la révolution iranienne* (Paris: Gallimard) in 2011.

Michael McConnell is a doctoral candidate at the University of Tennessee. His work focuses on examining how the merger of German counter-insurgency practices developed in Nazi-occupied Europe with domestic policing encouraged violence inside Germany at the end of the Second World War. The project was featured in an article published in the spring 2012 issue of the journal *Central European History*, and his research has been generously supported by the German Academic Exchange Service, the University of Tennessee, the Central European History Society, and the Center for Advanced Holocaust Studies, United States Holocaust Memorial.

Esteban Pontoriero is a doctoral researcher at the National University of General San Martín in Argentina. Recent publications include 'Pensar la "guerra revolucionaria": doctrina antisubversiva francesa y legislación de defensa en la Argentina (1958–1962)', *Cuadernos de Marte*, 3 (July 2012).

Mario Ranalletti is a Lecturer at the Institute of Historical Studies of the National University of Tres de Febrero, Buenos Aires, Argentina, and Head of the University's Programme of Studies on the History of the Present. He is currently working on the functioning and internal organization of clandestine detention centres under the last Argentine dictatorship (1976–83), using judicial sources. He also has an interest in the cinematographic writing of Argentina's recent past. His publications include *La escritura fílmica de la historia: problemas, recursos, perspectivas* (Buenos Aires: Editorial Eduntref, 2013); 'Filmic writing of history in Argentine cinema (1983–1990)', in Robert A. Rosenstone & Constantin Parvulescu (eds), *A Companion to the Historical Film* (Malden: Blackwell Publishing, 2013); 'Denial of the reality of state terrorism in Argentina as narrative of the recent past: a new case of "negationism"?', *Genocide Studies and Prevention: An International Journal*, 5:2 (2010); and 'Aux origines du terrorisme d'État en Argentine (1955–1976)', *Vingtième Siècle: Revue d'Histoire*, 105 (2010).

Nicky Rousseau teaches history at the University of the Western Cape in Cape Town, South Africa. She is a former researcher for the South African Truth and Reconciliation Commission (TRC), and was part of the team that wrote the TRC's seven-volume report. Subsequently she worked as a research consultant to South Africa's National Prosecuting Authority on post-TRC investigations, prosecutions, and missing persons. She has published a number of articles on the TRC, and more recently has returned to her TRC research with a view to rethinking questions of the national security state and counter-revolutionary warfare. Her current research interests include truth commissions, violence, histories of liberation, and human remains.

Robert Jan van Pelt is University Professor in the School of Architecture at the University of Waterloo. He is an expert on the construction history of Auschwitz in general and the crematoria in particular. He testified in the trial *Irving v. Lipstadt* in London. His books include: an edition of David Koker's concentration camp diary, published as *At the Edge of the Abyss* (Evanston: Northwestern University Press, 2012); *The Case for Auschwitz* (Bloomington: Indiana University Press, 2002); and three books written with Debórah Dwork, *Flight from the Reich*, *Holocaust* and *Auschwitz*, all published by W. W. Norton (New York: 2009, 2002, 1996).

Acknowledgements

We would like to thank everyone who has contributed to the development of this book and appreciate the time spent by all those dedicated to the *Corpses of mass violence and genocide* programme. We must also thank the many people who met and welcomed us during our field trips and, although it would not be possible to mention them all, we would particularly like to thank: Luis Fondebrider, Mirna Goransky, Belen Rodriguez Cardoso, Carolina Varsky, and Marcello in Buenos Aires; José López Mazz, Alvaro Rico, the members of the Commission for Peace, and the mothers and family members of Uruguayan disappeared detainees in Montevideo; Anna Galinskaya, Vadim Akopyan, Galina Ladissova, and Vadim in Minsk; and the ICMP staff, Sabina and Mustapha Subasic, Amor Masovic, Reis-ul-ulema Husein ef. Kavazović, Tarik Samarah, Muamer, and Adi in Sarajevo. Each of them allowed us to widen our understanding of the mass violence processes, and of their country, with considerable and considered insight.

Without our dedicated team of researchers, Caroline Fournet, Jon Shute, and Sévane Garibian, we would not be able to pursue our research in such a dynamic and friendly environment, and for this we are most grateful. We are also indebted to Laurence Radford, with whose expertise and commitment to the publication process we were able to create this book so rapidly, efficiently, and successfully.

Finally, we would like to acknowledge the support provided by the European Research Council for generously funding our research programme and enabling us to pursue our academic interests with such freedom and encouragement.

Élisabeth Anstett & Jean-Marc Dreyfus

Introduction: the tales destruction tells[1]

Élisabeth Anstett & Jean Marc Dreyfus

The twentieth century was the century of mass violence and genocide. The size, diversity, and systematic character of the massacres, but also the inscription of killings in murderous ideologies and the use of new techniques for the systematic eradication of human groups, mark a new way of conceiving, justifying, and perpetrating crime. The role of states, as the totalitarian regimes formally defined by Hannah Arendt as well as 'traditional' dictatorships, was also a prominent feature of this century.[2] Forms of mass violence certainly differed, and continue to differ, widely from one country to another, from one system to another, from one continent to another; nevertheless, this 'age of extremes', in the words of historian Eric Hobsbawm,[3] has seen an outburst of violence that has produced, as its logical consequence, mass death, ideological mass death, and therefore millions of corpses.

It may seem a truism, since this aspect of human destiny is shared universally, that every human body ends marked by rigor mortis before the decomposition of the flesh, and then of the bones, as a result of a combination of biological and chemical processes influenced by a wide variety of factors, such as climatic conditions, the nature of the ambient environment, or human intervention.[4] Of course, the countless cultures and religions, small or great, have always treated bodies according to special rituals, the product of socio-cultural contexts but also of continual historical developments. One might even say that social anthropology, as a field of knowledge, was partially constituted around the study of funerary rituals and the social logics of their perpetuation.[5] However, despite mass violence and genocide increasingly appearing as structural elements of the legacy of the twentieth century, and despite research in the fields of Holocaust studies and genocide studies developing rapidly, the dead body seems to elude the attention of researchers, whether historians, anthropologists, or lawyers. Very few of them have taken an interest in what became of the millions of corpses produced by mass crimes or have asked by whom, how, and why these dead bodies were – or were not – handled.

To place the body, or rather the bodies, back at the centre of the attention of researchers working on extreme violence is the principal goal of a large-scale research programme that we launched in February 2012 (www.corpsesofmassviolence.eu) and which received a starting grant from the European Research Council. This volume is the result of the first annual conference of our academic programme,[6] which was held at the École des Hautes Études en Sciences Sociales in Paris, 12–14 September 2012. It presents original research, including a synthesis of the main results of a multidisciplinary study focusing on the first phase we have defined, relating to the treatment of bodies immediately after death. Its purpose is to consider the fate of the body in its diversity, at the time of the murder or just thereafter, against the tendency, too often observed in studies on mass violence, to remove the dead body from the scrutiny of research.

To accomplish this we built on a previous conference dealing with the central methodological aspects of the research. It is to be published in the same book series with Manchester University Press, titled *Human Remains and Mass Violence: Methodological Approaches*.[7] Bearing this in mind, we attempt here to compare areas that may, prima facie, appear very different, both in their historical context and in the forms and extents of the persecutions and massacres concerned. Indeed, how can we compare the treatment of the corpses of the 6 million Jews murdered in the Holocaust with the disappeared persons of the Argentine dictatorship in 1976, of whom fewer than 10,000 have been identified by name and fewer than 1,000 of their bodies found? This is the very aim of our work – to attend exclusively to the means deployed to handle the bodies, their intrinsic logics, and their purposes – which allows us to draw these comparisons in order to understand the production of extreme violence, while bearing in mind, of course, the enormous differences between, in that example, genocide on a continental scale and what was a cruel police repression, albeit politically motivated and very effectively organized.

This theme of the first phase of research, limited to the period during which the executioners dispose of the bodies (see below on the question of temporality), will continue through to the phases of our project concerned with the search for and identification of bodies and then with 'reconciliation', that is, political, social, or religious strategies aimed at inscribing the recovered bodies or human remains at the centre – or on the margin – of pacified societies.

What, then, have been the specific objectives of our initial research? What do we think we have shown and what have we revealed by this focus on the mass destruction of corpses? One of our initial questions concerned whether the treatment of corpses resulting from acts of mass violence (which we already know takes a variety of forms) proceeded from the same ideology of destruction that led to the murder itself. It was thus first a matter of describing the political and symbolic economy that motivates and structures the treatment of the dead, and second a matter of placing it within a more general economy of the production of mass death. Thus if, in the eyes of their executioners, Jews killed in the Holocaust should disappear not only from Europe but even from European history, then a perfect cremation of the corpses, erasing the last trace of the lives destroyed, was required.

Many questions were raised immediately, while others have arisen from the papers presented at the 2012 conference and fed the exchanges that followed: How, by whom, and when were these bodies treated? Was this done at the time of killing or afterwards, by the perpetrators themselves or by other entities? What were the technical methods used? While technology has sometimes played a part in the process of annihilation, this has not always, or everywhere, been the case, as the Rwandan genocide demonstrates. The industrialization of the destruction process can even be seen as an exception. The different ways in which bodies have been destroyed also raise the question of what happens to human remains. Bones, skulls, hair, and skin are sometimes put on display, as in Buchenwald or during the great famine in China, or simply left out in the open air, as was sometimes the case in post-Soviet Russia or in Cambodia.[8] Exhibited, they can be made to serve as a political message of ultra-violence, as in Guatemala in the 1980s and in Eastern Europe during the Second World War (see chapter 3, by McConnell). Bodies have also been reused, as resources, giving death and the dead an ultimately utilitarian purpose. Hair was collected at Auschwitz II – Birkenau, and gold teeth at Treblinka.[9] Sometimes bodies have reappeared, without the knowledge of the murderers. This was the case with many of the bodies of victims of the Chinese Cultural Revolution that drifted to Hong Kong.[10] What different kinds of status are therefore conferred upon these remains? What uses are made of them? What do these practices of destruction tell us about the societies affected by mass violence?

That first conference focused on 'destruction'. While it has fallen to historians to document the precise historical and geographical contexts within which different methods of destruction have been employed and to examine their respective implications, legal scholars have concentrated on the charges relating to the destruction of bodies – and the legal status of the bodies themselves – with respect to both international criminal law and national legal systems. They also investigate the role played by corpses in the legal prosecution of perpetrators of mass violence, that is, as evidence of a crime; and when corpses are absent, legal issues arise regarding the status of the dead. Anthropologists, for their part, have addressed not only the question of how the destruction of bodies is integrated into the symbolic and social space of the societies in question, but also that of the hierarchies present among these corpses and of the dead more generally. Anthropological studies of blood and body parts are of immense value for an understanding of the role of societies in the process of collective destruction.

We have come to understand that it is possible to distinguish three distinct categories in the treatment of corpses in the initial phase. It can indeed be a matter of 'disposal', that is, an abandonment of the body, either at the massacre site, which in itself can be highly significant, or at another location. One of the most striking examples is the killing fields of the Cambodian genocide, the rice fields that served as places of execution, where the vast majority of the 2 million bodies of the victims of the Khmer Rouge were abandoned. The second category of treatment of the body is 'concealment', which can also take several forms, from an enforced disappearance under the seal of secrecy to a publicly orchestrated confiscation. The corpse is then removed from society, hidden, and sometimes buried, but not always; it can also be thrown into wells, caves, or lakes. It is therefore sometimes previously dismantled, cut into pieces to prevent its discovery, implicitly posing the question of the transportation of bodies and body parts. And the third category of treatment of bodies arises directly from the process of destruction itself: usually by incineration, as in the seminal examples of the Nazi concentration and death camps and the Soviet case, but also sometimes using corrosive chemicals, as in the Argentine and Uruguayan cases.[11]

These complex and multidimensional questions then allowed us to identify three avenues of study that have structured this work. The first concerns the agents of the treatment of the dead bodies. Who were they? How were they chosen? Were they the killers themselves or, rather, assistants? What uniforms did they wear: those of soldiers, police, or doctors? Can we observe, at least in some cases, a division of labour or a sharing of tasks leading to the production of social hierarchies and distinct criminal careers? It is within this first framework that the chapters comprising part I of the volume, 'Actors', fall: Max Bergholz's analysis of the role of the various agents of the mass violence committed in Bosnia in the 1940s, whose long and fatal posterity is well known (chapter 1), Elissa Mailänder's study of Erich Muhsfeldt, crematorium director of the concentration and extermination camps at Majdanek (chapter 2), and Michael McConnell's study of the agents of Nazi atrocities in Eastern Europe and their representations of violence (chapter 3).

A second avenue concerns the procedures for handling bodies. In association with lethal expertise and techniques, it is crucial to take this aspect of the production of death into account. This is a matter of examining the techniques and technologies used to treat the dead body, and to question both in the context of their production as well as their transmission and circulation from one massacre site to another, or even from one criminal sphere to another. How did the perpetrators handle corpses numbering in the tens, the hundreds, or sometimes hundreds of thousands? Can we observe phases of learning, of improving procedures for handling bodies? Part II of the volume, 'Practices', comprises the contributions of Raymond Kévorkian (chapter 4), who shows the extent and variety of the means used to make the bodies of the victims of the Armenian genocide disappear, Robert Jan van Pelt (chapter 5), who analyses the sources that shaped the conception of the Nazi crematoria, and Mario Ranalletti (chapter 6), who reconstructs the logics that came to legitimize the production of political violence in Argentina through a typology of the treatments inflicted on the bodies of the disappeared.

Our third avenue of study, finally, concerns the issues that arise in the differences between the ways in which corpses are handled.

Why are the bodies of the victims each time the subject of a singular treatment, and for what purpose? How do the three categories of disposal, concealment, and destruction come to resonate with one another? When we study the ideological, identitarian, political, or religious aspects associated with the confiscation, annihilation, or exhibition of bodies, do we not see a blurring of the distinctions between these categories, an overrunning of the boundaries between them, and the revelation of more complex logics? This third context is the subject of part III, 'Logics', in which we place Chowra Makaremi's contribution showing that the treatment of the bodies of Iranian dissidents forms part of the logic of building a revolutionary state (chapter 7), Nicky Rousseau's contribution highlighting of the properly political aspects of the breaking up of the body in apartheid South Africa (chapter 8), and Rémi Korman's nuanced reconstruction of the ideological and symbolic foundations of the massacre of victims in Rwanda, and particularly of the dismemberment of their bodies (chapter 9).

It is already possible to suggest that some research hypotheses have been confirmed. This is true of the link between the ideology that led to the mass murder and the modality of the treatment of corpses, which can be seen perfectly clearly in the cases of Rwanda, Argentina, South Africa, Iran, and Armenia, as well as in that of the Holocaust. Certainly, looking at the case studies in this volume, we can say that human ingenuity has no limits when it comes to defiling, dismembering, concealing, or destroying a body, to instrumentalizing and exploiting it. But the various outrages perpetrated upon the corpses do not constitute a simple outburst of sadism: they are thoroughly engaged with the ideological engine that has set in motion the destruction of lives, as demonstrated in most of the chapters. Let us merely note here the 'renaturalization' of the corpses, their return, in a denial of the religious ritual of the group to which they belong, to nature, caves, deserts, fields, natural pits. Physical geography is important, as is the landscape and the use made of rivers or mountainous areas, as we can see from the cases of Armenia, Argentina, and Bosnia with its karst caves, its crevices, its chasms, but also its peaks. Of crucial importance here is the contribution of anthropology, which can read the signs of fire (note that the human body is cooked by means of devices – ovens or grills – which are also used for the ordinary consumption of food, in a striking parallel with cannibalistic rituals of consumption), water (note that the corpses have been dumped in the sea, in lakes, rivers, or streams, such as the disappeared in the Argentine dictatorship, thrown from aircraft into the Rio de La Plata, which offered one of the most effective and easily accessible spaces for symbolic purification and cleansing), and earth, as seen in the disposal of the corpses of the Armenian genocide.

Another achievement of our research programme lies in recognizing the importance of temporality in the treatment of the body. While most of the treatment and mistreatment suffered by corpses is carried out immediately after the murder – as was the case in the cremation of corpses at Auschwitz or Majdanek, or the desecrations perpetrated in Rwanda – it can also take place a number of days later, as in the case of Bosnia analysed by Max Bergholz, or even many years afterwards, as in the famous case of Operation 1005.[12] Usually, the killers or their proxies have to conceal or destroy the corpses, as they are tangible evidence of past violence and potential proof in the event of an investigation. This delayed treatment of the body reveals that the victims and their murderers are engaged in a long-term relationship that prompts us, in part, to consider the violence not as an event but as a long, diachronic process, of which death and the treatment of the body are distinct but intrinsically linked steps. This long-term linkage also leads us to enquire more systematically into what the treatment of the body reveals about the killers' consciousness of participating in a criminal enterprise.

It seems important to conclude by looking at the utility of the concept of biopower for the study of mass corpses. The theory, as taken up and transformed by Michel Foucault, is often cited in studies of mass violence and genocide.[13] Placing the body at the centre of issues of control of the modern state, this theory seems attractive for the study of mass corpses a priori. But Foucault himself has written little – if at all – about mass murder, and instead refers much more broadly to policies of segregation and confinement. And the limits of this theory have to be stated.[14] We agree with Enzo Traverso's recent analysis, which emphasizes that while we may concede that Foucault's theory of pastoral power helps us to understand the Nazi vision of the people's community (*Volksgemeinschaft*), for example, it must also be admitted that the theory of biopower 'does not provide the key to understanding the Holocaust', as it is true that Foucault is not concerned with genocidal configurations.[15] We therefore lack a theoretical approach that takes into account the intentionally criminal nature of projects of mass destruction that would explain why victims' bodies remain for so long (well beyond their death, and sometimes as part of denialist strategies) an instrument in the murderers' hands. One of the key contributions of our research may, then, be to highlight the systematic exploitation of victims' bodies by their executioners in the extremely diverse configurations of mass crime and extermination that were the Armenian or Rwandan genocides, the Holocaust, or the Argentine, South African, or Iranian dictatorships, and thereby to reveal the heuristic dimensions of the study of the fate of the dead and the afterlife of corpses.

Highlighting the scale and complexity of this instrumentalization allows us to show the highly globalized processes through which criminal methods are transmitted, including both the circulation of knowledge (as is the case with the doctrine of counter-insurgency warfare, the effects of which we can trace from Indochina and Algeria, where it was forged by the French military, to South America's Plan Condor and South Africa's apartheid) and the transfer of technologies and 'know-how'. The latter include for example the crematoria of the German engineering company Topf & Söhne, of which the first version designed to work day and night was delivered to the NKVD (the People's Commissariat for Internal Affairs) in Moscow in 1926, before the development of the ovens commissioned for Auschwitz-Birkenau in 1943,[16] or the death flights developed in the Bay of Algiers during the Algerian War of Independence and adopted by the Argentine military during the dictatorship as one of the safest ways to dispose of the bodies of political opponents.

In light of the complexity of the process of producing mass death, the concepts of hygienic biopolitics and the immunization of the body politic, as defined by Robert Esposito, may be of more help than the simple notion of biopolitics on its own.[17] These notions are indeed relevant in their illumination of the Rwandan or Argentine case, as well as of the anti-partisan war during the Second World War in the European East. Here, Nazi officials were reprimanded because their execution of murder was both unsanitary and inefficient (i.e. it did not sweep up all the witnesses), their practices becoming explicitly a question of the sanitization of battle fields and beyond, as well as of society as a whole. But this hygienic dimension of biopolitics also enlightens the Armenian genocide, where, by disposing of corpses, the perpetrators intended not so much to conceal their crimes as to purge the new state of any 'foreign' material in a properly organicist sense.

This analysis of what is politically at stake in the treatment of corpses could thus be expanded to the entire destruction process from a necropolitical perspective, as defined by Giorgio Agamben.

More than an echo of *Remnants of Auschwitz*[18] can thus be found in the present volume, informing for example the treatment of dying victims at the hands of the South African police forces during apartheid, and enticing us to draw comparisons to the way South American juntas dealt with the corpses of the *desaparecidos*, the disappeared.

However, these well-researched theories on bodies and power do not exhaust the issues raised by the treatment of corpses themselves. Properly anthropological approaches to notions such as purity, dirtiness, cleanliness, or pollution, in their relation to collective representations of danger as described, among others, by Mary Douglas, may in these cases open an even wider scope of analysis.[19] Practices of sorting bodies, or of specifically treating corpses, body parts, and human remains, thus appear in most of the cases presented in our volume. These ways of dealing with issues of purity and danger, while producing mass crime, reveal astonishing and strong symbolic oppositions, with structuralist resonances to these sorting practices. Thus, in post-revolutionary Iran, religious and ideological discriminations have been enacted in the treatment of corpses of political opponents and their burial, in contexts in which the state and its death apparatus bring forth differences between the undeserving 'dangerous others'. Traditional Muslim Shiite funerary rituals have therefore been not only performed and transformed in these situations, but also inversed in order to desacralize these bodies.

Moreover, all the cases analysed in this volume illustrate the emergences of rituals – among them bureaucratic practices – and specific norms of social behaviour elaborated for facilitating and legitimizing the destruction of the other. Some can be understood as a direct reinforcement of state identity which questions whether the treatment of corpses should mirror nationalism and even community, nation, or empire building. And if all the contributions ultimately show the extent to which the treatments of corpses are indeed political, this is demonstrated not only at the macro level of empire building, which has already been demonstrated by genocide scholars such as Mark Levene,[20] but also at a regional or even local level. This extends to the pursuit of controlling space, not necessarily aimed at territorial expansion, as well as, on a more intimate level, embodying a relation of domination between murderers and their victims. In the end, given the apparent links among the actors, methods, and stakes underlying the production of mass death, it is a complex and interconnected understanding of the political dimensions in the production of extreme violence that we must now adopt, while taking into account the irreducible singularity of each event of mass atrocity, and of the fate of each victim.

Notes

1 The text of this chapter was translated from the authors' French by Cadenza Academic Translations.
2 H. Arendt, *The Origins of Totalitarianism* (New York: Harcourt, Brace, 1951).
3 E. Hobsbawm, *Age of Extremes: The Short Twentieth Century, 1914–1991* (London: Abacus, 1994).
4 S. H. James & J. J. Nordby (eds), *Forensic Science: An Introduction to Scientific and Investigative Techniques* (Boca Raton: Taylor & Francis, 2005).
5 R. Hertz, 'A contribution to the study of the collective representation of death', in *Death and the Right Hand* (Glencoe: Free Press, 1960), pp. 27–86.
6 It is within the framework of this programme that the series 'Human Remains and Violence' has been established, published by Manchester University Press, of which this volume is one of the first.
7 É. Anstett & J.-M. Dreyfus (eds), *Human Remains and Mass Violence: Methodological Approaches* (Manchester: Manchester University Press, 2014).
8 F. Dikötter, *Mao's Great Famine: The History of China's Most Devastating Catastrophe, 1958–1962* (London: Bloomsbury, 2010); É. Anstett & L. Jurgenson, *Le Goulage en héritage, pour une anthropologie de la trace* (Paris: Pétra, 2009).
9 R. J. Van Pelt, *The Case for Auschwitz* (Bloomington: Indiana University Press, 2002); J. Wiernik, *Une année à Treblinka* (Paris: Vendémiaire, 2012).
10 S. Leys, *The Chairman's New Clothes: Mao and the Cultural Revolution* (New York: St Martin's Press, 1977).
11 Van Pelt, *The Case for Auschwitz*; L. Fondebrider, 'The materialization of sadism: archaeology of architecture in clandestine detention centers (Argentinian military dictatorship, 1976–1983)', in P. Funari, A. Zarankin & M. Salerno (eds), *Memories from Darkness: Archaeology of Repression and Resistance in Latin America* (New York: Springer, 2009), pp. 57–77; C. Demasi, A. Marchesi, V. Markarian, R. Alvaro & J. Yaffe (eds), *La dictadura Cívio-Militar Uruguay 1973–1985* (Montevideo: Banda Oriental, 2009).
12 J. Hoffmann, *Das kann man nicht erzählen: 'Aktion 1005', wie die Nazis die Spuren ihrer Massenmorde in Osteuropa beseitigen* (Hamburg: KVV Konkret, 2008). Operation 1005 was launched by Heinrich Himmler in May 1942 to erase the traces of the massacres of Jews. A

Introduction 11

  special commando unit was systematically deployed at all the sites of the massacres to exhume the corpses and cremate them.
13 M. Foucault, 'The meshes of power', trans. G. Moore, in J. W. Crampton & S. Elden (eds), *Space, Knowledge and Power: Foucault and Geography* (Aldershot: Ashgate, 2007), pp. 153–68.
14 Y. Alsheh, 'Corpses of genocide and biopower – how corpses challenge the biopolitical paradigm in genocide research', in E. Anstett & J.-M. Dreyfus (eds), *Human Remains and Mass Violence: Methodological Approaches* (Manchester: Manchester University Press, 2014).
15 E. Traverso, *L'Histoire comme champ de bataille: Interpréter les violences du XXe siècle* (Paris: La Découverte Poche, 2012), p. 200.
16 J.-C. Pressac, *Auschwitz: Technique and Operation of the Gas Chambers* (New York: Beate Klarsfeld Foundation, 1989).
17 R. Esposito, *Bios: Biopolitics and Philosophy* (Minneapolis: University of Minnesota Press, 2008).
18 Giorgio Agamben, *Remnants of Auschwitz: The Witness and the Archive. Homo Sacer III* (New York: Zone Books, 1999).
19 M. Douglas, *Purity and Danger: An Analysis of Concepts of Pollution and Taboo* (London: Routledge and Kegan Paul, 1966).
20 The idea of genocide as intrinsic to the development of the nation state and of empire is developed by M. Levene, *Genocide in the Age of the Nation State: Vol. I, The Meaning of Genocide, Vol. II, The Rise of the West and the Coming of Genocide* (London: I. B. Tauris, 2005, 2008).

Bibliography

Agamben, G., *Remnants of Auschwitz: The Witness and the Archive. Homo Sacer III* (New York: Zone Books, 1999)

Alsheh, Y., 'Corpses of genocide and biopower – how corpses challenge the biopolitical paradigm in genocide research', in E. Anstett & J.-M. Dreyfus (eds), *Human Remains and Mass Violence: Methodological Approaches* (Manchester: Manchester University Press, 2014)

Anstett, É., *Une Atlantide russe: anthropologie de la mémoire en Russie postsoviétique* (Paris: La Découverte, 2007)

Anstett, É. & J.-M. Dreyfus (eds), *Human Remains and Mass Violence: Methodological Approaches* (Manchester: Manchester University Press, 2014).

Anstett, É. & L. Jurgenson, *Le Goulage en héritage, pour une anthropologie de la trace* (Paris: Pétra, 2009)

Arendt, H., *The Origins of Totalitarianism* (New York: Harcourt, Brace, 1951)

Blau, S. & Ubelaker, D. H. (eds), *Handbook of Forensic Anthropology and Archaeology* (Wallnut Creek: Left Coast Press, 2009)

Demasi, C., A. Marchesi, V. Markarian, R. Alvaro & J. Yaffe (eds), *La dictadura Cívio-Militar Uruguay 1973–1985* (Montevideo: Banda Oriental, 2009)

Dikötter, F., *Mao's Great Famine: The History of China's Most Devastating Catastrophe, 1958–1962* (London: Bloomsbury, 2010)

Douglas, M., *Purity and Danger: An Analysis of Concepts of Pollution and Taboo* (London: Routledge and Kegan Paul, 1966)

Esposito, R., *Bios: Biopolitics and Philosophy* (Minneapolis: University of Minnesota Press, 2008)

Fondebrider, L., 'The materialization of sadism: archaeology of architecture in clandestine detention centers (Argentinian military dictatorship, 1976–1983)', in P. Funari, A. Zarankin & M. Salerno (eds), *Memories from Darkness: Archaeology of Repression and Resistance in Latin America* (New York: Springer, 2009), pp. 57–77

Foucault, M., 'The meshes of power', trans. G. Moore, in J. W. Crampton & S. Elden (eds), *Space, Knowledge and Power: Foucault and Geography* (Aldershot: Ashgate, 2007), pp. 153–68

Hertz, R., 'A contribution to the study of the collective representation of death', in *Death and the Right Hand* (Glencoe: Free Press, 1960), pp. 27–86

Hobsbawm, E., *Age of Extremes: The Short Twentieth Century, 1914–1991* (London: Abacus, 1994)

Hoffmann, J., *Das kann man nicht erzählen: 'Aktion 1005', wie die Nazis die Spuren ihrer Massenmorde in Osteuropa beseitigen* (Hamburg: KVV Konkret, 2008)

James, S. H. & J. J. Nordby (eds), *Forensic Science: An Introduction to Scientific and Investigative Techniques* (Boca Raton: Taylor & Francis, 2005)

Joyce, C. & E. Stover, *Witnesses from the Grave: The Stories Bones Tell* (Boston, Little, Brow, 1991)

Levene, M., *Genocide in the Age of the Nation State: Vol. I, The Meaning of Genocide, Vol. II, The Rise of the West and the Coming of Genocide* (London: I. B. Tauris, 2005, 2008)

Leys, S., *The Chairman's New Clothes: Mao and the Cultural Revolution* (New York: St Martin's Press, 1977)

Pressac, J.-C., *Auschwitz: Technique and Operation of the Gas Chambers* (New York: Beate Klarsfeld Foundation, 1989)

Traverso, E., *L'Histoire comme champ de bataille: Interpréter les violences du XXe siècle* (Paris: La Découverte Poche, 2012)

Van Pelt, R. J., *The Case for Auschwitz* (Bloomington: Indiana University Press, 2002)

Wiernik, J., *Une année à Treblinka* (Paris: Vendémiaire, 2012)

Xun, Z. (ed.), *The Great Famine in China 1958–1962: A Documentary History* (New Haven: Yale University Press, 2012)

Part I: Actors

1
'As if nothing ever happened': massacres, missing corpses, and silence in a Bosnian community

Max Bergholz

This chapter is based on a book-length study, currently in progress, on the dynamics of mass violence in a Bosnian community in 1941 and the post-conflict silence that emerged about some of the killings after 1945. Here, I deal with two subjects that are relevant to the 'Corpses of Mass Violence and Genocide' project: first, the concrete methods of mass killing that various groups in this region employed, and specifically the symbolism and ramifications of how they treated the bodies of their victims; second, how these methods of killing, and treatment of victims and corpses, helped to create conditions for a post-war silence, in particular about the Muslim civilian war victims.[1] The main argument is that a micro-level analysis of the dynamics of local violence reveals a causal relationship between the encounters with corpses of victims and survivors of violence, and the triggering of further killings, whose scale and ferocity rapidly increased. This research suggests a new way in which scholars of mass violence can productively build on the insights of recent influential work on political violence, which has highlighted the importance of the local dimensions of that violence, and especially their frequent disjuncture with those of the 'master cleavage' of a conflict.[2] The discussion that follows shows that one fruitful path forward is to pay increased attention to a largely understudied dynamic of mass violence, particularly in times of civil war, which is largely discernable only at the micro level: the relationship between the warring factions' experience with corpses, particularly those of their relatives, neighbours, and fellow fighters, and the ebb and flow of mass killing.

The community in question lived in the Kulen Vakuf region of north-western Bosnia, approximately 50 km from the city of Bihać. On the eve of the Second World War, the municipality of Kulen Vakuf comprised a section of the Una River valley and its surrounding hills. In the valley were Muslim villages and the town of Kulen Vakuf. Its population was nearly entirely Muslim, while in the surrounding hills were many Serbian and a few Croatian villages.[3] The community's pre-war history, though not without conflict, due in part to the agrarian question, which pitted Muslim landlords against their predominately Orthodox Christian tenants, reveals a long-term history of inter-communal peace and manageable discord. Prior to the Second World War, serious inter-communal violence had occurred only once in the region, during the peasant uprising of 1875–78.[4] During the 1920s and 1930s, the population generally divided along religious and national lines when it came to politics.[5] Yet most people were friendly with one another, in the host of venues that made up their everyday existence, such as the weekly Thursday market in Kulen Vakuf, and soccer matches, during which Muslim and Serb men played on the same teams.[6]

This changed with the German invasion of the Kingdom of Yugoslavia on 6 April 1941. The region was incorporated into the newly established Independent State of Croatia (Nezavisna Država Hrvatska, or NDH), whose fascist leadership, known as the Ustašas, was committed to creating a state exclusively for Croats. As for the many Muslims who found themselves citizens of the new state, the Ustašas considered them to be Croats of the Islamic faith. Aside from Jews and Roma, the main population who stood in the way of the Ustašas' vision of an ethnically pure Croatian state was the Serb Orthodox community, which comprised nearly one-third of the population.[7]

Archival documents indicate that at least fifty-one local men joined the Ustašas in the Kulen Vakuf region, of whom thirty-two were Muslim and nineteen Croat. These men constituted less than 1 per cent of the region's population of Croats and Muslims. While it is difficult to determine what exactly led each of these men to join, the evidence suggests that most were from relatively poor families and thus they appear to have been attracted to the Ustašas out of a desire to quickly attain material wealth, and in some cases to settle personal scores with pre-war enemies among the Serb Orthodox population.[8] Only a handful, such as the local Croat Miroslav Matijević, who owned a tavern in Kulen Vakuf, appeared to have had connections to the Ustaša movement prior to the German invasion.[9]

Initially, the leadership of the NDH considered a number of potential policies to deal with the large Serb minority, such as rapidly converting a sizeable part of the Serb population (aside from its educated elite) to Catholicism, to make them 'Croat'.[10] It also sought to quickly expel large numbers of Serbs outside the borders of the state to Serbia, where the German army was ruling with a local collaborationist government. But the policy of transferring the Serb minority east proved difficult to realize in the context of the broader war. With the German army preparing for the invasion of the Soviet Union, it was not possible in the early summer of 1941 to devote sizeable resources to the deportation of nearly 2 million people considered to be Serbs. The NDH authorities were simply not equipped for the rapid transfer of so many people, nor were their counterparts in Serbia in a position to receive them, and the German army had more important priorities, given their mobilization to attack the Soviet Union.[11] The regional NDH authorities did attempt during late June and early July 1941 to transfer the Serb (as well as Jewish) population out of north-west Bosnia. Most notably, on 14 June they emptied the city of Bihać of those they considered to be members of these groups.[12] But it was much more difficult to implement the resettlement policy among the large number of Serb villages throughout the region. The NDH authorities thus looked to the heartland of their new state, which included north-western Bosnia, where the Kulen Vakuf region was located, and saw large numbers of Serbs whom they considered a threat. And so, by mid to late June, the regional NDH authorities in north-western Bosnia made the decision to use mass violence to physically eliminate part of the Serb population and to induce the rest to flee.[13]

Because they lacked strong popular support among the non-Serb population for committing mass violence against their Serb neighbours, the local Ustašas in the Kulen Vakuf region decided to carry out the bulk of the mass killing of Serbs at a pit about 10 km west of Kulen Vakuf, not far from the Croatian village of Boričevac. This way, they hoped that no one in the town would know where the killings were taking place, and no one would be able to discover the bodies. It appears that this strategy was designed to avoid alarming the non-Serb population, while sowing fear and uncertainty among the Serbs who remained in their villages, and inducing them to flee the region. In addition to 'Croatianizing' the region, which was the most important objective for the regional and national political elites, the attacks on Serbs, and the hoped-for emptying of their towns and villages, was appealing to some local leaders and most Ustaša foot soldiers, who seem to have been more concerned with plundering Serb property. Beginning in late June 1941, the local Ustašas went to the Serb villages, arrested the most influential men, demanded money from them, and then murdered many with a gunshot to the head, and dropped their bodies in the pit. The Ustašas had reason to fear a popular backlash from local Muslims and Croats who opposed these killings. There were many instances between June and August 1941 of Croats and Muslims warning their Serb neighbours that the Ustašas were going to attack them. In doing so, they saved many lives.[14]

The Ustašas were unable to carry out all the killings at the pit, and ended up murdering a number of Serbs near the local Orthodox Church in the town of Kulen Vakuf, as well as near the town's primary school. They carried out these killings by cutting the throats of the victims, and they buried the bodies in shallow graves and ditches. They also killed large numbers of Serbs, not only men but also women and children, in a number of villages in the wider region, such as Doljani, Osredci, Bubanj, Nebljusi, and Suvaja. These killings often wiped out entire extended families, such as the Keča clan of Suvaja, of which the local Ustašas murdered 45 members on 1 July 1941, along with 116 of their neighbours. If the Ustašas did not manage to throw the bodies into pits, then they tended to bury them in shallow mass graves.[15] In other cases, they left the corpses in the open. 'The bodies of men, women, and children killed on 2–3 July were laying everywhere', as one Ustaša described what he saw in a village in the region, 'which made for a terrible stench. Pigs and dogs were chewing on the corpses.'[16] This created an atmosphere of 'infectious fear' among the remaining Serb population, who immediately fled into the nearby forests.[17]

The differing treatment of the corpses seems to have been dependent in large part on the ethnic composition of the population where the killings took place. In mixed regions, such as the immediate vicinity of Kulen Vakuf, the Ustašas tended to lead their victims away from the non-Serb population, many of whom did not support violence against their Serb neighbours, in order to kill them and then drop their bodies into pits, where they disappeared from view. Killing and disposing of the corpses in this way appear to have been employed to avoid destabilizing the non-Serb population and provoking resistance. In regions where Serbs made up most or all of the population, by contrast, the Ustašas seem to have been much more willing to leave the mutilated and decomposing corpses in the open, so as to terrify the remaining Serb population, and, it was hoped, to induce them to flee, thus 'cleansing the terrain'.

After such massacres, local NDH military personnel wrote reports to their superiors in Zagreb, noting that sometimes survivors would return to their villages after the mass killings – which they euphemistically referred to as 'cleansings' – only to discover horrific scenes with bodies. 'This has created fear among the people, as well as indignation, all of which makes any kind of reconciliation [between the Serb and non-Serb population] unthinkable.'[18] One can only imagine the experience of finding the murdered bodies of parents and siblings, with limbs being chewed off by livestock and dogs. For one local man, who as a ten-year-old endured finding the bodies of his mother and younger brother in this condition after a massacre in July 1941, it was simply 'the greatest tragedy that could happen to a person'.[19] NDH military analysts noted the dramatic results of these 'Ustaša cleansing actions' on inter-communal relations: 'It is difficult to conceive of collective life of the Croat–Muslim part of the population with the Serb part. The chasm that now exists is too big.'[20] Thus, in a matter of weeks, the violence of the local Ustašas shattered the long-term, inter-communal bonds of friendship and neighbourliness that had existed for many in the region. They accomplished this by brutally murdering at least 600 Serbs in the Kulen Vakuf region between late June and late July 1941. The first victims were mostly men, and especially merchants, village elders, heads of households, priests, and others of influence, but later waves of killing included many women and children.[21]

The mass killings of Serbs caused the Serb survivors to organize an insurgency at the end of July 1941. Shortly thereafter, the Communist Party issued a call for an uprising. The local guerrilla fighters, who referred to themselves for the most part as 'insurgents' (*ustanici*), immediately overran at least four villages and towns, killed several Ustašas and other NDH police and military personnel, burned their commands to the ground, and captured their weapons and ammunition.[22] They attacked more villages during the last few days of July, with varying degrees of success.[23] However, the handful of Serb communists in the Kulen Vakuf region encountered difficulties trying to organize the peasant insurgents into a unified guerrilla army. Their numbers were exceptionally small and they lacked the necessary authority that other prominent local Serbs had, such as former gendarmes and military officers. None of these incipient insurgent units in the region had Communist Party organizations during the summer of 1941.[24]

Another point of tension was the issue of collaborating with Muslims and Croats. The communists hoped that fighters of all nationalities would join the uprising and fight together for the liberation of the country and socialist revolution. But for many of the Serb insurgents, their Muslim and Croat neighbours, only a small number of whom had joined the Ustašas, had now become their main collective enemy. Many of the Serb survivors of the massacres that the Ustašas committed suddenly viewed all Muslims and Croats as Ustašas, which instilled in them an intense desire to exact blood vengeance on their non-Serb neighbours.[25] Encounters between local Serbs and Croats during and after Ustaša attacks in the region earlier in July attest to these sentiments. In the village of Bubanj, where Ustašas, among whom were several Muslims from Kulen Vakuf, had murdered at least 150 Serbs on 3 July, local Croat villagers remembered hearing from surviving Serbs: 'You Croats are now filling bottomless pits [*bezdanke*] with us, but when our time comes we will do the same with you'.[26] This pledge to take revenge became real during attacks on a number of Croatian villages in late July and early August 1941, when Serb insurgents burned the villages and massacred all Croats, including women and children.[27] The massacres vividly revealed how little control the small number of communists had over the revenge-seeking peasant fighters. As one insurgent remembered after the attack on the village of Vrtoče: 'Hatred toward the Ustašas and the desire to take revenge on them for the relatives and friends [of the insurgents] they had killed dominated during the attack.'[28]

During these killings the Serb insurgents treated their victims and their corpses in ways that deserve closer examination in order to better understand what fuelled the intensity of violence in the region, and shaped its dynamics. In some cases they sought to physically obliterate the Croat community, as in the village of Brotnja, where, at the end of July, they rounded up nearly the entire Croat population, who all happened to be of the Ivezić family, and proceeded to throw them one at a time, while still alive, to their deaths in a deep vertical cave.[29] But often they tortured their victims before finally killing them, such as a local Catholic priest in the village Krnjeuša, whose nose and ears they cut off, and whose eyes they poked out. They then locked him and others inside a Catholic church and set it on fire, which finally killed all of them. In order to take revenge, the insurgents sought out the relatives of Ustašas who had killed Serbs, and in some cases made a point of mutilating the bodies in ways that would sow fear and anger. In one case, they captured the father of Miroslav Matijević, the local Ustaša leader in Kulen Vakuf who had been the main organizer of the violence against the Serb community in the region earlier in the summer. They cut off his head. They then placed it on top of a stick that they carried around the village of Vrtoče while killing others, including his wife, and at least eight further members of his family.[30]

The symbolic meaning of placing the head of Matijević's father on the stick can be better understood if one situates the act within the context of the history of violent practices in the region. The Ottoman authorities, as well as the local *kapetani* (Muslim military commanders who were in charge of the fortifications along the Ottoman–Habsburg military border) in the Kulen Vakuf region, used such techniques on those whom they considered to be enemies, including both Christians and Muslims. This was not merely a way of executing an enemy and taking revenge; it also was a form of communication with the rest of the population, designed to transmit fear, to clearly show who was in control, and to publicly demonstrate that the enemy had been killed in a shameful and humiliating way. Beheading had been standard practice in the Kulen Vakuf region at least through the first third of the nineteenth century. The head was placed on a stick and then positioned on or near the site of an Ottoman military fortification to look like a gravestone, which would be visible to all local villagers. Being executed in this way, and having one's head displayed on a stick, was considered to be a disgrace.[31] Based on the nearly identical style of execution of Matijević's father in early August 1941, and the subsequent placing of his head on a stick, it seems as though the insurgents preserved the memory of these Ottoman-era practices and employed them to take revenge on their neighbours and humiliate them. As for the rest of the Croats whom the insurgents killed in the village of Vrtoče, they made a point of killing most by cutting their throats in the same way they would slaughter their livestock, as most of these Serb insurgents were peasants who made their livelihoods from animal husbandry. This method may have been simply rooted in the lack of ammunition among the Serb insurgents; but it may also have been a way of reducing their victims in death to the level of animals, which could be seen as a further humiliation.[32]

What these killings and mutilations demonstrated was a complex mixture of discriminate and indiscriminate violence, to use the distinction of the political scientist Stathis Kalyvas.[33] On the one hand, the insurgents chose very specific targets, such as the local Catholic priest and the father of the local Ustaša leader, whom they viewed as intimately connected to the Ustašas and the local Croat community. They made a point of killing and mutilating each in very horrific and public ways, which communicated a sense of fear and humiliation, as well as disgracing their enemies. On the other hand, these discriminate acts of violence seemed to set the stage for what quickly became mass indiscriminate killings, in which the insurgents sought out their victims less because of their perceived connection to the Ustašas, and more because of whom they understood their victims to be (i.e., Croats). Ultimately, it appeared that both approaches to the killing led towards the same objective: exacting blood vengeance on the entire local Croat community for the killings the Ustašas had carried out during the previous weeks.

Unlike the Ustašas, who often tried to throw the bodies of their victims into pits or to bury them in mass graves so as to hide the evidence of their killings, the Serb insurgents tended to leave the bodies of their Croat victims in plain view so that, it seems, those who later found them would be horrified by the blood vengeance that the Serb insurgents had taken. And this was exactly what happened. Archival documents from the NDH military indicate that those who found these mutilated bodies of Croats were enraged. When a regiment of Domobrani (i.e., the 'Home Guards', the official army units of the NDH) made their way into the destroyed village of Krnjeuša a few days after the insurgents had tortured and murdered all of its Croat inhabitants who did not flee, they were aghast at the sights of mutilated and burned bodies. 'No one could remain indifferent to the horrible sight. The soldiers could barely contain themselves from going out and killing every Serb.'[34] But this kind of experience did not just bring about a desire to kill; it also compelled at least some to go out and murder more Serbs.[35] After learning that Serb insurgents had decapitated his father, Miroslav Matijević went immediately to the primary school in Kulen Vakuf, where a number of Serb prisoners were being held. With two other Ustašas he took nineteen of them to the Serbian Orthodox Church in Kulen Vakuf and proceeded to butcher them inside it, as an act of revenge.[36] This part of the violence was symbolic, as the church was not only a place of worship but also the main repository of the community's history and identity. So the specific methods of killing and the treatment of corpses in what was now a civil war had the result of ratcheting up the intensity of the mass violence, most especially through revenge killings that were carried out in ways intended to be both physically and symbolically destructive.

The radicalizing effects of finding bodies of victims, as well as interacting with injured survivors of massacres, swung in the other direction as well. In early August 1941 Serb insurgents overran the Croatian village of Boričevac, near the pit where the local Ustašas had murdered hundreds of Serbs from the Kulen Vakuf region. Around the entrance of the pit they found several severed heads with the eyes poked out, as well as other body parts, and pools of semi-dried blood.[37] Then they yelled down into the pit to see if anyone was alive. After a few moments voices called for help, and the insurgents pulled out two men who had been in the pit, in the midst of a large number of corpses, for several days and nights. One had been shot in the head, but had managed to survive, while the other had jumped in on his own after watching Matijević kill his son, two brothers, and three uncles.[38] Several insurgents later noted that the experience of finding these survivors and listening to their stories about how Serbs had been killed at the pit instilled in them a desire for revenge that was 'all consuming'.[39] At the same time, seeing the pits that the Ustašas had used may have given some insurgents an idea as to how such deep vertical caves could be used in the future, for the purpose of taking this revenge. Again, the encounter between those committing violence with the bodies of victims, as well as with survivors, had the effect of intensifying the desire to commit more violence.

The desire for revenge among many insurgents only intensified when the fighters left the area immediately around Boričevac and came across the destroyed houses of Serb peasants near the village of Kalati, which the local Ustašas had recently ransacked and burned after they had fled from Boričevac. Under the summer sun, the decomposing corpses of massacred women, children, and elderly lay inside the burned houses, and strewn throughout the yards and gardens.[40] The methods of torture and mutilation prior to killing were clear to see on the corpses: the bodies of women and girls showed signs of their having been raped prior to killing; murdered children were missing eyes, while others had been stabbed with pitchforks and leaned up against fences and walls around houses; the Ustašas had apparently impaled some victims on sticks while they were still alive, and let them suffer excruciating deaths.⁴¹ As one insurgent later wrote: 'What we saw there was very difficult for us, and we could barely wait to find the Ustašas'.⁴² But no Ustašas remained in the immediate vicinity to take revenge on, as they had already fled to Kulen Vakuf when the insurgents attacked, taking the entire local Croat population with them. Many of the Serb fighters then laid waste to what the Ustašas left behind. They returned to the empty Croatian village of Boričevac and set every building on fire, including the Catholic Church. The whole village burned to the ground within an hour.⁴³ So once again, it was the encounter between those committing violence with the bodies of victims, as well as with survivors, that had the effect of fuelling the desire to commit more violence.

During late August 1941, in the aftermath of these massacres in the Croatian villages in the region, the local NDH authorities realized that they would not be able to hold their position in the town of Kulen Vakuf, as well as defend the local Muslim population in the vicinity, if the insurgents launched an attack. The Serb peasant fighters had amassed a considerable amount of weapons and ammunition after each of their attacks on the Croatian villages, and now had nearly 1,000 men under arms, which was many times more than their opponents in the region. They had encircled the town of Kulen Vakuf, which meant that neither supplies nor reinforcements could reach the Ustašas and NDH soldiers.⁴⁴ And so the Ustašas decided to flee while evacuating the region's entire Muslim population of about 5,600 people to the nearby city of Bihać, about 50 km away.

Early in the morning of 6 September 1941 they left. But not far from Kulen Vakuf the Serb insurgents, who were hiding in the forests, opened fire. While some fought against the armed NDH soldiers and Ustašas, others turned their rifles on the unarmed Muslim refugees, killing perhaps as many as 500. The bodies of these victims, many of whom were women and children, were left in the open along a 2 km stretch of dirt road.⁴⁵ The Ustašas and NDH soldiers returned fire and eventually managed to break through the Serb insurgent ambush after several hours of fierce fighting, bringing with them about 3,100 of the refugees.⁴⁶ The insurgents captured the remaining 2,000. One group of insurgents immediately took about seventy Muslim men to a nearby pit and, without making any attempt to determine if they had been Ustašas, shot each in the head and then dropped their bodies into the hole, killing them in exactly the same way as the Ustašas had killed Serbs earlier in the summer. The arrival of the small number of communist commanders put a stop to these executions and they ordered that the rest of the Muslims be taken back to Kulen Vakuf.⁴⁷

Once they returned to the town, the insurgents divided the prisoners into three groups, two for women and children and one for men and teenage boys. Some of the insurgents then began breaking into shops and homes. Others opened up the many taverns in Kulen Vakuf and started drinking. Another group demanded that several of the male Muslim prisoners show them the location of the mass graves of Serb victims in Kulen Vakuf. They found a shallow grave near the primary school where the Ustašas had murdered Serbs in August 1941. The insurgents ordered several Muslims to begin unearthing the bodies. As each corpse was dragged out of the hole the insurgents tried to identify their relatives and neighbours. Other local Serbs came down from villages in the hills and joined in this process of exhuming these bodies and identifying them. This experience of touching the corpses of their murdered neighbours and relatives appears to have aroused in many what one insurgent later called 'a wild and uncontrollable desire for revenge'.⁴⁸ The encounter with these corpses seems to have marked a decisive turning point for many insurgents and peasants. With the bodies of murdered Serbs on display for all to see, the local Ustašas and the entire Muslim population seem to have merged into one entity. For many insurgents and peasants, all their Muslim neighbours now appeared guilty for the killings of their relatives and neighbours, and now all of them would need to be destroyed. What seemed to suddenly take hold among many was, in the words of one fighter who was an eyewitness, 'a psychosis of revenge'.⁴⁹ Like the killings in the previous weeks in the Croatian villages, the insurgents began with targeted killings of Muslim men suspected of having been Ustašas. They circulated among the Muslim prisoners and could be heard yelling out: 'This one is an Ustaša! He killed my brother and father',⁵⁰ and the individual would be led away and executed, sometimes with a gunshot to the head, sometimes by cutting the victim's throat, and sometimes by cutting off the victim's head.⁵¹

Not long after these targeted killings, the violence in Kulen Vakuf progressively shifted into wholesale slaughter. The insurgent commander in charge of guarding the Muslim men and boys, Petar 'Pero' Đilas, ordered that they all be taken to the nearby Serbian village called Martin Brod, where they would await some kind of improvised trial to determine their fate. Then the insurgents, along with a number of Serb peasants who had arrived to plunder the property of the Muslims, set the town of Kulen Vakuf on fire, with many fighters drinking heavily while doing so. Soon after, they began murdering the Muslim women and children. Serb insurgents and peasants cut their throats using knives and other farm tools, or simply beat them to death with sticks. Others they chased to the edge of the Una River, and in particular to a bridge over the Una, and watched as the women threw their children and then themselves into the water, where most drowned.[52] This meant that a large number of the bodies of these victims soon disappeared without a trace. Other Muslim women and children tried to hide in nearby cornfields, but Serb insurgents and peasants later found most of them, and it appears that there were instances of mass rape of Muslim women prior to their killing.[53]

As for the over 400 Muslim men and boys whom the insurgents had taken to the Serbian village of Martin Brod to stand trial, the commander, Đilas, arrived at the village on a horse and yelled out to the insurgents guarding them that all of the prisoners were Ustašas and should be killed.[54] A local Serb communist, Ranko Šipka, condemned this order and demanded that the insurgents ignore it. But it appears that nearly all refused to listen to him.[55] A group of insurgents then proceeded to march the Muslim prisoners in small groups to a nearby pit, which was known to Serbs in the area as 'Golubnjača' ('the pigeon cave'). Many local Serbs believed that this pit was home to witches, vampires, and devils, and that the pigeons that were often seen around its entrance were actually angels that God had sent in order to prevent the evil spirits inside the cave from leaving and attacking people. One local Serb communist, Gojko Polovina, later told how, when he was a child, he once asked his grandfather whether such stories were true. His grandfather answered:

> What kinds of devils and what kinds of witches? In Golubnjača lie the bones of rebels who were killed without trial and outside the law. They were thrown into the pit so no one would know where their graves are.[56]

The Serb insurgents apparently had this understanding of the Golubnjača pit in mind when they marched the Muslim men and boys to its entrance. They bound their hands with wire and brought them in small groups to the edge of the pit. They cut the prisoners' throats and then dropped their bodies into the darkness. Only one man managed to get his hands free and escape. He ran several hundred metres into the forest and hid silently for the next hour and a half, listening to the screams of his neighbours as the insurgents murdered them one by one.[57]

Before going on, it is worth pausing for a moment to sum up the overarching dynamics of mass killing and the treatment of the corpses of the victims. The Ustašas killed with gunshots to the head and they cut throats. In more ethnically mixed areas they tended to throw the bodies of their victims into pits or to bury them in mass graves, with the intention of concealing the evidence of their violence so as to not provoke resistance from the non-Serb population, many of whom opposed violence against their Serb neighbours. In other instances, the Ustašas killed and left the corpses of Serbs in plain view to decompose and be eaten by wild animals and livestock, in order to terrorize the remaining Serb population into fleeing the region. These acts of killing caused the Serb insurgency, which, initially, led to killings by Serbs of Croats, primarily by the cutting of throats. The Serb insurgents intentionally left the mutilated bodies of their Croat victims in plain view to humiliate their enemies, by showing that they had taken revenge in brutal ways, such as through decapitation and the cutting off of facial features. The discovery of these corpses and acts of mutilation further radicalized the Ustašas, who intensified their violence against the Serb community. At the same time, the experience of finding the corpses of Serb victims, as well as discovering survivors of Ustaša killings, further radicalized the Serb insurgents. This radicalization culminated in the mass killing of Muslims, whom many of the Serb insurgents, along with many local peasants, saw collectively as Ustašas. In a desire to wipe out the local Muslim population once and for all, they killed with gunshots but especially with farm tools, such as axes. They threw the vast majority of the bodies into pits and rivers, which meant that a large number of the corpses of Muslims literally disappeared. This fitted the objective of the insurgents, which was to take complete revenge on their perceived enemies, by totally erasing their presence from the community, including the presence of their corpses. In short, once the violence began, there was a causal relationship between encounters with corpses of victims and survivors of violence, and the triggering of further killings, whose scale and ferocity rapidly increased.

To return to early September 1941. In the end, of the approximately 5,600 Muslims and a handful of Croats who left Kulen Vakuf on the morning of 6 September 1941, around 3,100 arrived at the city of Bihać, along with most of the local Ustašas, whose violence had set off the successive waves of mass killing earlier in the summer. Of the other 2,500 Muslims, it appears that Serb communists, non-communist insurgents, and Serb peasants managed to save around 500. It seems that many of those Serbs who saved their Muslim neighbours did so because of the lengths that some Muslims, as well as Croats, had gone to save Serbs earlier in the summer.[58] Serb insurgents and peasants murdered the rest – nearly 2,000 men, women and children – between 6 and 8 September 1941.

Despite the shock and disgust of local communist commanders with the massacres, no investigation was ever conducted to determine who was responsible for the killings and no one was ever punished. In September 1941, the communists could not risk alienating large numbers of insurgents at a time when they lacked sufficient authority over them.[59] Nonetheless, in the weeks that followed the massacres, communist insurgent leaders in the wider region sent out directives to local commanders in which they called attention to the need to take all possible measures to punish those who engaged in stealing, burning, and killing.[60] Such letters illustrate both the more proactive stance that the communists were taking, and the ongoing destructive behaviour of more than a small number of the fighters they sought to command. Even before the massacres in and around Kulen Vakuf, several communist leaders, such as Marko Orešković Krntija, had already issued extremely blunt statements, arguing that the killings of innocent people by the insurgents made them look no different from 'the Ustaša hordes'.[61]

By 1942, the communists began to carry out more intensive political work among their predominately Serb fighters, in which they emphasized that not all Muslims and Croats were Ustašas, and that Serbs needed to cooperate with their neighbours of different nationalities in the fight for liberation.[62] This prompted a relatively small number of insurgents to abandon their communist-led units, now increasingly called 'the partisans', and seek out the Chetniks, who were loosely organized groups of Serb nationalist insurgents. Notable among these were two of the insurgent commanders who were largely responsible for the massacres of the Muslims in and around Kulen Vakuf.[63]

But the departure for the Chetniks of a handful of insurgents who were directly involved in the massacres of Muslims did not mean that partisan units in the Kulen Vakuf region were suddenly cleansed of those who had murdered Muslims. The vast majority of the Serbs who had participated in the massacres, of which there appear to have been at least several hundred, were still with the partisans. Vividly demonstrating this dynamic was what occurred after the liberation of the city of Bihać in November 1942, when the partisans defeated the NDH military and Ustašas. Well over a year had passed since the communist leadership of the partisan movement began its intensive political work among its fighters, constantly stressing the importance of building 'Brotherhood and Unity' among Serbs, Croats, Muslims, and others in the struggle for liberation. Yet this multi-ethnic mind-set seemed still to have very shallow roots among many partisans. When one Serb fighter from the Kulen Vakuf region came upon Huso Šabić in Bihać, who was a teenager and communist sympathizer, his first question was to ask where the boy came from. Šabić replied that he was a refugee from the town of Kulen Vakuf, having fled on 6 September 1941. Upon hearing the name of the boy's hometown, the Serb partisan immediately executed him. In another instance, several partisans arrested the Muslim Halil Omanović, who was from the village of Orašac in the Kulen Vakuf region. One fighter, who was from Oraško Brdo, a Serbian village in the hills just above the Muslim village of Orašac, whose population suffered at the hands of local Muslim Ustašas, approached him. Omanović asked his former Serb neighbour why his hands had been bound. The Serb partisan looked him in the eyes and said: 'I personally killed seven members of the Omanović family [in September 1941], and now I'm going to kill you!' Several other partisans in the vicinity heard this exchange and immediately intervened to save Omanović's life.[64]

So, even more than a year after the massacres of Muslims in the Kulen Vakuf region, the partisan ranks still contained former insurgents who had murdered large numbers of their non-Serb neighbours, and who intended to take revenge upon them. In certain moments, such as those during the liberation of Bihać, it was clear that the local origins and dynamics of violence, and specifically the desire to take revenge, had not faded away.[65] Instead, they could be suddenly triggered, the dynamics of which researchers can better understand only through further micro-level research on the local origins and dimensions of violence. Most of the Serb perpetrators remained with the communist-led partisans at this time, and, aside from those who went over to the Chetniks or were killed in battle between 1942 and 1945, they were still with them when the war ended.[66]

After the war, neither the local communist authorities nor the rest of the local population publicly discussed the September massacres of the Muslims. The dominant type of communication about the killings was silence. People made a conscious choice not to talk about the massacres, about which they had intimate knowledge, because of a certain constellation of political, social, and psychological factors that made it virtually impossible to speak about them publicly. This led, during the initial years after the war, to the formation of a public culture of silence that crystallized in at least two distinct ways.[67]

The first and most basic element was that the authorities prohibited the returning Muslim refugees from searching for and burying the bodies of their relatives and neighbours.[68] Many of the Serbs who had carried out the killings, as well as their commanding officers, who had either participated or opposed the killings, but who were nonetheless in positions of authority when the massacres took place, had, for the most part, become partisans during the war. After the war, many of these individuals occupied positions in local government. More than a few had become officers in the Yugoslav People's Army.[69] To locate and bury the bodies of the Muslims, whose deaths these individuals were directly and indirectly responsible for, would call into question their positions of authority. It would raise the issue as to whether such individuals were war criminals. Burials and reburials of the Muslim victims of the 1941 massacres were therefore prohibited.

Prohibiting the exhumation and burial of the bodies of the Muslims was made easier by the fact that the methods of killing and treatment of the corpses during the war made retrieval of the bodies very difficult. Many corpses had been washed away in the Una River. Many more were in deep pits. Even if the political will for exhumations and burials had existed, these would have been very difficult to carry out. So the absence of bodies, which made the practice of traditional death rituals nearly impossible, greatly impaired the capacity of the surviving Muslims to engage in concrete acts of remembrance, and was thus a cornerstone in the creation of a public silence about the massacres of Muslims.

A second element of the silence was that there were no post-war investigations of the killings, and therefore no trials were ever held of those responsible. This was also true of the killings of Croats in the region. Again, the basic reason for this was that the majority of Serb insurgents who participated in the massacres had become partisans during the course of the war. This dynamic resulted in the survivors having no choice but to endure regular encounters with a number of the perpetrators. Most of these encounters unfolded in silence. Muslim men would sometimes go to the many taverns in Kulen Vakuf and see Serbs who had participated in the massacres drinking brandy or wine. They sat down at tables, ordered drinks for themselves, and drank without saying a word to those who had killed their relatives and neighbours.[70] Other Muslims worked on the railroad each day with the Serbs who had murdered their parents, yet never said a word about the killings.[71] And in the weekly market Muslim women would regularly pass silently by their Serb neighbours who had tried to beat them to death in September 1941.[72] These usually silent encounters between perpetrators and survivors were a regular part of daily post-war life. For the Muslim survivors, seeing such individuals not only walking freely, but also in a number of cases holding positions of political authority, communicated that those responsible for the massacres would not be held accountable. The absence of any war crimes investigation, and the regular encounters between unpunished perpetrators and generally silent survivors were thus central aspects in the creation of the silence.[73]

How was it possible for such high levels of mass violence, and such brutal treatment of victims and their corpses, to result in post-war silence? First, the particular dynamics of the war, namely, the incorporation of many Serb insurgents, who had previously murdered Muslims and Croats, into the communist-led partisan movement meant that their killings would not be spoken of after 1945. The insurgents obviously did not wish to implicate themselves in the mass murder of innocent civilians. The communist authorities refused to speak of these killings out of fear of de-legitimizing their performance in the Second World War, which was a cornerstone of their 'Socialist Revolution'. So too was their desire to forge 'Brotherhood and Unity' among the country's war-torn, multi-ethnic population.

Second, the concrete methods of mass killing and the treatment of the corpses during September 1941 meant that this post-war silence was easier to enforce. Most of the bodies of Muslims in the Kulen Vakuf region had been washed away in the crystal-clear waters of the Una River and lay deep within the Golubnjača pit, as well as others. The grandfather of the local Serb communist Gojko Polovina told him long before the Second World War that bodies had been thrown into that vertical cave so that no one would know where the graves were of those 'killed without trial and outside the law'.[74] The communists found this use of the pit to be in their political interest after 1945. The local history of the war – when communists, who fought for a multi-ethnic socialist state, joined forces during the summer and autumn of 1941 with revenge-seeking Serb insurgents, many of whom were intent on slaughtering their Croat and Muslim neighbours, whom they saw collectively as 'Ustašas' – was politically indigestible after 1945. The absence of the corpses of Muslims meant that fewer questions could be asked about this dark history. And this allowed the memories of those bloody months, an accurate and public record of which would have been deeply threatening the post-war communist authorities, to be pushed more easily into the shadows.

What was paramount to the communists in the first decades following the war was not confronting the complex nature of the mass violence during war. Rather, their main task was to construct a heroic master narrative about that conflict as a titanic struggle of the partisans versus foreign fascist occupiers and their domestic collaborators. The reality of the intimate mass killing among neighbours, the traumatic experience of seeing the mutilated bodies of loved ones, of pulling relatives and neighbours out of pits full of corpses, of seeing decapitated heads of parents and children on the top of sticks, and the cascading cycle of revenge killings that these experiences provoked – all this deeply divisive and potentially destabilizing history had to be tightly guarded and, for the most part, silenced after the war.

The imposition of the heroic master narrative, with its portrayal of the conflict as a macro-level conflict among rival ideological camps, has affected how scholars have studied and interpreted the mass violence in Bosnia during the war. Until very recently, the tendency was to argue for a top-down causation for the mass killing. This approach has produced many valuable studies on the macro dimensions of the mass violence.[75] Yet this dominant top-down approach has obscured the local dimensions of the violence, and in particular the history of the intimate relationship between the corpse and the escalation of mass killing, the dynamics of which come into focus only at the micro level. This chapter has tried to excavate this concealed history by taking the local dynamics of killing, the treatment of corpses, and their effects on further instances of violence as the focus of analysis. A further methodological approach here has been to disaggregate the killing in a single community so that the dynamics of the local violence can be carefully seen over time, very slowly, massacre by massacre, reaction by reaction. These modes of analysis have made it possible to discern a local causal relationship between the methods of killing and the discovery of corpses and survivors, with the intensification of violence. Most of this violence does not appear to be very closely linked with any explicit overarching ideological agenda, such as the creation of an ethnically pure Croatian nation state, or the decisions of political elites. Rather, the initial Ustaša killings, which certainly could not have taken place without an elite committed to using mass violence to sculpt and mould the ethnic composition of the population, were nevertheless carried out by local residents who seem to have been primarily motivated by a desire to plunder their neighbours and to settle scores for past conflicts. In short, the main motivations of the foot soldiers committing the initial killings were not very similar to those of the political elites who empowered them to engage in violence. The main conclusion here, however, is that this locally executed violence then set off a complex dynamic of interconnected, cascading revenge killings, whose intensification cannot be adequately explained without taking close account of how individuals responded to the ever-growing presence in their communities of the mutilated corpses of their neighbours and relatives. This chapter argues for the need not merely to pay more attention to the dynamics of local violence, and how they often diverge from the central master cleavage of a given conflict, which is a subject that many scholars have recently called attention to.[76] Rather, we need to build on this important insight by paying more attention to a difficult-to-discern dynamic *within* the complex world of local violence: the relationship between the treatment of the corpse and the ebb and flow of revenge killings.

In the Kulen Vakuf region, the end result of the revenge-driven mass killings was the existence of a strange silence, whereby everyone knew that large numbers of Muslims and Croats had been murdered, as well as who had done the killing. Yet nearly everyone quickly learned how *not* to speak of these victims, because many of the perpetrators had become partisans during war, which made the history of the killings deeply threatening to the communist authorities after 1945. What greatly facilitated this silence was that the physical evidence of the violence – the corpses – had, for the most part, vanished. One local man succinctly summed up the atmosphere during the decades that followed the massacres simply as: 'It was as if nothing ever happened'.[77]

Notes

1. There was also a silence about the Croat civilian war victims in the region, which I briefly discuss here, but that is not the main subject of this chapter.
2. The key work here that has shaped the field in recent years is Stathis Kalyvas, *The Logic of Violence in Civil War* (New York: Cambridge University Press, 2006); for an illuminating discussion of some recent studies on local violence, which suggests a number of new questions for future research, see Evgeny Finkel, 'Mass killing and local context', *Comparative Politics*, 45:1 (October 2012), 107–24.
3. The ethnic structure of the region prior to the Second World War was approximately as follows: 5,600 Muslims, 8,600 Serb Orthodox, and 1,600 Croat Catholic. On these numbers, see Hamdija Kreševljaković, *Kulen Vakuf* (Sarajevo: Islamska dionička štamparija, 1935).
4. For examples of this violence, much of which local Muslims, under the command of land-holding elites (*begovi*), committed against Orthodox Serb peasants in the villages near Kulen Vakuf, see Sir Arthur J. Evans, *Illyrian Letters: A Revised Selection of Correspondence from the Illyrian Provinces of Bosnia, Herzegovina, Montenegro, Albania, Dalmatia, Croatia, and Slavonia, Addressed to the 'Manchester Guardian' During the Year 1877* (New York: Cosimo Classics, 2007 [1878]), pp. 39, 77–81, 85, 90–1; for examples of violence that Serb Orthodox rebels committed against local Muslims, see Esad Bibanović, *Stanovništvo Kulen Vakufa i okoline kroz istoriju* (unpublished manuscript, Sarajevo, 1980), pp. 92–5.
5. For a discussion of local politics in the region during the inter-war period, see Bibanović, *Stanovništvo Kulen Vakufa*, pp. 112–70.
6. On cordial relations between Serbs and Muslims during the weekly Thursday market, see Jovica Keča, 'Ustanički dani u okolini Kulen Vakufa', in *Bosanski Petrovac u NOB: Zbornik sjećanja. Knjiga IV* (Bosanski Petrovac: Opštinski odbor SUBNOR-a, 1974), pp. 199–200; on the ethnically mixed soccer teams in the region, see Bibanović, *Stanovništvo Kulen Vakufa*, pp. 128–9.
7. For an introduction to the history of the Independent State of Croatia, see Fikreta Jelić-Butić, *Ustaše i Nezavisna Država Hrvatska, 1941–1945* (Zagreb: Liber, 1977). The population of the NDH was approximately 6 million. Just over half were Croat Catholics. The rest included 1.9 million Orthodox Serbs, about 500,000 Muslims, 140,000 ethnic Germans, 70,000 Hungarians, 40,000 Jews, and 150,000 'others' (e.g. Roma). On these statistics, see Tomislav Dulić, *Utopias of Nation: Local Mass Killing in Bosnia and Herzegovina, 1941–1942* (Uppsala: Uppsala Universitet, 2005), p. 79.
8. On the numbers and names of local Ustašas in the region, as well as on some of their motivations for joining, see: Arhiv Jugoslavije (AJ), Fond 110, Državna komisija za utvrđivanje zločina okupatora i njihovih pomogača (DKUZ), kut. 817, Okružni sud Bihać, Pojedinačne optužnice i presude, 1946, dos. br. 817-320, Javno tužioštvo za Okrug

Bihać, Krivični predmet protiv Burzić Avde, 27 May 1946; ibid., dos. br. 817-376, Javno tužioštvo za Okrug Bihać, Krivični predmet protiv Kadić Bege, 23 September 1946; ibid., dos. br. 817-403, Javno tužioštvo za Okrug Bihać, Krivični predmet protiv Kozlice Agana, 12 October 1946; ibid., dos. br. 817-421, Javno tužioštvo za Okrug Bihać, Krivični predmet protiv Kulenović Mahmuta, 26 August 1946; ibid., dos. br. 817-469, Javno tužioštvo za Okrug Bihać, Krivični predmet protiv Pehlivanović Ibrahima, 30 May 1946; ibid., dos. br. 817-534, Javno tužioštvo za Okrug Bihać, Krivični predmet protiv Sušnjar-Vukalić Mujage, 15 October 1946; ibid., kut. 531, dos. broj. 5361, Zapisnik br. 14, Mjesni odbor: Vrtoče, 31 July 1946; ibid., Zapisnik br. 10, Mjesni odbor: Kalati, 5 August 1946; ibid., Zapisnik br. 20, Mjesni odbor: Rajinovci, 7 August 1946; ibid., Zapisnik br. 21, Mjesni odbor: Veliki Stjenjani, 8 August 1946; ibid., Zapisnik br. 22, Mjesni odbor: Kulen Vakuf, 9 August 1946; Arhiv Bosne i Hercegovine (ABiH), Fond Zemaljska komisija za utvrđivanje zločina okupatora i njihovih pomagača (ZKUZ BiH), kut. 91, Zapisnik br. 22, Mjesni odbor: Malo Očijevo, 9 August 1946; ibid., kut. 68, Srez Bosanski Petrovac, Zapisnik br. 18, Mjesni odbor: Prkosi, 4 August 1946; ibid., kut. 14, Srez Bihać, Zapisnik br. 21, Mjesni odbor: Veliki Stjenjani, 8 August 1946.

9   Bibanović, *Stanovništvo Kulen Vakufa*, p. 129.
10 It appears that the Ustašas did not seriously begin to pursue a policy of religious conversion until the autumn of 1941, once their more violent policies towards the Serb community had provoked a Serb insurgency that threatened the existence of the NDH. On the Ustaša policy of forced religious conversions, see Mark Biondich, 'Religion and nation in wartime Croatia: reflections on the Ustaša policy of forced religious conversions, 1941–1942', *Slavonic and East European Review*, 83:1 (January 2005), 71–116.
11 On the wider context that framed Ustaša decision making towards the Serb community in the NDH during the early summer of 1941, see Jozo Tomasevich, *War and Revolution in Yugoslavia, 1941–1945: Occupation and Collaboration* (Stanford: Stanford University Press, 2001), p. 395.
12 'Izvještaj Zapovjedništva bosanskog diviziskog područja od 10. srpnja o pripremama naroda za ustanak i raseljavanju srpskog stanovništva u Bosanskoj Krajini', Br. 235, in *Zbornik dokumenata i podataka o Narodnooslobodilačkom ratu jugoslovenskih naroda, tom IV, knjiga 1, Borbe u Bosni i Hercegovini 1941. god.* (Beograd: Vojno-istoriski institut Jugoslovenske Armije, 1951), pp. 523–4; on state-wide orders to set up offices for the resettlement of certain populations of the NDH, see 'Okružnica Državnog ravnateljstva za ponovu od 2. srpnja 1941. svim Kotarskim predstojništvima o osnivanju ureda za iseljavanje, njegovoj organizaciji i zadacima', Br. 93, in *Zločini na jugoslovenskim prostorima u Prvom i Drugom svetskom ratu. Zbornik dokumenata* (Beograd: Vojnoistorijski institut, 1993), pp. 183–8.
13 Milan Vukmanović, *Ustaški zločini na području Bihaća u ljeto 1941. godine* (Banja Luka: Institut za istoriju u Banjaluci, 1987).

14 For examples of inter-communal rescue during the summer of 1941, see Esad Bibanović, *Kulen Vakuf: Svjedočanstvo jednog vremena* (unpublished manuscript, Sarajevo, 2008), pp. 48–50; Bibanović, *Stanovništvo Kulen Vakufa*, pp. 120–4; Esad Bibanović, 'Kulenvakufski komunisti u radničkom pokretu i ustanku', in *Bihać u novijoj istoriji (1918-1945) Tom I* (Banja Luka: Institut za istoriju u Banjaluci, 1987), pp. 432–4; Abas Mušeta, *Kulen Vakuf. Tragedija od 10.04 do 06-18.09 1941: godina* (unpublished manuscript, 2004), p. 36.
15 Milan Obradović, 'Zločini na kotaru Donji Lapac od 1941. do 1945', in *Kotar Donji Lapac u Narodnooslobodilačkom ratu 1941-1945* (Karlovac: Historijski arhiv u Karlovcu, 1985), p. 833.
16 Ibid., p. 836.
17 'Desetodnevni izveštaj Stožer vrbaskog divizijskog područja od 8. srpnja 1941. o stanju na svojoj teritoriji i zločinima ustaša u selima Lički Osredci i Suvaja', Br. 103, in *Zločini na jugoslovenskim prostorima u Prvom i Drugom svetskom ratu. Zbornik dokumenata*, p. 217.
18 'Izvještaj Zapovjedništva prve hrvatske okružičke pukovnije od 16. kolovoza 1941. o zločinima ustaša i akcijama partizana u Kordunu', Br. 132, in *Zbornik dokumenata i podataka o Narodnooslobodilačkom ratu jugoslovenskih naroda, tom V, knjiga 1, Borbe u Hrvatskoj 1941. god.* (Beograd: Vojno-istoriski institut Jugoslovenske Armije, 1951), p. 343.
19 Rade Dubajić Čkaljac, 'Tragično djetinjstvo', in *Kotar Donji Lapac u Narodnooslobodilačkom ratu 1941-1945*, pp. 862–3.
20 Hrvatski Državni Arhiv (HDA), Fond 1450, Ministarstvo oružanih snaga Nezavisne Države Hrvatske (MINORS NDH), D-2229, 'Izvještaj o vanjskoj i unutarnjoj situaciji za treću deseticu', 19–29 July 1941, p. 1.
21 This approximate figure was arrived at by consulting the documents in note 8.
22 These villages and towns included: Oštrelj, Drvar, Rmanj Manastir (Martin Brod), and Grkovac. For an NDH report about these attacks, which included an urgent request for the deployment of reinforcements to crush the insurgency before it became any larger, see HDA, Fond 1450, MINORS NDH, D-2229, 'Vrhovno oružničko zapovjedništvo Zapovjedništvu kopnene vojske', 28 July 1941; see also ibid., 'Izvještaj o vanjskoj i unutarnjoj situaciji za treću deseticu', 20–31 July 1941, pp. 6–7; ibid., D-2121, 'Telefonska obavjest primljena', 27 July 1941, p. 1.
23 These villages included Doljani, Nebljusi, Palanka, and Drenovo Tijesno. See ibid., D-2121, 'Situacija, 30. srpnja 1941. godine prije podne, Bihać u 12.05 časova', 30 July 1941, p. 1.
24 On the origins of the Serb insurgency in the region, see: Jovo Reljić, 'Martin Brod 1941. godine', in *Drvar, 1941-1945: Sjećanja učesnika, knjiga 2* (Drvar: Skupština opštine Drvar, 1972), pp. 393–4; Nikola Karanović, 'Sadjejstvo sa ličkim ustanicima', in ibid., p. 410; Đoko Jovanić, *Ratna sjećanja* (Beograd: Vojnoizdavački i novinski centar, 1988), p. 119; Milan Majstorović, 'Kulen Vakuf opština u NOR-u', in *Bosanski Petrovac u NOB: Knjiga III* (Bosanski Petrovac: Opštinski odbor SUBNOR-a, 1974), p. 379; Keča, 'Ustanički dani u okolini

Kulen Vakufa', p. 201. On the weakness of the communists throughout Bosnia-Herzegovina in asserting control over the Serb insurgents during the first year of the war, which nearly caused the failure of their resistance movement, see Rasim Hurem, *Kriza Narodnooslobodilačkog pokreta u Bosni i Hercegovini krajem 1941. i početkom 1942. godine* (Sarajevo: Svjetlost, 1972), pp. 33–71.

25 For examples of the rapid emergence of this sensibility in the aftermath of the Ustaša mass killings in the Kulen Vakuf region during the summer of 1941, see Bibanović, *Kulen Vakuf*, pp. 54–5; Vukmanović, *Ustaški zločini na području Bihaća*, p. 130; Mara Kecman-Hodak, 'Sjećanje na Bušević, Kestenovac, Bosanske Štrpce i Kalate', in *Bosanski Petrovac u NOB: Zbornik sjećanja. Knjiga III* (Bosanski Petrovac: Opštinski odbor SUBNOR-a, 1974), pp. 199–200; Karanović, 'Sadjejstvo sa ličkim ustanicima', p. 410.

26 'Izveštaj Krilnog oružničkog zapovjedništva Gospić od 12. srpnja 1941. Zapovjedniku 1. hrvatske oružničke pukovnije o klanju, ubijanju, paljenju i pljački srpskog življa u selu Bubanj', Br. 123, *Zločini na jugoslovenskim prostorima u Prvom i Drugom svetskom ratu. Zbornik dokumenata*, pp. 319–21.

27 The Croatian villages included Boričevac, Brotnja, Vrtoče, and Krnjeuša. On these killings, see Dane Ivezić, 'Brotnja: ustanici istrijebili Iveziće', in Josip Pavičić (ed.), *Dossier Boričevac* (Zagreb: Naklada Pavičić, 2012), pp. 343–52; Josip Jurjević, *Pogrom u Krnjeuši 9. i 10. kolovoza 1941. godine* (Zagreb: Vikarijat Banjalučke biskupije, 1999); Ana Došen, *To je bilo onda* (Zagreb: A. Došen, self-published, 2006); Ana Došen, *Krnjeuša u srcu i sjećanju* (Opatija: Matica Hrvatska Ogranak Rijaka i Tvrtka SCH, 1994); Josip Pavičić (ed.), *Dossier Boričevac* (Zagreb: Naklada Pavičić, 2012); *Odmetnička zvjerstva i pustošenja u Nezavisnoj državi Hrvatskoj u prvim mjesecima života Hrvatske Narodne Države* (Zagreb: Ministarstvo vanjskih poslova NDH, 1942), p. 38.

28 Lazo Radošević, 'Vrtoče u ustanku', in *Bosanski Petrovac u NOB: Knjiga II* (Bosanski Petrovac: Opštinski odbor SUBNOR-a, 1974), p. 470.

29 Ivezić, 'Brotnja', pp. 343–52. For what appears to be only a partial list of the victims who are said to have been killed by 'pro-Chetnik elements' responding to the killings that local Ustašas (from the same village) committed earlier in July 1941, see 'Žrtve fašističkog terora i rata s područja kotara Donji Lapac 1941–1945', in *Kotar Donji Lapac u Narodnooslobodilačkom ratu 1941–1945* (Karlovac: Historijski arhiv u Karlovcu, 1985), pp. 1126–7.

30 HDA, Fond 1450, MINORS NDH, D-2232, 'Izvješće Aleksandra Seitza Poglavniku', 20 August 1941. See also *Odmetnička zvjerstva i pustošenja u Nezavisnoj državi Hrvatskoj u prvim mjesecima života Hrvatske Narodne Države*, pp. 38–42.

31 Lični arhiv Esada Bibanovića (LAEB), Lični fond Esada Bibanovića, Hamdija Kreševljaković, *Kulen Vakuf* (Sarajevo: Islamska dionička štamparija, 1935), p. 15.

32 On the notion that killing by cutting of throats, rather than shooting, places victims on the level of animals, see John Allcock, *Explaining*

Yugoslavia (New York: Columbia University Press, 2000); for a different interpretation, which stresses the lack of ammunition among Serb fighters as a possible reason for killing by cutting throats, see Dulić, *Utopias of Nation*, pp. 356-7.

33 On the notion of discriminate and indiscriminate violence, see Kalyvas, *The Logic of Violence in Civil War*.

34 HDA, Fond 1450, MINORS, D-2121, 'Izvještaj o selu Krnjeuša, 14.VIII.1941. u 20.50 sati', 14 August 1941; on reactions to the killings in Krnjeuša, see also ibid., 'Glavni stožer, Stanje 14. kolovoza', 14-15 August 1941, p. 1.

35 Ibid., D-2121, 'Glavni stožer, Stanje 14. kolovoza', 14-15 August 1941, p. 1.

36 Bibanović, *Kulen Vakuf*, p. 65; Bibanović, *Stanovništvo Kulen Vakufa*, p. 210.

37 Nikola Plećaš-Nitonja, *Požar u Krajini* (Chicago: Plećaš-Nitonja, self-published, 1975), pp. 78-9.

38 Pero Pilipović, 'Borba Cvjetnićana na petrovačkom području', in *Bosanski Petrovac u NOB: Zbornik sjećanja. Knjiga I* (Bosanski Petrovac: Opštinski odbor SUBNOR-a, 1974), p. 589.

39 Milan Štikavav, 'Krvavo lapačko ljeto', in *Ratna sjećanja iz NOB, knjiga II* (Beograd: Vojno-izdavački zavod, 1981), p. 616.

40 Milan Majstorović & Mićo Medić, *Prve iskre: Doljani u NOB* (Zagreb: Lykos, 1961), p. 41.

41 Danilo Damjanović-Danić, *Ustanak naroda Hrvatske 1941. u Srbu i okolini* (Zagreb: IP Progres, 1972), pp. 121-2; Sava Mileusnić, 'Donji Lapac u ustanku', in *Lika u NOB: Zbornik. Pišu učesnici* (Novi Sad: Budućnost, 1963), p. 390.

42 Majstorović & Medić, *Prve iskre*, p. 41.

43 Nikola Knežević, 'Cvjetnićani u akciji', in *Drvar, 1941-1945. Sjećanja učesnika, knjiga 2* (Drvar: Skupština opština Drvar, 1972), p. 457.

44 On how the local Serb insurgents better armed themselves after each of their attacks during July and August 1941, see Pilipović, 'Borba Cvjetnićana na petrovačkom području', p. 593.

45 On these killings, see 'Izvještaj Štaba partizanskih odreda u Brdu Oraškom drvarske brigade od 9. septembra 1941. god. o borbama za oslobođenje Kulen Vakufa', 9 September 1941, Br. 114, in *Zbornik dokumenata i podataka o Narodnooslobodilačkom ratu jugoslovenskih naroda, tom IV, knjiga 1, Borbe u Bosni i Hercegovini 1941. god.*, pp. 253-4; 'Komanda 3. Žandarmerijske pukovnije Banja Luka Vrhovnoj komandi Žandarmerije NDH Zagreb', 12 September 1941, in Vladimir Dedijer & Antun Miletić (eds), *Genocid nad Muslimanima, 1941-1945: zbornik dokumenata i svjedočenja* (Sarajevo: Svjetlost, 1990), p. 66.

46 Bibanović, *Kulen Vakuf*, pp. 95-6.

47 For the testimony of Bećo Šiljdedić, a man who survived these executions, see ibid., pp. 97-9.

48 Karanović, 'Sadjejstvo sa ličkim ustanicima', p. 413. On the exhumation of these bodies, and the reactions to them, see Dušan Lukač, *Ustanak u Bosanskoj Krajini* (Beograd: Vojno-izdavački zavod, 1967), pp. 191-2;

'Izvještaj Štaba gerilskih odreda za Liku koncem rujna 1941. god. Štabu drvarske brigade o vojno-političkoj situaciji', undated but appears to have been written on or about 15 September 1941, Br. 42, in *Zbornik dokumenata i podataka o Narodnooslobodilačkom ratu jugoslovenskih naroda, tom V, knjiga 1, Borbe u Hrvatskoj 1941. god*, p. 134.
49 Radošević, 'Vrtoče u ustanku', p. 472.
50 Jovanić, *Ratna sjećanja*, p. 128.
51 On this phase of the killings, see Bibanović, *Kulen Vakuf*, pp. 100 1; see also ABiH, Fond ZKUZ BiH, kut. 88, Svjedočenje Altića Aijše i Kadića Zejne, undated and handwritten document, most likely from the summer of 1946.
52 For the recollections of a woman who jumped into the water with her three children, of whom two quickly drowned, see the testimony of Hana Štrkljević in Bibanović, *Kulen Vakuf*, p. 101; see also, AJ, Fond 110, DKUZ, kut. 531, dos. br. 5361, Zapisnik br. 10, Mjesni odbor: Kalati, 5 August 1946, p. 7.
53 Derviš Kurtagić, *Zapisi o Kulen Vakufu* (Bihać: Derviš Kurtagić, self-published, 2005), p. 32; Mušeta, *Kulen Vakuf*, p. 48. It appears that there were instances in which insurgents took Muslim girls, particularly those from the families of former Muslim land-holders, and kept them prisoner for days while passing them around from insurgent to insurgent to be raped. On this subject, see Bibanović, *Stanovništvo Kulen Vakufa*, p. 290.
54 Bibanović, 'Kulenvakufski komunisti', p. 452; see also the testimony of Mujo Dervišević, who was among the prisoners when this order was given, in Bibanović, *Stanovništvo Kulen Vakufa*, p. 287.
55 Bibanović, *Kulen Vakuf*, p. 105.
56 Gojko Polovina, *Svedočenje. Prva godina ustanka u Lici* (Beograd: Izdavačka radna organizacija Rad, 1988), pp. 91–2.
57 For the testimony of the sole survivor, Mujo Dervišević, see Ibrahim Kajan, 'Pakao Vakuf Golubnjača', *Ogledalo*, 1:2 (December 1990), p. 27.
58 On instances of inter-communal rescue during the massacres of Muslims between 6 and 8 September 1941, see Abaz Mušeta, 'Tužan gledam kako moj Vakuf tiho gori i umire, više ne mogu ni plakati', in J. Pavičić, (ed.), *Dossier Boričevac* (Zagreb: Naklada Pavičić, 2012), p. 404; Ilija Rašeta, *Kazivanje pobjednika smrti* (Zagreb: Grafički zavod Hrvatske, 1988), pp. 173–80.
59 For communist reactions to the massacres of Muslims in and around Kulen Vakuf, see 'Izvještaj Štaba gerilskih odreda za Liku koncem rujna 1941. god. Štabu drvarske brigade o vojno-političkoj situaciji', Br. 42, undated but appears to have been written on or about 15 September 1941, in *Zbornik dokumenata i podataka o Narodnooslobodilačkom ratu jugoslovenskih naroda, tom V, knjiga 1, Borbe u Hrvatskoj 1941. god.*, p. 134; 'Izvještaj Štaba partizanskih odreda u Brdu Oraškom drvarske brigade od 9. septembra 1941. god. o borbama za oslobođenje Kulen Vakufa', 9 September 1941, Br. 114, in *Zbornik dokumenata i podataka o Narodnooslobodilačkom ratu jugoslovenskih naroda, tom IV, knjiga 1, Borbe i Bosni i Hercegovini 1941. god.*, pp. 253–4; 'Naređenje

Štaba prvog bataljana "Sloboda" od 8. septembra 1941. god. Komandama četvrog odreda u Boboljuskama, Velikom i Malom Cvjetniću i Osredcima za raspored snaga', 8 September 1941, Br. 106, in *Zbornik dokumenata i podataka o Narodnooslobodilačkom ratu jugoslovenskih naroda, tom IV, knjiga 1, Borbe u Bosni i Hercegovini 1941. god.*, p. 237.

60 See, for example, HDA, Fond 1194, Zbirka dokumenata NOR i Partizanskih odreda Jugoslavije, kut. 22, 'Štab gerilskih odreda za Srez Korenicu i okolinu Operativnim oficirima na položaju', 23 September 1941.

61 Ibid., Marko Orešković Krntija, 'Uloga i zadaci partizanskih odreda', undated document but appears to have been written at the end of August 1941, p. 7.

62 On this political work by the communists, see Hurem, *Kriza Narodnooslobodilačkog pokreta*, p. 95; Lukač, *Ustanak u Bosanskoj Krajini*, p. 307.

63 These two were Mane Rokvić and Petar 'Pero' Đilas. On Rokvić, see ABiH, Fond ZKUZ BiH, kut. 91, Zapisnik br. 22, Mjesni odbor: Malo Očijevo, 9 August 1946, p. 2; ibid., kut. 68, Srez Bosanski Petrovac, Zapisnik br. 18, Mjesni odbor: Prkosi, 4 August 1946, p. 3. On Đilas, see Reljić, 'Martin Brod 1941', pp. 404–5; Polovina, *Svedočenje*, pp. 92–3; Pero Pilipović, 'Istina o jednom zločinu', in *Bosanski Petrovac u NOB. Zbornik sjećanja. Knjiga II* (Bosanski Petrovac: Opštinski odbor SUBNOR-a, 1974), p. 605; 'Izvještaj Štaba gerilskih odreda za Liku koncem rujna 1941. god. Štabu drvarske brigade o vojno-političkoj situaciji', undated but appears to have been written on or about 15 September 1941, Br. 42, in *Zbornik dokumenata i podataka o Narodnooslobodilačkom ratu jugoslovenskih naroda, tom V, knjiga 1, Borbe u Hrvatskoj 1941. god.*, p. 134. On the history of the Chetniks in the region more generally during the Second World War, see Simo Lukić, 'Četnici u kotaru Donji Lapac od 1941. do 1945', in *Kotar Donji Lapac u Narodnooslobodilačkom ratu 1941–1945* (Karlovac: Historijski arhiv u Karlovcu, 1985), pp. 865–8.

64 Bibanović, *Stanovništvo Kulen Vakufa*, pp. 331–2.

65 For another example of the settling of scores that went on during the partisan takeover of Bihać in 1942, when some local Serbs from the Kulen Vakuf region sought out former Muslim neighbours whom they believed had been Ustašas, see Kurtagić, *Zapisi o Kulen Vakufu*, p. 37.

66 For examples of Serbs who were absorbed into the partisans after having participated in the massacres of Muslims, see ibid., p. 32; see also the testimony of Mujo Derviševića in Kajan, 'Pakao Vakuf Golubnjača', p. 27.

67 On the notion of silence as a form of communication, and how it often becomes dominant in the aftermath of traumatic events when no social and political framework exists to support alternative modes of expression, see Ruth Wajnryb, *The Silence: How Tragedy Shapes Talk* (Crows Nest: Allen & Unwin, 2001), p. 96.

68 Interviews with: Derviš Kurtagić, 9 November 2006, in Kulen Vakuf; Sead Kadić, 3 November 2008, in Bihać; Derviš Derviševič, 1 and 5 October 2008, in Klisa; Maho Vazović, 24 September 2008, in Kulen Vakuf; Ale Galijašević, 12 October 2008, in Kulen Vakuf.

A Bosnian community 41

69 Two such individuals were Jovo Reljić and Nikola Karanović, both of whom were said to have made attempts to save Muslims during the killings in and around Kulen Vakuf. For basic biographical information on Reljić, see Arhiv Unsko-sanskog Kantona (AUSK), Fond Sreski komitet (SK) Saveza komunista (SK) Bosne i Hercegovine (BiH), Bihać, kut. 172, biografski podaci, Jovo Reljić, 14 February 1959, p. 2; on his apparent attempts to oppose the killings of Muslims, see Damjanović-Danić, *Ustanak naroda Hrvatske 1941 u Srbu i okolini*, pp. 195–7; for basic information on Karanović, see 'Likovi boraca iz revolucije: Nikola Karanović', *Krajina: list Saveza socijalističkog radnog naroda bihaćkog sreza*, 1 June 1961, p. 5.
70 Interview with Adem Derviševič, 6 October 2008, in Klisa. The drinking of alcohol was not uncommon among some Muslims in Bosnia-Herzegovina, particularly those who were not religiously observant.
71 Interview with Sead Kadić, 3 November 2008, in Bihać.
72 Interview with anonymous informant, 24 September 2008 (location withheld).
73 For a more extensive analysis of the post-war silence in the Kulen Vakuf region about Muslim civilians massacred by Serb insurgents in 1941, see Max Bergholz, 'The strange silence: explaining the absence of monuments for Muslim civilians killed in Bosnia during the Second World War', *East European Politics and Societies*, 24:3 (summer 2010), 408–34.
74 Polovina, *Svedočenje*, pp. 91–2.
75 See, for example, Jelić-Butić, *Ustaše i Nezavisna Država Hrvatska, 1941–1945*; Tomasevich, *War and Revolution in Yugoslavia, 1941–1945*; see also Dulić, *Utopias of Nation*, which is a newer study that purports to study local mass killing in Bosnia during 1941–42, but nonetheless ends up portraying the violence in various regions as essentially the result of the decisions of nationalist political elites. The locality is portrayed here as impacted from the outside, rather than a place whose own dynamics of history and violence, even if shaped in significant ways by outsiders, are worthy of being the central analytical focus.
76 See Kalyvas, *The Logic of Violence in Civil War*.
77 Interview with Adem Derviševič, 6 October 2008, in Klisa.

Bibliography

Archives

Arhiv Bosne i Hercegovine (ABiH) [Archive of Bosnia-Herzegovina], Sarajevo: Fond Zemaljske komisije za utvrđivanje zločina okupatora i njihovih pomagača (ZKUZ BiH) [Commission for Determining the Crimes of the Occupiers and Their Collaborators of Bosnia-Herzegovina]

Arhiv Jugoslavije (AJ) [Archive of Yugoslavia], Belgrade: Fond 110, Državna komisija za utvrđivanje zločina okupatora i njihovih pomogača (DKUZ) [State Commission for Determining the Crimes of the Occupiers and Their Collaborators]

Arhiv Unsko-sanskog kantona (AUSK) [Archive of the Una-Sana Canton], Bihać: Fond Sreskog komiteta (SK) Saveza komunista (SK) Bosne i Hercegovine (BiH), Bihać [League of Communists of Bosnia and Herzegovina for the Bihać Region]

Hrvatski Državni Arhiv (HDA) [Croatian State Archive], Zagreb: Fond 1450, Ministarstvo oružanih snaga Nezavisne Države Hrvatske (MINORS NDH) [Ministry of the Armed Forces of the Independent State of Croatia]; Fond 1194, Zbirka dokumenata NOR i Partizanskih odreda Jugoslavije [collection of documents from the People's Liberation War and Partisan Units of Yugoslavia]

Lični arhiv Esada Bibanovića (LAEB) [personal archive of Esad Bibanović], Sarajevo: Lični fond Esada Bibanovića [personal collection of Esad Bibanović]

Interviews

Anonymous informant, 24 September 2008 (location withheld)
Adem Dervišević, 6 October 2008, in Klisa
Derviš Dervišević, 1 and 5 October 2008, in Klisa
Ale Galijašević, 12 October 2008, in Kulen Vakuf
Sead Kadić, 3 November 2008, in Bihać
Derviš Kurtagić, 9 November 2006, in Kulen Vakuf
Maho Vazović, 24 September 2008, in Kulen Vakuf

Newspapers

Krajina: list Saveza socijalističkog radnog naroda bihaćkog sreza

Memoirs, unpublished manuscripts, books, chapters, and articles

Allcock, J., *Explaining Yugoslavia* (New York: Columbia University Press, 2000)

Bergholz, M., 'The strange silence: explaining the absence of monuments for Muslim civilians killed in Bosnia during the Second World War', *East European Politics and Societies*, 24:3 (summer 2010), 408–34

Bibanović, E., *Kulen Vakuf: Svjedočanstvo jednog vremena* (unpublished manuscript, Sarajevo, 2008)

Bibanović, E., 'Kulenvakufski komunisti u radničkom pokretu i ustanku', in *Bihać u novijoj istoriji (1918–1945) Tom I* (Banjaluka: Institut za istoriju u Banjaluci, 1987), pp. 432–4

Bibanović, E., *Stanovništvo Kulen Vakufa i okoline kroz istoriju* (unpublished manuscript, Sarajevo, 1980)

Biondich, M., 'Religion and nation in wartime Croatia: reflections on the Ustaša policy of forced religious conversions, 1941–1942', *Slavonic and East European Review*, 83:1 (January 2005), 71–116

Damjanović-Danić, D., *Ustanak naroda Hrvatske 1941. u Srbu i okolini* (Zagreb: IP Progres, 1972)

Dedijer, V. & A. Miletić (eds), *Genocid nad Muslimanima, 1941–1945: zbornik dokumenata i svjedočenja* (Sarajevo: Svjetlost, 1990)

Došen, A., *Krnjeuša u srcu i sjećanju* (Opatija: Matica Hrvatska Ogranak Rijaka i Tvrtka 'SCH', 1994)

Došen, A., *To je bilo onda* (Zagreb: Došen, self-published, 2006)

Dubajić Čkaljac, R., 'Tragično djetinjstvo', in *Kotar Donji Lapac u Narodnooslobodilačkom ratu 1941–1945* (Karlovac: Historijski arhiv u Karlovcu, 1985), pp. 862–3

Dulić, T., *Utopias of Nation: Local Mass Killing in Bosnia and Herzegovina, 1941–1942* (Uppsala: Uppsala Universitet, 2005)

Evans, Sir A. J., *Illyrian Letters: A Revised Selection of Correspondence from the Illyrian Provinces of Bosnia, Herzegovina, Montenegro, Albania, Dalmatia, Croatia, and Slavonia, Addressed to the 'Manchester Guardian' During the Year 1877* (New York: Cosimo Classics, 2007 [1878])

Finkel, E., 'Mass killing and local context', *Comparative Politics*, 45:1 (October 2012), 107–24.

Hurem, R., *Kriza Narodnooslobodilačkog pokreta u Bosni i Hercegovini krajem 1941. i početkom 1942. godine* (Sarajevo: Svjetlost, 1972)

Ivezić, D., 'Brotnja: ustanici istrijebili Ivezića', in J. Pavičić (ed.), *Dossier Boričevac* (Zagreb: Naklada Pavičić, 2012), pp. 343–6

Jelić-Butić, F., *Ustaše i Nezavisna Država Hrvatska, 1941–1945* (Zagreb: Liber, 1977)

Jovanić, Đ., *Ratna sjećanja* (Beograd: Vojnoizdavački i novinski centar, 1988)

Jurjević, J., *Pogrom u Krnjeuši 9. i 10. kolovoza 1941. godine* (Zagreb: Vikarijat Banjalučke biskupije, 1999)

Kajan, I., 'Pakao Vakuf Golubnjača', *Ogledalo*, 1:2 (December 1990), 27

Kalyvas, S., *The Logic of Violence in Civil War* (New York: Cambridge University Press, 2006)

Karanović, N., 'Sadjejstvo sa ličkim ustanicima', in *Drvar, 1941–1945: Sjećanja učesnika, knjiga 2* (Drvar, Skupština opštine Drvar, 1972), pp. 407–14

Keča, J., 'Ustanički dani u okolini Kulen Vakufa', in *Bosanski Petrovac u NOB: Zbornik sjećanja. Knjiga IV* (Bosanski Petrovac: Opštinski odbor SUBNOR-a, 1974), pp. 199–201

Kecman-Hodak, M., 'Sjećanje na Bušević, Kestenovac, Bosanske Štrpce i Kalate', in *Bosanski Petrovac u NOB: Zbornik sjećanja. Knjiga III* (Bosanski Petrovac: Opštinski odbor SUBNOR-a, 1974), pp. 199–200

Knežević, N., 'Cvjetnićani u akciji', in *Drvar, 1941–1945: Sjećanja učesnika, knjiga 2* (Drvar: Skupština opština Drvar, 1972), p. 457

Kreševljaković, H., *Kulen Vakuf* (Sarajevo: Islamska dionička štamparija, 1935)
Kurtagić, D., *Zapisi o Kulen Vakufu* (Bihać: Kurtagić, self-published, 2005)
Lukač, D., *Ustanak u Bosanskoj Krajini* (Beograd: Vojno-izdavački zavod, 1967)
Lukić, S., 'Četnici u kotaru Donji Lapac od 1941. do 1945', in *Kotar Donji Lapac u Narodnooslobodilačkom ratu 1941-1945* (Karlovac: Historijski arhiv u Karlovcu, 1985), pp. 865-88
Majstorović, M., 'Kulen Vakuf opština u NOR-u', in *Bosanski Petrovac u NOB: Knjiga III*. (Bosanski Petrovac: Opštinski odbor SUBNOR-a, 1974), pp. 374-80
Majstorović, M. & Medić, M., *Prve iskre: Doljani u NOB* (Zagreb: Lykos, 1961)
Mileusnić, S., 'Donji Lapac u ustanku', in *Lika u NOB: Zbornik. Pišu učesnici* (Novi Sad: Budućnost, 1963)
Mušeta, A., *Kulen Vakuf. Tragedija od 10.04 do 06-18.09 1941: godina* (unpublished manuscript, 2004)
Mušeta, A., 'Tužan gledam kako moj Vakuf tiho gori i umire, više ne mogu ni plakati', in J. Pavičić (ed.), *Dossier Boričevac* (Zagreb: Naklada Pavičić, 2012), p. 404
Obradović, M., 'Zločini na kotaru Donji Lapac od 1941. do 1945', in *Kotar Donji Lapac u Narodnooslobodilačkom ratu 1941-1945* (Karlovac: Historijski arhiv u Karlovcu, 1985), pp. 821-47
Odmetnička zvjerstva i pustošenja u Nezavisnoj državi Hrvatskoj u prvim mjesecima života Hrvatske Narodne Države (Zagreb: Ministarstvo vanjskih poslova NDH, 1942)
Pavičić, J. (ed.), *Dossier Boričevac* (Zagreb: Naklada Pavičić, 2012)
Pilipović, P., 'Borba Cvjetnićana na petrovačkom području', in *Bosanski Petrovac u NOB: Zbornik sjećanja. Knjiga I* (Bosanski Petrovac: Opštinski odbor SUBNOR-a, 1974), pp. 585-602
Pilipović, P., 'Istina o jednom zločinu', in *Bosanski Petrovac u NOB. Zbornik sjećanja. Knjiga II* (Bosanski Petrovac: Opštinski odbor SUBNOR-a, 1974), pp. 603-5
Plećaš-Nitonja, N., *Požar u Krajini* (Chicago: Plećaš-Nitonja, self-published, 1975)
Polovina, G., *Svedočenje. Prva godina ustanka u Lici* (Beograd: Izdavačka radna organizacija Rad, 1988)
Radošević, L., 'Vrtoče u ustanku', in *Bosanski Petrovac u NOB: Knjiga II* (Bosanski Petrovac: Opštinski odbor SUBNOR-a, 1974), p. 470
Rašeta, I., *Kazivanje pobjednika smrti* (Zagreb: Grafički zavod Hrvatske, 1988)
Reljić, J., 'Martin Brod 1941. godine', in *Drvar, 1941-1945: Sjećanja učesnika, knjiga 2* (Drvar: Skupština opštine Drvar, 1972), pp. 389-406
Štikavav, M., 'Krvavo lapačko ljeto', in *Ratna sjećanja iz NOB, knjiga II* (Beograd: Vojno-izdavački zavod, 1981), p. 616
Tomasevich, J., *War and Revolution in Yugoslavia, 1941-1945: Occupation and Collaboration* (Stanford: Stanford University Press, 2001)

Vukmanović, M., *Ustaški zločini na području Bihaća u ljeto 1941: godine* (Banja Luka: Institut za istoriju u Banjaluci, 1987)
Wajnryb, R., *The Silence: How Tragedy Shapes Talk* (Crows Nest: Allen & Unwin, 2001)
Zbornik dokumenata i podataka o Narodnooslobodilačkom ratu jugoslovenskih naroda, tom IV, knjiga 1, Borbe u Bosni i Hercegovini 1941. god. (Beograd: Vojno-istoriski institut Jugoslovenske Armije, 1951)
Zbornik dokumenata i podataka o Narodnooslobodilačkom ratu jugoslovenskih naroda, tom V, knjiga 1, Borbe u Hrvatskoj 1941. god. (Beograd: Vojno-istoriski institut Jugoslovenske Armije, 1951)
Zločini na jugoslovenskim prostorima u Prvom i Drugom svetskom ratu. Zbornik dokumenata (Beograd: Vojnoistorijski institut, 1993)
'Žrtve fašističkog terora i rata s područja kotare Donji Lapac 1941–1945', in *Kotar Donji Lapac u Narodnooslobodilačkom ratu 1941–1945* (Karlovac: Historijski arhiv u Karlovcu, 1985), pp. 1126–7

2

A specialist: the daily work of Erich Muhsfeldt, chief of the crematorium at Majdanek concentration and extermination camp, 1942–44[1]

Elissa Mailänder

In the context of the invasion of the Soviet Union, due to begin on 22 June 1941, Heinrich Himmler, visiting Lublin on 20 June that year, ordered a camp to be built in this Polish city situated in the south-east of occupied Poland, the so-called Generalgouvernement. Officially run as the 'Lublin Waffen-SS prisoner of war camp', the camp – which the prisoners named after the Lublin suburb of Majdan Tatarski – was nevertheless revealed after inspection to be a concentration camp,[2] although, for as long as it existed, from 1941 to 1944, it fulfilled many different functions. It served as a prisoner of war camp for Soviet soldiers (1941–44), as a labour camp primarily for Jewish, but also for Polish, prisoners (1941–42), as a hostage and internment camp for the Polish and Soviet rural population, and as a concentration camp principally for Polish political prisoners (1942–44). In October 1942 a women's camp was set up within the men's camp, for Polish and Jewish women, where Jewish infants were also occasionally held. The Jewish prisoners – women, men, and children – were systematically murdered, since Majdanek was, between June 1942 and November 1943, one of the extermination camps for European Jews from all over Europe.

The history of the camp is directly linked with the National Socialist policy of occupation and extermination in occupied Poland, as well as with the course of the war on the Eastern Front. Majdanek was a place of political and racist persecution and forced labour, and, at the same time, it was a place of systematic extermination.³ The Polish historian Tomasz Kranz coined the phrase 'multifunctional provisional arrangement'⁴ to describe Majdanek, as its multifunctionality and improvisational character make it difficult to compare with other concentration camps. The nearest parallel is Auschwitz, which was also a concentration camp and extermination camp combined. I follow the French historian and sociologist Jacques Sémelin, and I make use of his social science oriented concept of 'destruction'.⁵ Destruction is a broader and less normative concept than the judicial concepts of 'murder' and 'genocide', and it may be the result of any method of killing, whether it involves fire, water, gas, hunger, or cold, or whether direct and fast or stealthy and slow.⁶ This concept is useful in examining the mass murder that took place at Majdanek concentration and extermination camp since it can be used to analyse the systematic murder of European Jews as well as the mass extermination of prisoners of different nationalities. This makes it possible to see how concentration camp violence went hand in hand with genocidal violence.

The SS killed the prisoners in Majdanek and destroyed their bodies in many different ways. Because of poor material provision and poor maintenance of the camp's infrastructure by the SS, epidemics were rife and killed thousands of prisoners. Instead of resolving the problem and providing better living conditions, the SS killed prisoners who were, or were suspected of being, ill. They were killed, or 'injected' (*abgespritzt*) as it was called in SS language, in the medical section with carbolic acid or petrol injections. Larger groups were shot in a nearby forest area. The systematic murder of Jewish prisoners began in June 1942, and the murdering did not only take place in the gas chambers. Most were killed in mass shootings, the last of these being the massacre of 3 November 1943, the so-called Aktion Erntefest (Operation Harvest Festival), in which 18,000 Jews were murdered.⁷ The genocide of the European Jews was carried out as 'Geheime Reichssache' (secret Reich business). The SS were scrupulous in ensuring that virtually no administrative evidence of it was produced and that even less was left.

According to Thomas Kranz, because of limited source material, the exact number of fatalities at Majdanek can no longer be established. Today the research assumes that between summer 1941 and summer 1944, some 78,000 people lost their lives at Majdanek, of whom 59,000 were of Jewish origin.⁸ The analysis of occupancy at the camp showed that, in comparison with Auschwitz, the SS committed a relatively high percentage of Jewish prisoners to the camp (i.e. let them live at the selections). According to Kranz, over 60 per cent of those who died did not die in the gas chambers but rather because of extremely poor supplies and living conditions, malnutrition, forced labour, illness, or violent treatment by camp staff.[9] In this sense, it was not only the camp commanders who bore considerable responsibility for the lethal living conditions: it was also the female supervisors and SS men who, in the way they conducted themselves in their daily duties, controlled and decided the lives and deaths of the prisoners.

It is precisely this daily work, with its protagonists and social dynamics, that deserves our attention in all its complexity and presumed normalcy, for it points us towards the social practices of concentration camp supervisory staff, the ambiguity of their actions, and the production and organization of social norms. For this purpose, an everyday historical approach is useful because it no longer focuses on the elites,[10] but rather on the everyday work of 'normal' perpetrators in terms of a history of experience. In our case this group is the subordinate SS staff[11] of the Majdanek concentration and extermination camp. To ask questions about daily realities and daily practices has the 'controversial consequence', to quote Alf Lüdtke, 'that not only the people in "high command" become visible as historical agents'.[12]

Taking a closer look at daily work at the camp reveals how closely work and extermination were bound, for violence on a massive scale does not imply the suspension of the everyday; rather, in the daily practice of violence, and even in exceptional circumstances – at the workplace of the concentration camp – a particular kind of banality emerges, and this should be explored and scrutinized. My thesis is that the enormous scale of violence and extermination at the Majdanek concentration and extermination camp cannot solely be explained by the National Socialist policy of persecution and extermination, or the 'institution' of the concentration camp. The SS men and women's actual modes of behaviour on site, and the emotional background to these, are also determining factors. As we will see, in the context of daily work, material interests, and individual states of mind or needs are interwoven with the National Socialist policy of persecution and extermination.

In this chapter I analyse the working practices at Majdanek, using statements made in court during the Krakow Auschwitz trial (1946–47) by Erich Muhsfeldt (also spelt Muβfeldt), the chief of the crematorium at Majdanek, as well as statements made by his

Erich Muhsfeldt, chief of the crematorium   49

deputy, Robert Seitz, as part of the investigations for the Düsseldorf Majdanek trial.[13] Even though the judicial statements of former SS staff are in many respects problematic (the discourse of exculpation, refusing to speak about acts of violence, extenuation, etc.), they are nonetheless very useful for a study focused on everyday history. The depositions that have been recorded enable the historian to semantically analyse the former SS staff members' argumentation and their justification of their actions. If we examine their statements in their cultural, social, and historical context we can reconstruct the SS men's internal logic and value system from statements made during their interrogations. Ultimately, we are also able to analyse the social dimension of their actions. By linking historical setting and ethnological analysis we should gain an insight into the way of life and the practice of violence at Majdanek.

The assignment

Extermination was carried out as a professional work process that entailed many different steps and that actively involved a multitude of agents, male and female. The prisoners had to be selected, some of them bathed and stripped of all their valuables, supervised, and eventually killed. Finally, the corpses were transported off site and – again via several procedures – removed.[14] Whereas the processes of killing and the cremation work at Auschwitz have been thoroughly researched by Robert Jan van Pelt,[15] there has been no such study of Majdanek.

As in Auschwitz, the 'removal' of corpses was an important job within the extermination process at Majdanek. First, it had to be carried out as efficiently as possible, for reasons of hygiene and the threat of epidemics, and, second, this work had political significance, for it was, of course, about removing evidence of mass murder. The job was done by special squads in Majdanek, as in Auschwitz. Jewish and Soviet prisoners worked under the command of prisoners who were 'citizens of the Reich' (*Reichsdeutsche*) and under the strict supervision of SS staff. The two men who led this squad were the chief of the crematorium, Senior Squad Leader Erich Muhsfeldt, and his deputy, Junior Squad Leader Robert Seitz.

Muhsfeldt was born in Brandenburg in 1913, and he was a qualified baker in terms of his civilian profession. He joined the SA in 1933, and in 1939 he became a member of the Nationalist Socialist Party. In 1940 he switched to the SS, where he first completed a short training course in Sachsenhausen and was then transferred to the main camp at Auschwitz in August of the same year.[16] At first, he led various prisoner work squads there, and soon he became a block commander (*Blockführer*).

According to his own statements, Junior Squad Leader (*Unterscharführer*) Muhsfeldt was moved to Majdanek on 15 November 1941, where he again worked as a commander of a block. He recounts that a few months after his arrival, in the summer of 1942, the then camp commander, Karl-Otto Koch, transferred to him the so-called 'funeral squad'. He stated that he took on this job reluctantly.[17] To provide him with assistance, Muhsfeldt was given Junior Squad Leader Robert Seitz as his deputy. Seitz was born in 1911 in Liedolsheim and transferred to Majdanek in late 1941 or early 1942.

Initiation into extermination 'work' and further professionalization

According to Muhsfeldt's statements, between November 1941 and June 1942 the corpses were hastily buried in mass graves on a plot of land behind the area where Field V was later constructed. Due to the high mortality rates in the camp, the mass graves were constantly expanded.[18] Seitz, too, indicated in his interrogation that the corpses were 'buried'[19] in the beginning. 'For the transport and burial of the corpses there was a special squad consisting of Polish Jewish prisoners of war',[20] Muhsfeldt explained at the 1947 Krakow Auschwitz trial. But this method was uneconomical and too time-consuming in the long run, since corpses had to be transported to the graves in trucks.

In June 1942 the first crematorium, made by the Kori company in Berlin, was built between Fields I and II, diagonally opposite the bathing barracks which later became the gas chambers. This crematorium was known in the camp as the 'old crematorium'. The Kori company was a rival of the renowned firm Topf & Söhne, based in Erfurt, which supplied material to Auschwitz and other camps. Both companies specialized in heating systems, delousing equipment, and combustion furnaces for incineration and waste.[21]

Because both furnaces at the Majdanek crematorium came from the Sachsenhausen camp, the camp command sent Muhsfeldt there to be trained in incineration before the Majdanek crematorium was put into operation. He spent a week with the squad leader of

Erich Muhsfeldt, chief of the crematorium 51

the crematorium there, Chief Squad Leader (*Hauptscharführer*) Klein, learning how to operate the furnaces. According to his own statements, Muhsfeldt performed this duty unwillingly:

> But I didn't like the work. This is why, after I returned to Lublin and had to show Kommandant Koch how I operated the furnaces, I started a fire, where the roof of the barrack where the two furnaces were housed burned down.[22]

We have no way of knowing today whether he really felt this way. His immediate reluctance, however, was dispelled. Because this crematorium work was of national-political importance, and probably also in order to motivate Muhsfeldt, he was immediately promoted on 1 September 1942 to SS Squad Leader (*Scharführer*).[23]

As Seitz explained in his interrogation, at the time of the implementation of the 'funeral squad' it was assigned a new team, which means that the previous prisoner crew had been killed.[24] At the Krakow Auschwitz trial Muhsfeldt gave a detailed description of how the crematorium was operated:

> It consisted of two iron furnaces which held fire clay bricks inside. Each furnace functioned independently, had its own chimney and was heated with oil.... Each crematorium furnace had only one combustion chamber. 2–5 corpses could fit into a combustion chamber like this. Around 100 corpses could be burned in each furnace every day if they were in constant operation for 24 hours.... The first crematorium was in operation up to the end of October 1942. From June 1942 until October 1942 I always led the work in the crematorium, and so I can say that during this period around 5,000 corpses were burned in the crematorium.[25]

Any remains of corpses were ground up in the so-called 'bone mills' and scattered in the surrounding woods or used as fertilizer in the nursery at the Fellin storage facility. Magnificent cabbages thrived there, and this remained a vivid memory for all the camp's survivors.[26]

It must be noted here that the cremation that took place in Majdanek, as in all other concentration and extermination camps, was not 'professional' in terms of civil cremation standards for the time. Unlike in civil cremation, where only one corpse is burned sequentially per oven, so that the ashes can be attributed to this person, the SS burned several corpses at once in one furnace chamber, meaning that the ash could not be attributed unequivocally to any one person. The ash and other remains of the burned corpses were mixed together in metal containers under the grills. 'If sometimes Germans from the Reich requested the ashes of their dead relatives, they were just given something from the large mound',[27] explained the Polish prisoner and former 'Clerk of the Dead' Julian Gregorowicz before the Düsseldorf regional court.

The first crematorium in Majdanek was powered by oil, and because there was soon a shortage of oil the SS stopped operating the combustion furnaces as early as November 1942.[28] According to Muhsfeldt's statements, the crematorium team then returned to the old method, of burying the corpses.[29] If we believe the chief of the crematorium's estimates, his squad buried around 2,000 corpses in the Krepiecki forest between November 1942 and January 1943. The corpses were taken into the forest by the SS men in trucks. Again, the crematorium replaced its prisoner team: 'I was assigned 20 French and German Jews', Muhsfeldt explained to the Krakow court. 'Apart from these 20 Jews, I also had 3 Russian prisoners of war and a German overseer working in my squad.'[30]

Yet the mass graves could be only a temporary solution. On 19 February 1943 Muhsfeldt was sent for further training: this time he was to learn how to burn corpses in open pits at Auschwitz, that is, at Birkenau. We will see in the next section how this was a technique he was to develop and perfect.

Muhsfeldt travelled to Auschwitz together with the SS medic and future manager of the Majdanek gas chamber Anton Endreß (also spelt Entress), who was sent to view the delousing institute and to familiarize himself with the killing of people by gas. At Auschwitz Muhsfeldt reported to Camp Commandant Höss, who referred him to the Protective Custody Camp Leader (*Schutzhaftlagerführer*) Hans Aumeier.[31] 'Aumeier showed me the site plan of a corpse-burning pit, explained the map to me and added that corpses burned excellently in the open pit',[32] Muhsfeldt recalled in Krakow. In the end, the Protective Custody Camp Leader sent Endreß and Muhsfeldt to Maximilian Grabner, the chief of the political division. He placed a subordinate SS man, Bogner, at the disposal of the two delegates from Majdanek, who took them to the open pits where the corpses of people who had been gassed were burned.[33]

> There, the squad leader who was in charge of the work explained to us the process of gassing and the burning of the corpses. The corpses were burned right there in the pit, and the gas chamber was empty. It was a walled building, a farmhouse that had been converted into a gas chamber.[34]

Auschwitz started operating its first crematorium from the firm Topf & Söhne, with a performance rate of more than 100 corpses a day, as early as summer 1940, and was well ahead of Majdanek, with many more years of cremation experience.³⁵ As Robert van Pelt has so powerfully portrayed, as the mass killings and mortality rates at Auschwitz increased, the incineration facilities were gradually extended, and already by autumn 1941 they had reached a throughput of up to 1,440 corpses every day. In the course of the mass extermination of the Jews with gas, it was decided as early as February 1942 that a new, large crematorium should be set up at Birkenau. The farmhouse that Muhsfeldt describes in his interrogation was converted according to the most modern standards and was, like all the crematoria in Auschwitz, both gas chamber and incineration facility in one. In the late winter of 1943, when Muhsfeldt came for his training at Auschwitz-Birkenau, it was serving mainly as a crematorium. At this time the killings had reached an average of 800 every day, and the bodies were disposed of in four crematoria altogether. Yet it seems they could barely cope with the corpses, which meant that open incineration pits had to be used concomitantly.

The day after the short, intensive period of training at Auschwitz, Endreβ, and Muhsfeldt returned to Lublin and started their work straightaway. Endreβ took on the management of the gas chamber, while Muhsfeldt and his team, on the orders of the new commandant, Hermann Florstedt, had to exhume the corpses in the Krepiecki forest, dig up the graves on the edge of Field V, and then burn the remains on funeral pyres.³⁶ This massive exhumation operation, which went under the code name Special Operation 1005, involved the cremation of all the Jews in the General Government for the Occupied Polish Territories and Soviet prisoners of war who were executed and buried during Operation Reinhardt. Special Operation 1005 was carried out in order to remove all traces of this crime. People who had been gassed or who had died in other ways in the concentration camp were also 'disposed of' in this way from thereon. In 1961 Seitz described this cremation work as follows:

> I went to the forest about twice with the squad myself. On these occasions 20 Jewish workers were deployed. I estimated that the forest area was about 8 kilometres from Majdanek concentration camp. The cremation site was in the middle of the forest. A grill had been made out of hollowed out railway track. The fuel was the oil already mentioned. At any one time I had four or five members of the SS security force with me to guard the prisoners.³⁷

Over the following months, like his colleagues in Auschwitz, Muhsfeldt and his crew developed a system that optimized the cremation process: corpses with fatty tissue burned better, so they were put at the bottom on the grill to kindle the fire. Muhsfeldt explained the technique in detail at the Krakow Auschwitz trial:

> First, I dug a pit. But because I could not kindle the fire in the pit, I built myself the following construction for cremating the corpses themselves: I mounted old truck undercarriages onto large stones, laid the corpses on top and poured methanol over them. I put layers of wood under the undercarriages and lit them. About 100 corpses were cremated each time in one go. These were corpses from the pits as well as freshly dead bodies from the camp. Once one load had been burned, it was pounded into meal, and then it was poured into the pit where the corpses were stored for cremation. An iron board and an iron pounder were used to pound the bones. This is the operative method I used up to the end of October 1943 to cremate all the corpses buried in the forest and the corpses from the pits behind camp Field V.[38]

According to Muhsfeldt's statements, he cremated around 6,000 corpses in the forest and around 3,000 behind Field V. As we can see, Muhsfeldt clearly became reconciled to his work over time; in fact, he developed not only expertise but also ambition. His work was esteemed by his superiors, and on 1 June 1943 the departing Commandant Florstedt promoted Muhsfeldt to SS Senior Squad Leader (*Oberscharführer*).[39]

The specialist

In November 1943 his expertise was needed again, this time with particular urgency. The day after the massacre of 3 November 1943 (in Operation Harvest Festival), on the orders of the departing Commandant Florstedt and his successor, Weiss, Muhsfeldt's squad set about cremating 18,000 corpses behind the crematorium, in the pits. Here, the chief of the crematorium used the cremation technique he had learned in Auschwitz, and which he explained in detail at an interrogation:

> On the 4th I collected wood and planks and on 5 November 1943 I began cremating the corpses. Because the part of the ditch where the victims entered did not have corpses in it, I filled it with some soil so that the ditch was a bit flatter and had a better draught. Then I built a kind of grill out of wood on the ground. The prisoners placed the corpses from the ditches in layers on top. Once there was a stack of corpses it was covered in methanol and set alight. The next corpses were then constantly piled up in the ditch in the places where corpses

had been taken away for cremation. Once the ash had cooled after the cremation it was brought to the top by prisoners in my squad, where it was ground with a special petrol-powered mill and turned into bone meal. The bone meal was put into paper sacks and taken by car to SS land near the camp.[40]

It was a matter of removing traces of evidence, and this was of great political importance in the context of the Front moving closer and closer. The fact that – according to Muhsfeldt's descriptions – an official of the SD (*Sicherheitsdienst*) Lublin was closely supervising the cremation workers indicates the top political priority of this whole operation. The SD officer wanted to a make sure that all the corpses were cremated.

Muhsfeldt came up to the expectations of his superiors and had shown, once again, he could work efficiently. In Krakow he explained, not without pride: 'I completed the cremation of 17,000 murdered Jews, which began on 3 November 1943, before Christmas 1943'.[41] After that, the ditches were filled with soil and levelled off.

Former female supervisors vividly remembered the cremation work, which lasted just under two months. 'It went on day and night, and it smelled terrible',[42] said Anna M. at the Düsseldorf Majdanek trial. In a documentary film, Luzie H. similarly remembered the stench that accompanied these cremations in their daily work:

> After the shootings they filled in the ditches, you know, and then they always burned the corpses. That really stank! That really stank! The smoke came over the camp street where we walked to work. Then we walked like this [covers nose and mouth with left hand – EM] with a handkerchief over our faces through the smoke to work.[43]

Meanwhile, in September 1943 the building of a new crematorium had begun, but it was ready for operation only in January 1944. This new crematorium, which, like the old one, came from the Kori company in Berlin, had five chambers and therefore a larger capacity, was cheaper to heat, as it was fuelled with coke, and was meant to create less of a stench. Coke, the solid carbonic remainder from bituminous coal, is low in ash and sulphur, and burns with an almost invisible blue flame. Ideally, it does not produce any rust or visible smoky gases when it burns. Muhsfeldt set about testing the new material as soon as the crematorium was up and running:

> Only one corpse was put into one combustion chamber. The cremation took around 1 hour. I burned one corpse after another in all the furnaces in order to try them out. The corpses burned only very slowly, for the

furnace had a weak chimney draught. Because the one chimney had to serve all combustion points, it had a poor draught and the burning happened very slowly.[44]

Not least, this draught defect once again caused a dreadful smell, which continued to leave its mark on the daily work of all the staff at Majdanek.

However, according to Muhsfeldt's statements, once the evacuation of the camp began in January 1944, 'fewer corpses accrued, so I could no longer keep trying out the daily capacity of this crematorium in my work at Majdanek'.[45] We might be tempted to think that he was bored in this final phase at Majdanek, before he was transferred to Auschwitz in May 1944.

The end of a (successful) career

Once he arrived at Auschwitz, Muhsfeldt worked under the direction of Otto Moll, leader of the two special squads of crematoria I and II. However, seemingly at Auschwitz as initially at Majdanek, Muhsfeldt did not enjoy the work anymore, as he complained at the Krakow trial that the equipment at Auschwitz had become dilapidated since he had last been there: 'The chimneys in these crematoria at that time were already so burnt-out and worn that you had to be prepared for the operation to stop at any minute'.[46]

Muhsfeldt worked only during the day: 'Then in the mornings I came across corpses in the gas chamber and I started cremating them'.[47]

> 14 days after beginning my duties there, I started cremating the corpses in crematoria I and II, which were under my control. These were the corpses of Jews who had been gassed in the crematoria. At this time only those Jews who came to the camp at night with the transports were gassed in crematoria I and II with the aid of gas. Prisoners who arrived by day were gassed and cremated in crematoria III and V as well as in the farmhouse behind the new sauna and the pits behind the house.[48]

This shows how Muhsfeldt was significantly involved in the extermination of the Hungarian Jews, a killing operation that was coordinated by the former camp commandant, Rudolf Höss, who was specially delegated from Oranienburg to Auschwitz for this purpose. As squad leader, Muhsfeldt had at his side ten men who changed guard duty shifts by day and night. Prisoners had to do the main work. We only have to look at the number of workers in the team for the two crematoria to see just how extensive the killings were. According to Muhsfeldt there were 180 in the teams, including twenty Russians from Lublin and some Poles and French Jews, but the majority were Greek Jews.

According to some estimates, Muhsfeldt cremated 10,000 12,000 corpses altogether during his time working in Auschwitz, between the end of May and the beginning of August 1944. Despite his initial lament about the state of the equipment, he acknowledged before the court the relatively high performance of the Auschwitz furnaces:

> In these crematoria three adult corpses could be put into each combustion chamber. The corpses of children were classed as extras. It took about half an hour to cremate a load like this. The furnaces in these crematoria were more efficient than those in Majdanek. They were merely heated up and then switched off, so the corpses burned in their own flames which were formed as the corpses burned.[49]

The SS men and the medics on duty who served in the special squads were given vouchers for extra provisions for their hard work: they could get an extra half a litre of schnapps, ten extra cigarettes, and a piece of sausage and bread.[50]

Muhsfeldt had already requested to be transferred to the Front while at Majdanek because he was enjoying his work less and less. By mid-August his request was finally granted, and he was assigned to a combat unit of the Waffen SS in Bohemia and Moravia, where he first fought in Hungary and then finally, up to May 1945, in the Alsace and Lorraine.[51] After being wounded he was again sent into service in a concentration camp – against his will.

> On my arrival in Oranienburg I registered in Office Group D. The officer who received me there severely reproached me for registering myself at the Front as a person entrusted with confidential information, telling me that there was no question of me commanding such divisions and that I was to continue to serve in a concentration camp, more specifically at Flossenbürg.[52]

At this camp in Franconia, for about four weeks, Muhsfeldt undertook his last concentration camp duty, now as roll-call leader. During the evacuation and the death march[53] he was to prove his ability and use his expertise in the disposal of corpses one last time in the service of the SS, as the leader of the funeral squad.

Conclusion: a man for all phases

Despite his initial reluctance, Muhsfeldt developed in Majdanek broad-ranging expertise, indeed talent, in everything related to corpse disposal. In the first phase (November 1941 to June 1942) he buried the corpses near the camp. From June to October 1942 he cremated them in the so-called 'old' crematorium. In the third phase (November 1942 to January 1943), because of lack of materials, he went on to bury the corpses in the Krepiecki forest again. The fourth and fifth phases were the greatest challenge to his professional performance and his expertise: between February and the end of October 1943 Muhsfeldt cremated the corpses on funeral pyres, while from 5 November to 24 December 1943 he burned the cadavers in open pits. In the final months (January to May 1944) he operated a crematorium again. In his own estimation, he and his team cremated 33,000 corpses during his two and a half years of employment at Majdanek, that is, between November 1941 and May 1944.[54] Then there are the 10,000–12,000 corpses he cremated at Auschwitz between May and August 1944. Altogether, in just under three years of his 'undertaker career', Muhsfeldt destroyed at least 43,000 cadavers.

As this example of the chief of the crematorium Erich Muhsfeldt precisely shows, even after initial reluctance – Muhsfeldt let it be known at the Krakow Auschwitz trial that he was at first anything but pleased to be assigned to the Majdanek funeral squad – it was possible to come to enjoy one's work. It was specifically the 'manual skill' and expertise required that motivated a dynamic approach to work and gave the work meaning. His work and career correspond to sociological professionalization criteria. The work of a chief of the crematorium was a monopolized field that was strictly separated from other activities and functions. It required qualifications, training, and constant professional development, but it was also characterized by a certain degree of autonomy in executing the work. Gratifications (promotions) and economic incentives (extra rations) had a motivating effect.[55]

It is clear from the court interrogations that his professional self-image and his professional ambition were based on the importance and value attached to his work. This is because, along with specialist knowledge, Muhsfeldt also developed professional-ethical principles. For Muhsfeldt, the mass murder of Jews was primarily a 'logistical problem', and solving it was a great challenge for him, for of course he had to fulfil the quota and 'master' the constantly rising number of corpses. As Sémelin details, the extermination of people on a massive scale always requires a certain degree of organization; however, this does not exclude improvisations, accelerations, pauses, or radicalizations by the agents doing the actual work on site. These daily challenges demanded of the camp's SS staff 'professionalism', a 'performance mentality',[56] and emotional hardness. Ambition (Alf Lüdtke speaks of 'professional appeal' or 'momentum of specialized professionalism') connected killing with a professional understanding of work.[57] 'Quality work' produced, not least, satisfaction, 'even when the aim or result was destruction, not production'.[58]

The macro perspective does not do justice to the extermination work on the ground. A phenomenological perspective on daily extermination at Majdanek shows, rather, that the 'system' in the General Government did not function almost perfectly – as, for instance, Timothy Snyder claims, or as the metaphor of the 'death factory' suggests.[59] The gas chambers in Majdanek, but also in other camps, were not able to cope with the number of people who had to be killed, which is why firing squads often had to be brought in again. Even with its numerous crematoria the cremation work could not keep up, and breakdowns delayed the quota, which was difficult to fulfil anyway. In the camps, mountains of corpses were accumulating, adding to the already serious danger of epidemics. SS staff were overworked, and this exacerbated the level of violence.

We should not assume that the everyday just means routine. It actually means the multi-layered reality of life, not just as it is found to be, but also as it is perpetually appropriated, that is, interpreted, confirmed, constructed, and changed by its protagonists. The everyday and everyday behaviours are interesting moments of crystallization, within which we can not only comprehend individuals in their actions but also observe human beings living together, and establish tangibly how historical protagonists relate to one another, how they treat one another, how they live and work together, how they joke and quarrel.

Central to the everyday history, as developed by Lüdtke, is the question of domination (*Herrschaft*) or, rather, domination as a social practice.[60] Everyday life is not an apolitical vacuum; rather, it is everyday life that is the principal generator of mastery, through the social practice of all those affected, through their perceptions and interpretations, their actions and modes of expression. The institution of the concentration camp created the framework and the National Socialist ideology created the goal for violent action.

However, the male and female protagonists on site appropriated these 'framework conditions' on their own terms (*eigensinnig*; cf. Alf Lüdtke). State interests or the National Socialist ideology did not play the prominent role in violent actions or the 'work' of killing that most research claims. Nobody worked for years in a concentration camp in order to serve an idea. It was precisely in the practice of their daily duties that the protagonists adopted conceptions of the enemy and ideological patterns as their own, and imbued them with meaning. The kaleidoscope of daily work quotas, minor and major breakdowns, 'problem' solving, incentives, and the SS staff's feelings that they were succeeding in something, and indeed creating something, had a motivating and even radicalizing effect. From an everyday historical perspective it is clear that violence and extermination were not only ordered 'from above', but rather – if not primarily – generated by the complex interaction between the agents on the ground.

This is why this study has focused less on the ideological reading of violent practices and more on the chief of the crematorium's work-based actions and forms of appropriation. This does not mean we are fundamentally ruling out the influence of ideology on the actions of the perpetrators as an explanation for these. The materials reviewed here, and the close attention to the micro perspective, have, however, drawn attention to another important aspect: the staff of the concentration camp understood their duty as work they had to carry out 'well', and the SS men and the female supervisors experienced the camp primarily as a workplace. The violent behaviour of the protagonists was a multi-layered process that was in no sense linear but multi-causal. Violence and extermination arose out of complex normative, institutional, social, and situational dynamics. In this respect, the everyday historical approach, in spite of the ideological context, allows us to take into account the individual working experiences and violent practices of the concentration camp staff. At the same time, it becomes apparent that even in an institution like the Majdanek concentration and extermination camp, staff could still choose how to act. Staff rarely refused violence or extermination 'work'; rather, as in Muhsfeldt's case, they went about it energetically, and added their own personal touch.

Notes

1. The text of this chapter was translated from the author's German by Cadenza Academic Translations.
2. The central administration of the concentration camps was in Oranienburg, and from 1933 to 1942 it was under the control of the central Inspection of Concentration Camps (IKL). From 1942 the IKL was replaced by Department Group D of the Main Economic and Administrative Department (WVHA). See J. Tuchel, *Die Inspektion der Konzentrationslager, 1938-1945: Das System des Terrors. Eine Dokumentation* (*The Inspection of the Concentration Camps, 1938-1945. The System of Terror. A Documentation*) (Berlin: Hentrich & Hentrich, 1994); J. E. Schulte, *Zwangsarbeit und Vernichtung: das Wirtschaftsimperium der SS: Oswald Pohl und das SS-Wirtschafts-Verwaltungshauptamt 1933-1945* (*Forced Labour and Extermination: The Economic Empire of the SS: Oswald Pohl and the SS Main Economic and Administrative Department 1933-1945*) (Paderborn: Schöningh, 2001).
3. B. Schwindt, *Das Konzentrations- und Vernichtungslager Majdanek: Funktionswandel im Kontext der 'Endlösung'* (*The Majdanek Concentration and Extermination Camp. Functional Change in the Context of the 'Final Solution'*) (Würzburg: Königshausen & Neumann, 2005); E. Mailänder, *Gewalt im Dienstalltag. Die SS-Aufseherinnen des Konzentrations- und Vernichtungslagers Majdanek (1942-1944)* (*Violence in Daily Work. The Female Overseers at Majdanek Concentration and Extermination Camp (1942-1944)*) (Hamburg: Hamburger Edition, 2009).
4. T. Kranz, 'Das KL Lublin – zwischen Planung und Realisierung' ('The Lublin concentration camp – between planning and realisation'), in U. Herbert, K. Orth & C. Dieckmann (eds), *Die nationalsozialistischen Konzentrationslager. Entwicklung und Struktur* (*The National Socialist Concentration Camp. Development and Structure*) (Göttingen: Wallstein Verlag, 1998), pp. 363–7, at p. 369.
5. J. Sémelin, 'Du massacre au processus génocidaire', *Revue Internationale des Sciences Sociales*, 147 (2002), 483–92; see also J. Sémelin, *Purify and Destroy: The Political Uses of Massacre and Genocide* (New York: Columbia University Press, 2009).
6. Sémelin, 'Du massacre au processus génocidaire', pp. 486–7.
7. T. Kranz, 'Das Konzentrationslager Majdanek und die "Aktion Reinhardt"' ('The Majdanek Concentration Camp and "Operation Reinhardt"'), in B. Musial (ed.), *'Aktion Reinhardt': Der Völkermord an den Juden im Generalgouvernement 1941-1944* (*'Operation Reinhardt': The Genocide of the Jews in the General Government 1941-1944*) (Osnabrück: Fibre Verlag, 2004), pp. 233–55.
8. T. Kranz, 'Ewidencja Zgonow i Smiertelnosc Wiezow KL Lublin' (Records of deaths and mortality at KL Lublin), *Zeszyty Majdanka*, 23 (2005), 7–53.
9. Kranz, 'Das KL Lublin', p. 381.

10. See A. Lüdtke, *The History of Everyday Life: Reconstructing Historical Experiences and Ways of Life* (trans. W. Templer) (Princeton: Princeton University Press, 1995).
11. In contrast to Karin Orth, who has studied the male functionary elite in the form of the camp commandant, by 'subordinate' I mean the 'common' or subordinate male and female security staff. K. Orth, *Die Konzentrationslager-SS: Sozialstrukturelle Analysen und biographische Studien* (*The Concentration Camp SS: Socio-structural Analyses and Biographical Studies*) (Göttingen: Wallstein Verlag, 2000).
12. A. Lüdtke, *Eigen-Sinn: Fabrikalltag, Arbeitererfahrung und Politik vom Kaiserreich bis in den Faschismus* (*Self-Will: Daily Factory Work, Workers' Experience and the Politics of the German Empire up until Fascism*) (Hamburg: Ergebnisse Verlag, 1993), p. 15; A. Lüdtke, '"German work" and "German workers": the impact of symbols on the exclusion of Jews in Nazi-Germany. Reflections on open questions', in D. Bankier (ed.), *Probing the Depths of German Antisemitism* (New York: Berghahn Books, 2000), pp. 296–311; A. Lüdtke, 'People working: everyday life and German Fascism', *History Workshop Journal*, 50 (2000), 75–92.
13. Muhsfeldt was sentenced to death and hanged in Krakow, while on 11 July 1975 the Cologne Public Prosecutor's Office accused Seitz of premeditated joint murder and murder in several individual cases in Lublin Majdanek concentration camp between December 1941 and early 1944. Seitz was, however, declared unfit to stand trial before the case could begin.
14. Andreas Kilian, Eric Friedler, and Barbara Siebert have researched this process of extermination at Auschwitz in detail. To what extent Majdanek differed from this is still in question, for there is as yet no study of the special squads there. It is probable, however, that the division of work between SS and prisoner squads, as well as the allocation of the different procedural steps, was largely similar. E. Friedler, B. Siebert & A. Kilian, *Zeugen aus der Todeszone: Das jüdische Sonderkommando in Auschwitz* (*Witnesses from the Death Zone: The Jewish Special Squad in Auschwitz*) (Munich: Deutscher Taschenbuch Verlag, 2005). See also *Die Auschwitz-Hefte. Texte der polnischen Zeitschrift 'Przeglad Lekarski' über historische, psychische und medizinische Aspekte des Lebens und Sterbens in Auschwitz* (*The Auschwitz Books. Texts from the Polish Magazine 'Przeglad Lekarski' on Historical, Psychiatric and Medical Aspects of Living and Dying in Auschwitz*) (Weinheim: Hamburger Institut für Sozialgeschichte, 1987); R. Glazar, *Die Falle mit dem grünen Zaun: Überleben in Treblinka* (*The Trap with the Green Fence: Surviving in Treblinka*) (Frankfurt am Main: Fischer Taschenbuch Verlag, 1992); G. Greif, '*Wir weinten tränenlos*'. *Augenzeugenberichte des jüdischen 'Sonderkommandos' in Auschwitz* ('*We cried without tears*': *Witness Reports by the Jewish 'Special Squads' in Auschwitz*) (Frankfurt am Main: Fischer Verlag, 2001).
15. R. J. van Pelt, *The Case for Auschwitz: Evidence from the Irving Trial* (Bloomington: Indiana University Press, 2002).

Erich Muhsfeldt, chief of the crematorium 63

16 See Muhsfeldt, Bundesarchiv-Berlin (Federal Archive), Berlin Document Centre (henceforth BDC), N0008.
17 See Erich Muhsfeldt, Interrogation, 14 August 1947, in Krakow, Landesarchiv Nordrhein-Westfalen, former Hauptsstaatsarchiv (henceforth HStA) Düsseldorf, Ger. Rep. 432 No. 204, p. 96.
18 Ibid.
19 Robert Seitz, Interrogation, 17 March 1965, in Liedolsheim, HStA Düsseldorf, Ger. Rep. 432 No. 266, p. 140,
20 Erich Muhsteldt, Interrogation, 14 August 1947, in Krakow, HStA Düsseldorf, Ger. Rep. 432 No. 204, p. 95.
21 See also Advertising and Information Material, HStA Düsseldorf, Ger. Rep. 432 No. 420, pp. 539–50. There is now detailed research on the firm Topf & Söhne: see E. Schwarzenberger, *Topf & Söhne: Arbeiten an einem Täterort* (*Topf & Söhne: Working at a Criminal Scene*) (Erfurt: Förderkreis Topf & Söhne, 2001); A. Assmann, F. Hiddemann & E. Schwarzenberger (eds), *Firma Topf & Söhne: Hersteller der Öfen für Auschwitz. Ein Fabrikgelände als Erinnerungsort?* (*The Firm Topf & Söhne: Manufacturers of Furnaces for Auschwitz. A Factory Site as a Place of Memory?*) (Frankfurt am Main: Campus, 2002); R. J. van Pelt, 'Auschwitz', in G. Morsch & B. Perz (eds), *Neue Studien zu nationalsozialistischen Massentötungen durch Giftgas: Historische Bedeutung, technische Entwicklung, revisionistische Leugnung* (*New Studies on National Socialist Mass Killings with Poisonous Gas: Historical Meaning, Technical Development, Revisionist Denial*) (Berlin: Metropol, 2011), pp. 196–218.
22 Erich Muhsfeldt, Interrogation, 14 August 1947, in Krakow, HStA Düsseldorf, Ger. Rep. 432 No. 204, p. 100.
23 Muhsfeldt, Federal Archive, BDC, N0008.
24 Robert Seitz, Interrogation, 17 March 1965, in Liedolsheim, HStA Düsseldorf, Ger. Rep. 432 No. 266, p. 140.
25 Erich Muhsfeldt, Interrogation, 14 August 1947, in Krakow, HStA Düsseldorf, Ger. Rep. 432 No. 204, pp. 99–100.
26 E. Fechner, *Der Prozess: Eine Darstellung des Majdanek-Verfahrens in Düsseldorf* (*The Trial: A Portrayal of the Majdanek Proceedings*), parts 1–3, documentary film, Norddeutscher Rundfunk, 1984.
27 Statement by Julian Gregorowicz, 19 April 1977, Main hearing, HStA Düsseldorf, Ger. Rep. 432 No. 283, p. 4.
28 Erich Muhsfeldt, Interrogation, 14 August 1947, in Krakow, HStA Düsseldorf, Ger. Rep. 432 No. 204, p. 100. According to Muhsfeldt, the two furnaces were dismantled and transferred to Plaszow at the beginning of 1943.
29 The guard Otto Z. also recalled that prisoners dug mass graves because, apparently, the death quota in the camp was so high that the corpses could not all be cremated in the crematorium. See Otto Z., Interrogation, 20 February 1970, LKA-NW, Munich, HStA Düsseldorf, Ger. Rep. 432 No. 204, p. 30.
30 Erich Muhsfeldt, Interrogation, 14 August 1947, in Krakow, HStA Düsseldorf, Ger. Rep. 432 No. 204, p. 101. According to his statements,

the German overseer was a 'German Reich' prisoner or later a Jewish prisoner from Vienna. Ibid., p. 125.
31 Erich Muhsfeldt, Interrogation, 14 August 1947, in Krakow, HStA Düsseldorf, Ger. Rep. 432 No. 204, p. 102.
32 Erich Muhsfeldt, Interrogation, 8 September 1947, in Krakow, HStA Düsseldorf, Ger. Rep. 432 No. 204, p. 125.
33 Erich Muhsfeldt, Interrogation, 14 August 1947, in Krakow, HStA Düsseldorf, Ger. Rep. 432 No. 204, p. 102.
34 Erich Muhsfeldt, Interrogation, 8 September 1947, in Krakow, HStA Düsseldorf, Ger. Rep. 432 No. 204, p. 126.
35 van Pelt, 'Auschwitz'.
36 See also Adam Czuprin, Interrogation, 9 August 1944, by Russian-German commission, HStA Düsseldorf, Ger. Rep. 432 No. 274, pp. 114–18; Kazimierz Gagol, Interrogation, 9 August 1944, by Russian-German commission, HStA Düsseldorf, Ger. Rep. 432 No. 274, pp. 119–20.
37 Robert Seitz, Interrogation, 5 December 1961, in Karlsruhe, HStA Düsseldorf, Ger. Rep. 432 No. 266, pp. 85–6.
38 Erich Muhsfeldt, Interrogation, 14 August 1947, in Krakow, HStA Düsseldorf, Ger. Rep. 432 No. 204, pp. 101–2. See also Robert Seitz, Interrogation, 17 March 1965, in Liedolsheim, HStA Düsseldorf, Ger. Rep. 432 No. 266, p. 141.
39 See also Muhsfeldt, Federal Archive, BDC, N0008.
40 Erich Muhsfeldt, Interrogation, 16 August 1947, in Krakow, HStA Düsseldorf, Ger. Rep. 432 No. 204, p. 108.
41 Ibid., p. 110. In the research it is assumed that there were 18,000 victims of this massacre, rather than the 17,000 Muhsfeldt indicates here.
42 Anna M., Interrogation, 2 August 1961, Zentrale Stelle, Stuttgart, HStA Düsseldorf, Ger. Rep. 432 No. 234, p. 23f.
43 Luzie H., in Fechner, *Der Prozess*, part 3.
44 Erich Muhsfeldt, Interrogation, 16 August 1947, in Krakow, HStA Düsseldorf, Ger. Rep. 432 No. 204, pp. 110–11.
45 Ibid.
46 Erich Muhsfeldt, Interrogation, 19 August 1947, in Krakow, HStA Düsseldorf, Ger. Rep. 432 No. 204, p. 116.
47 Ibid., p. 120.
48 Ibid., pp. 119–20.
49 Ibid., p. 120.
50 Ibid., p. 123.
51 See also Muhsfeldt, Federal Archive, BDC, N0008.
52 Erich Muhsfeldt, Interrogation, 19 August 1947, in Krakow, HStA Düsseldorf, Ger. Rep. 432 No. 204, p. 124. Office Group D was the central administration of the concentration camp.
53 See D. Blatman, *The Death Marches: The Final Phase of Nazi Genocide* (Harvard: Harvard University Press, 2011).
54 See also Erich Muhsfeldt, Interrogation, 16 August 1947, in Krakow, HStA Düsseldorf, Ger. Rep. 432 No. 204, pp. 95, 97, 101, 103; Erich Muhsfeldt, Interrogation, 14 August 1947, in Krakow, ibid., pp. 112–13.

55 K. H. Jarausch, 'Higher education and social change: some comparative perspectives', in K. H. Jarausch (ed.), *The Transformation of Higher Learning 1860-1930: Expansion, Diversification, Social Opening and Professionalization in England, Germany, Russia and the United States* (Stuttgart: Klett Kotta, 1983), p. 29.
56 H. Buchheim, 'Befehl und Gehorsam' ('Command and obedience'), in H. Buchheim, M. Broszat, H.-A. Jacobsen & H. Krausnick (eds), *Anatomie des SS-Staates* (*Anatomy of the SS State*) (Munich: Deutscher Taschenbuch Verlag, 1999), pp. 215-320, at p. 242.
57 A. Lüdtke, '"Die Fiktion der Institution". Herrschaftspraxis und Vernichtung der europäischen Juden im 20. Jahrhundert' ('"The fiction of the institution". Ruling practice and extermination of European Jews in the 20th century'), in R. Blänkner & B. Jussen (eds), *Institutionen und Ereignis: Über historische Praktiken und Vorstellungen gesellschaftlichen Ordnens* (*Institutions and Event: On Historical Practices and Concepts of Social Ordering*) (VMPG 138) (Göttingen: Vandenhoeck & Ruprecht, 1998), pp. 355-79, at p. 369.
58 A. Lüdtke, '"Fehlgreifen in der Wahl der Mittel": Optionen im Alltag militärischen Handelns' ('"Mistakes in the choice of means": options in everyday military actions'), *Mittelweg*, 36:1 (2003), 61-75, at p. 68.
59 T. Snyder, *Bloodlands: Europe Between Hitler and Stalin* (New York: Basic Books, 2010), pp. 253-76, at p. 260.
60 In the last few years there have been some innovative studies in the area of National Socialist research. See, for instance, M. Koch, *Fahnenflucht: Deserteure der Wehrmacht im Zweiten Weltkrieg. Lebenswege und Entscheidungen* (*Desertion: Wehrmacht Deserters in the Second World War. Lives and Decisions*) (Paderborn: Schöningh, 2008); R. Mühlhäuser, *Eroberungen: Sexuelle Gewalttaten und intime Beziehungen deutscher Soldaten in der Sowjetunion 1941-1945* (*Conquests, Sexual Violence and Intimate Relationships of German Soldiers in the Soviet Union 1941-1945*) (Hamburg: Hamburger Edition, 2010); A. Oeser, *Enseigner Hitler: les adolescents allemands face au passé nazi. Appropriations, Interprétations et usages de l'histoire* (*Teach Hitler: German Teenagers Face the Nazi Past. Appropriations, Interpretations and Uses of History*) (Paris: Editions de la Maison des sciences de l'homme, 2010); M. Christ, *Die Dynamik des Tötens: Über die Ermordung der Berditschewer Juden. Ukraine 1941-44* (*The Dynamics of Killing: On the Murder of the Berditschew Jews. Ukraine 1941-44*) (Frankfurt am Main: Fischer, 2011).

Bibliography

Archives

Bundesarchiv-Berlin (Federal Archive), Berlin Document Centre (BDC)
Landesarchiv Nordrhein-Westfalen, former Hauptsstaatsarchiv (HStA) Düsseldorf

Film

Fechner, E., *Der Prozess: Eine Darstellung des Majdanek-Verfahrens in Düsseldorf*, parts 1-3, documentary film, Norddeutscher Rundfunk, 1984

Books, chapters, and articles

Allen, M. T., *Business and Industry in Nazi Germany* (New York: Berghahn Books, 2004)
Allen, M. T., *The Business of Genocide: The SS, Slave Labor, and the Concentration Camps* (Chapel Hill: University of North Carolina Press, 2002)
Assmann, A., F. Hiddemann & E. Schwarzenberger (eds), *Firma Topf & Söhne: Hersteller der Öfen für Auschwitz. Ein Fabrikgelände als Erinnerungsort?* (Frankfurt am Main: Campus, 2002)
Blatman D., *The Death Marches: The Final Phase of Nazi Genocide* (Harvard: Harvard University Press, 2011)
Buchheim, H., 'Befehl und Gehorsam', in H. Buchheim, M. Broszat, H.-A. Jacobsen & H. Krausnick (eds), *Anatomie des SS-Staates* (Munich: Deutscher Taschenbuch Verlag, 1999), pp. 215-320
Caplan, J. & N. Wachsmann, *Concentration Camps in Nazi Germany: The New Histories* (London: Routledge, 2010)
Christ, M., *Die Dynamik des Tötens: Über die Ermordung der Berditschewer Juden. Ukraine 1941-44* (Frankfurt am Main: Fischer, 2011)
Die Auschwitz-Hefte. Texte der polnischen Zeitschrift 'Przeglad Lekarski' über historische, psychische und medizinische Aspekte des Lebens und Sterbens in Auschwitz (Weinheim: Hamburger Institut für Sozialgeschichte, 1987)
Friedler, E., B. Siebert & A. Kilian, *Zeugen aus der Todeszone: Das jüdische Sonderkommando in Auschwitz* (Munich: Deutscher Taschenbuch Verlag, 2005)
Glazar, R., *Die Falle mit dem grünen Zaun: Überleben in Treblinka* (Frankfurt am Main: Fischer Taschenbuch Verlag, 1992)
Greif, G., *'Wir weinten tränenlos'. Augenzeugenberichte des jüdischen 'Sonderkommandos' in Auschwitz* (Frankfurt am Main: Fischer Verlag, 2001)
Herbert, U., K. Orth & C. Dieckmann (eds), *Die nationalsozialistischen Konzentrationslager: Entwicklung und Struktur*, vol. 2 (Göttingen: Wallstein Verlag, 1998)
Jarausch, K. H., 'Higher education and social change: some comparative perspectives', in K. H. Jarausch (ed.), *The Transformation of Higher Learning 1860-1930: Expansion, Diversification, Social Opening and Professionalization in England, Germany, Russia and the United States* (Stuttgart: Klett Kotta, 1983), pp. 9-36
Koch, M., *Fahnenflucht: Deserteure der Wehrmacht im Zweiten Weltkrieg. Lebenswege und Entscheidungen* (Paderborn: Schöningh, 2008)

Kranz, T., 'Das KL Lublin – zwischen Planung und Realisierung', in U. Herbert, K. Orth & C. Dieckmann (eds), *Die nationalsozialistischen Konzentrationslager: Entwicklung und Struktur* (Göttingen: Wallstein Verlag, 1998), pp. 363–7

Kranz, T., 'Das Konzentrationslager Majdanek und die "Aktion Reinhardt"', in B. Musial (ed.), *'Aktion Reinhardt': Der Völkermord an den Juden im Generalgouvernement 1941–1944* (Osnabrück: Fibre Verlag, 2004), pp. 233–55

Kranz, T., 'Ewidencja Zgonow i Smiertelnosc Wiezow KL Lublin', *Zeszyty Majdanka*, 23 (2005), 7–53

Lüdtke, A., '"Die Fiktion der Institution". Herrschaftspraxis und Vernichtung der europäischen Juden im 20. Jahrhundert', in R. Blänkner & B. Jussen (eds), *Institutionen und Ereignis: Über historische Praktiken und Vorstellungen gesellschaftlichen Ordnens* (VMPG 138) (Göttingen: Vandenhoeck & Ruprecht, 1998), pp. 355–79

Lüdtke, A., *Eigen-Sinn: Fabrikalltag, Arbeitererfahrung und Politik vom Kaiserreich bis in den Faschismus* (Hamburg: Ergebnisse Verlag, 1993)

Lüdtke, A., '"Fehlgreifen in der Wahl der Mittel": Optionen im Alltag militärischen Handelns', *Mittelweg*, 36:1 (2003), 61–75

Lüdtke, A., '"German work" and "German workers": the impact of symbols on the exclusion of Jews in Nazi-Germany: reflections on open questions', in D. Bankier (ed.), *Probing the Depths of German Antisemitism* (New York: Berghahn Books, 2000), pp. 296–311

Lüdtke, A., 'People working: everyday life and German Fascism', *History Workshop Journal*, 50 (2000), 75–92

Lüdtke, A., *The History of Everyday Life: Reconstructing Historical Experiences and Ways of Life* (trans. W. Templer) (Princeton: Princeton University Press, 1995)

Mailänder, E., 'Everyday life in Nazi Germany: a forum, moderated by Andrew Stuart Bergerson (University of Missouri-Kansas City)', *German History*, 27:4 (2009), 560–79

Mailänder, E., *Gewalt im Dienstalltag: Die SS-Aufseherinnen des Konzentrations- und Vernichtungslagers Majdanek (1942–1944)* (Hamburg: Hamburger Edition, 2009)

Mailänder, E., '"Going East": colonial experiences and practices of violence of the female and male camp guards in Majdanek (1941–1944)', *Journal of Genocide Research*, 10:4 (2008), 559–78

Mailänder, E., 'Work, violence and cruelty: an everyday historical perspective on perpetrators in Nazi concentration camps', *L'Europe en Formation*, 357 (autumn 2010), 30–51

Mühlhäuser, R., *Eroberungen: Sexuelle Gewalttaten und intime Beziehungen deutscher Soldaten in der Sowjetunion 1941–1945* (Hamburg: Hamburger Edition, 2010)

Oeser, A., *Enseigner Hitler: les adolescents allemands face au passé nazi. Appropriations, Interprétations et usages de l'histoire* (Paris: Editions de la Maison des sciences de l'homme, 2010)

Orth, K., *Die Konzentrationslager-SS: Sozialstrukturelle Analysen und biographische Studien* (Göttingen: Wallstein Verlag, 2000)

Pressac, J.-C., *Les crématoires d'Auschwitz: la machinerie du meurtre de masse* (Paris: CNRS Éditions, 1993)
Schulte, J. E., *Zwangsarbeit und Vernichtung: das Wirtschaftsimperium der SS: Oswald Pohl und das SS-Wirtschafts-Verwaltungshauptamt 1933-1945* (Paderborn: Schöningh, 2001)
Schwarzenberger, E., *Topf & Söhne: Arbeiten an einem Täterort* (Erfurt: Förderkreis Topf & Söhne, 2001)
Schwindt, B., *Das Konzentrations- und Vernichtungslager Majdanek: Funktionswandel im Kontext der 'Endlösung'* (Würzburg: Königshausen & Neumann, 2005)
Sémelin, J., 'Du massacre au processus génocidaire', *Revue internationale des sciences sociales*, 147 (2002), 483-92
Sémelin, J., *Purify and Destroy: The Political Uses of Massacre and Genocide* (New York: Columbia University Press, 2009)
Snyder, T., *Bloodlands: Europe Between Hitler and Stalin* (New York: Basic Books, 2010)
Tuchel, J., *Die Inspektion der Konzentrationslager, 1938-1945: Das System des Terrors. Eine Dokumentation* (Berlin: Hentrich & Hentrich, 1994)
van Pelt, R. J., 'Auschwitz', in G. Morsch & B. Perz (eds), *Neue Studien zu nationalsozialistischen Massentötungen durch Giftgas: Historische Bedeutung, technische Entwicklung, revisionistische Leugnung* (Berlin: Metropol, 2011), pp. 196-218
van Pelt, R. J., *The Case for Auschwitz: Evidence from the Irving Trial* (Bloomington: Indiana University Press, 2002)

3

Lands of *Unkultur*: mass violence, corpses, and the Nazi imagination of the East

Michael McConnell

On 1 June 1943 Herr Lange, a political advisor in the civilian administration of Generalkommissariat Weissruthenia, delivered a report regarding a recent *Bandenaktion*, or anti-partisan operation, to his superiors in Minsk.[1] He noted that during a punishment action in the district of Borrisow, German troops and their local collaborators had herded the inhabitants into a large barn. Once inside they were shot and the building was then set on fire. However, it only partially burned and when Lange visited the scene a few days later he found the unburned bodies of the victims still piled inside the half-ruined structure. Wild animals had dragged some of the corpses into the village streets and surrounding fields, and mutilated bodies were scattered over the landscape. Commenting further on the poor performance of the troops, upon later investigation he discovered some of the victims were merely wounded in the shooting. Despite their injuries these survivors had managed to drag themselves out from under the bodies of their neighbours and were later taken to a local hospital, where they told others about the atrocity.[2]

The report was not a protest against the brutality visited on the rural inhabitants of a Belarusian village. On the contrary, it simply assessed the operation and offered insights into what aspects needed to be corrected in future missions. Lange was undoubtedly repulsed by what he saw, and his superiors themselves noted in the transcription of the meeting that 'The verbal report from

Political Advisor Lange concerning an incident during a recent anti-partisan operation is hardly pleasant [*wenig erfreulich*]'.[3] This revulsion stemmed not only from the physical aftermath of the murders, but from the fact that the German-led operation was conducted in a manner allowing for a type of chaos and disorder which was not only unsanitary but also failed to conceal the crime, letting wounded civilians escape to tell their tale, encouraging the growing resistance movement in the region. Embedded in the report was the implicit idea that violence committed by the occupational authorities should be precise and efficient, embodying their self-perceived national character. As a *Kulturvolk*, or 'cultured people', Germans were obliged to kill in certain ways, which set them apart from their uncivilized, brutal enemies in the East.

Through an examination of the anti-partisan war in Generalkommissariat Weissruthenia, this chapter assesses how Germans' cultural stereotypes of Eastern Europeans drove the extreme forms of violence visited on the region. As historian Alon Confino has recently argued, scholars should begin to pay closer attention to the ways in which imagination and fantasy interacted with state ideology, to expose 'people's tendency to think outside, against, underneath, and above it'. Such efforts do not attempt to discount or minimize the role of ideology in mass violence, but rather underscore that ideology is a part of culture and therefore remains linked with a longer continuity of mentalities which feed into it, justify it, and form its foundation.[4]

This argument works well for the subject of the German vision of the East. As Vejas Liulevicius has noted, a longer trajectory of German thought vis-à-vis Eastern Europe existed prior to the Nazis, one largely articulated through notions of cultural struggle, with the supposed Germanic traits of order, proficiency, and cleanliness locked in a life-or-death battle with the allegedly disease-ridden, primitive, and morally corrupt East. Germans often described these lands as areas of *Unkultur*, literally 'devoid of culture', which were therefore enticing due to the seemingly unlimited possibilities they offered colonizers, as the land and its people could be shaped to fit their vision. As such, Eastern Europe had long provoked a plethora of fantasies, which merged with the Nazi vision of an eastern utopia to be won at the expense of the local inhabitants.[5]

Co-mingling with optimistic imaginings of the future were deep feelings of disgust, as the East was repulsive in its current, natural state. For example, during his post-war trial, a former member of a police unit stationed in the Generalkommissariat recalled, 'It was like the Wild West, a hundred years ago in America'. This ground-level vision of an untamed wilderness populated by unruly savages was also held at the highest echelons of the Nazi state. In August 1942, commenting on the rising resistance in the East, Hitler remarked: 'The struggle we are waging there against the partisans resembles very much the struggle in North America against the Red Indians ... at all costs we will establish law and order there'.[6] Such cultural fantasies regarding a lawless East, ironically encouraged by the efforts directed at mastering it, and the atrocities that occurred in Weissruthenia only served to perpetuate preconceptions of its inherent barbarity as they plunged the region into catastrophe.

The corpses of the occupation's victims played a key role in encouraging mass violence. As subhumans inhabiting the wilderness on the edge of Nazi empire, the dead of Eastern Europe were treated in ways which broke with European traditions regarding death and burial. Hung from trees or left to rot in the smouldering ruins of destroyed villages, the corpses were put on display, expressing the occupiers' contempt and marking them as something other than human. Aside from the deliberate attempt to dehumanize the indigenous population by desecrating the dead, the scattered, decaying remains generated disgust among those directly responsible for enforcing Nazi policies and reinforced the perception that the East was a primitive place in need of violent transformation. Over the course of the German anti-partisan war, a destructive dynamic emerged in which each brutal search-and-destroy operation failed to eliminate the partisan threat and only enhanced perceptions of Eastern Europe as a wild place beyond law and order. This perception called for ever more ruthless measures against the civilian population. The treatment and display of corpses contributed to the expansion of mass violence between 1941 and 1944.

The war against banditry

The anti-partisan war allows scholars to examine the reciprocal relationship between cultural fantasy and atrocity. Unlike Nazi persecutions of ethnic minorities such as the Jews and Roma, the anti-partisan war struck the entire population of Eastern Europe. It not only internalized these genocides, casting the victims as partisans alongside their Slavic neighbours. Efforts to eliminate resistance, perceived or otherwise, also caused widespread social and economic collapse, hindering efforts at colonial exploitation and thereby radicalizing notions of Eastern primitiveness. Furthermore, partisans were a central figure in the image of 'the Wild East', as they best embodied the supposed character of the local population.

The East was considered by the Nazis to be the cradle of so-called 'Judeo-Bolshevism', and even prior to 1933 German politicians and military leaders paid close attention to developments within the Soviet Union. Of prime interest was the Russian Civil War, and this conflict played a crucial role in shaping German thought regarding the civilian population of the Soviet state and its neighbours. The terror and forced population removals visited on regions such as the Don Basin and the western borderlands during this period projected the idea that the Soviet regime had jettisoned the civil-military distinctions governing the conduct of European militaries. These acts were interpreted as the removal of traditional forms of restraint, creating a new form of conflict the Germans termed *Volkskrieg*, or 'people's war', which involved the direct participation of the entire civilian population. Due to the manner in which it was conducted, *Volkskrieg* was interpreted by German military planners as barbaric. The Russian Civil War and the social engineering projects which followed also buttressed stereotypes of the Soviets as fanatics and Eastern peoples in general as desensitized to violence, able to respond only to brutal forms of governance. These tropes were later enhanced by the racial dogma of the Nazi regime after 1933, which biologized these notions and underscored the idea that a war in the East would be a conflict unparalleled in the history of warfare, in terms of both scope and violence.[7]

This was starkly evidenced by Directive Number 21, issued to German troops by the Wehrmacht High Command on the eve of the invasion of the Soviet Union in June 1941. It remarked, 'Bolshevism is the mortal enemy of the National Socialist German people ... this war demands the ruthless suppression of bolshevist snipers, guerrillas, saboteurs, Jews, and the complete elimination of active or passive resistance'.[8] The military clearly expected the entire population to resist the German advance, as this was a war of peoples rather than of militaries; the Germans thereby in effect launched a type of *Volkskrieg* of their own on the Soviet Union, by eroding the distinctions between civilians and combatants within its territory. Such orders highlighted the supposed fanatical, savage, and underhand nature of Eastern peoples.

Contrary to these expectations, however, the invaders initially found little resistance from the local population and Stalin's call on 1 July for scorched earth and a guerrilla war behind the Front went largely unanswered.⁹ During this period, the greatest threat to the occupiers came from members of the Red Army cut off during the opening days of the invasion, and, overall, the threat remained relatively small. Regardless, soldiers were ordered not to let their guard down. Commanders of rear-area garrison and police units spent the quiet autumn months formatting guidelines and honing tactics for the war they expected to fight. For example, in late September 1941, General Max von Schenkendorff held a conference in Mogilev for police and military commanders from the rear area of Army Group Centre. Over the course of the three-day meeting, officers shared their experiences to date and brainstormed plans for future confrontations with partisans. The meeting concluded with a demonstration of tactics, and the participants witnessed a company of police cordon off and search a village. Thirty-two of the inhabitants were executed, all of them Jewish, since actual partisans could not be found, exposing the relationship between genocide and the dictates of rear-area security.¹⁰

The outcome of such intellectual exchanges was a series of handbooks issued to soldiers and police stationed in the East. These publications quoted Stalin's call for a partisan war behind the Front and cast the Soviets as guerrilla fighters par excellence. They reiterated the message that the entire civilian population was suspect, as women, small children, and even the elderly, traditionally non-combatants, often worked for the partisans as spies and couriers. In order to drive home the message that the occupational troops were fighting an inhuman enemy, the manuals reprinted captured documents detailing partisan tactics, stressing their penchant for 'dirty' or 'unfair' attacks, such as ambushes and the mining of roadways. One such captured document instructed recruits to take the following oath: 'I, a citizen of the Soviet Union and loyal son of the heroic Russian people, swear to eliminate every fascist snake that stands on Russian soil'.¹¹

In the face of such apparent, and often manufactured, fanaticism, one document, drafted by Heinrich Himmler, the head of all anti-partisan operations in occupied Europe, advised German soldiers that 'The most important qualifications for combating this criminality are good nerves [and] a fearless heart'. Another document, drafted by an officer with experience of fighting partisans, encouraged troops to be 'tirelessly active, comradely, and hard', like their opponents. In short, Germans were to conduct themselves in ways similar to their supposedly merciless and barbaric enemies in the East, encouraging the pre-emptive use of ruthless violence out of proportion to the actual threat. This notion was encouraged by Hitler, who ordered, due the nature of the partisan war, that the military and police forego adherence to the Geneva Convention.[12]

The correspondence regarding the anti-partisan war further criminalized the activities of the enemy. As Jonathan Gumz has pointed out in his work on the anti-partisan war in the Balkans, German military and police personnel often used technocratic language in order to distinguish their violence from the supposedly irrational forms of atrocity committed by the indigenous population.[13] Reports from Generalkommissariat Weissruthenia also reflected this tendency. Officers described anti-partisan operations in clinical terms such as *Säuberung des Gelandes*, or 'cleansing the landscape', and those killed had been given 'special treatment' (*Sonderbehandelt*), populations were 'evacuated' (*Evakuierte*), as a euphemism for murder, and once a mission ended the targeted areas had been 'pacified' (*Befriedete Gebiete*), whereas the reality was that the local population had been either killed or forcibly removed.[14]

In contrast, the partisans and their activities were described in dramatic emotional terms; attacks were raids (*Überfallen*), cast at best as annoyances (*Unwesen*), or at worst as murder and robbery (*Mord und Raub*). The partisans were described as criminals; they allegedly plundered villages and towns and were described as bandits (*Banden*) or sometimes as a plague (*Pest*) haunting the land. Keeping in tandem with such quasi-biological language, locations deemed under their control were described as *Bandenverseuchtegebiete*, literally 'areas infested with bandits', conjuring the image of a dangerous and spreading menace. These medical tropes were also reflected in maps created by the security forces. Many were covered in circles with the numbers of suspected insurgents written within, and were constantly updated. To the observer, Weissruthenia appeared to be covered in shifting coloured splotches of various sizes and shapes, much like the body of an epidemic victim, calling to mind the imaginings of disease and contamination long associated with the East.[15]

In September 1942, Führer Directive Number 46, *Instructions for Intensified Action Against Banditry in the East*, institutionalized this language, ordering that the term 'bandit' replace the word 'partisan' in all correspondence, in an effort to coordinate policy and encourage aggressiveness.[16] This decree effectively criminalized resistance while simultaneously extending what was deemed to be part of the anti-partisan effort to action against common criminality such as black marketeering, petty theft, and smuggling, which were in fact caused by the occupation's exploitative economic policies. The term 'bandit' was vague enough to encompass a variety of meanings, and grew to encompass most of the civilian population. The definition also encouraged local initiative to pursue violent solutions, as it created a perception that Germans in the East were under siege at every turn. By its very definition, the word 'bandit' connoted outsiders who lived on the margins of civilization and attacked towns and villages, that is, attacked civilization itself. Hence this deliberate merging of political resistance with everyday criminality indiscriminately expanded the anti-partisan campaign to the entire civilian population of Generalkommissariat Weissruthenia and radicalized pre-existing stereotypes of the region as a lawless, merciless land of outlaws, and led to the unleashing of extreme forms of violence.

The atrocities encouraged the desecration and defilement of the corpses of the victims. Standing outside the boundaries of European cultural affinity in the eyes of the Germans, and demonized by racial dogma and the violent language of occupation, the dead bodies of civilians killed during anti-partisan sweeps were inscribed with the contempt of their killers, set on display or denied a proper burial, and simply left to lie where they fell. These acts themselves helped perpetuate and exacerbate the very stereotypes fuelling mass murder in the region.

Land and body: atrocity and aftermath in Generalkommissariat Weissruthenia

In spring 1942 the German doctrine on combating partisans shifted. The guerrilla threat was growing, due not only to the Soviet's increasing success at inserting reinforcements, advisors, and supplies behind the lines, but also to the economic policies of the occupational administration. Prior to this period, efforts to contain the partisan movement were sporadic, consisting mostly of foot patrols, the taking of hostages, fines against the civilian population, and select mass reprisals, such as executions and the burning of villages. Security forces complained about these methods, arguing they failed to comprehensively address the growing threat. Decisions were then made to conduct so-called 'large operations' (*Grossunternehmen*), in which Wehrmacht divisions would operate alongside police units and their local auxiliaries across wide stretches of territory in order extend the administration's control.[17]

This change was crucial, as these operations transferred military tactics into civilian areas, essentially waging war on the local population. Troops, working from information passed on by informers, bracketed off large swaths of the region, seeking to encircle partisan forces and cut off their escape routes. The space inside these 'cauldrons' was then reduced in size until units reached the centre, then swept their way outwards, hoping to catch any stragglers who might have escaped the first sweep. These areas were essentially free-fire zones, and although troops worked their way through the tangled forests looking for partisan camps, the operations' main targets were villages suspected of supporting the resistance.[18]

German guidelines for these assaults called for an overwhelming show of force, and aircraft and artillery often bombarded these locations prior to the start of the operation.[19] Shortly afterwards troops would arrive and surround the villages. Those villagers who attempted to escape or resisted were killed on the spot, and the rest of the population was gathered in the centre of the village and interrogated regarding the whereabouts of the partisans. Suspects were then executed on the scene, and the rest of the inhabitants were deported for slave labour; livestock and food supplies were usually removed. The villages were then set on fire, both to demonstrate the repercussions of assisting the enemy and to deny the partisans resources.[20]

At ground level these actions created chaos. German troops entered villages and rounded up the population, and beat them with whips, rifle butts, and sticks as they attempted to separate those deemed 'work capable' (*Arbeitsfähig*) from the elderly, sick, and very young, who were to be executed or deported to languish in special camps. Unsurprisingly, some villagers resisted and scuffles and gun shots rang out among shouted orders and the cries of children. The thick smoke emanating from burning thatch and straw increased the tense atmosphere. Interrogations were carried out on the scene, with inhabitants and their children threatened at gunpoint in an effort to extract information about local partisan groups. Those found to have missing adult male family members or without identity papers were considered 'partisan supporters' and executed. In some cases entire villages were wiped out, either for their perceived resistance to the raids, or simply because they were located on the edges of the forest, and thus associated with the partisans lurking within.[21]

In some locations the inhabitants were gathered together and forced to dig mass graves. At others, natural or pre-existing manmade depressions, such as gullies and ditches, were used. Other peasants were forced to fill them, underlining notions of collective punishment and reinforcing notions of their subhuman nature. However, during these operations units were under strict timetables to reach particular map coordinates by the end of each day, ensuring the area under assault would remain isolated. As a result, troops often dispensed with efforts to concentrate their victims at one prepared killing site, and massacres tended to decentralize into scattered, smaller shootings throughout the village. The bodies of the victims were left where they fell, for surviving members of the local population to attend to after the soldiers moved on.[22]

German doctrine also called for the hanging of 'bandits'. Here, the bodies of the victims were used most directly as a vehicle to convey the occupation's power. This technique served as a spectacular form of communication, to express the Germans' ability to discipline those who resisted. Each displayed body also helped craft the image of the civilian population and the partisans as one and the same in the minds of the occupiers. Many villagers died by this method, and few resistance fighters were caught during raids by the occupation's troops. Hanging criminalized these victims through an act of punishment historically associated throughout Europe with banditry. This point was driven home by the signs hung around their necks, proclaiming their alleged 'crimes', such as theft, robbery, or looting. Many of the corpses were also displayed prominently on the main thoroughfares of towns, or at important intersections or crossroads, ensuring their view by the local populace. These public executions also called for a kind of collective participation different from other forms of murder. Soldiers gathered to watch the executions or to observe the bodies afterwards, posing with them for photographs, further dehumanizing the suspended victims as macabre trophies. Each suspended corpse symbolically served to assert the occupation's authority, and underscored the supposed criminal nature of the entire population, as their public display implied that these so-called bandits hailed from the people.

In some cases, these acts of spectacle came in the wake of the partisans' own efforts to use the corpses of their attackers to convey resistance to the occupation. For example, during one anti-partisan operation, part of a group of Latvian police led by German officers was cut off from its detachment and annihilated. They were later found naked and mutilated in the woods, and when efforts were made to recover the bodies, the troops discovered they were mined. The unit which recovered the bodies a short time later burned several villages and killed their inhabitants in revenge for what they considered to be an especially underhand act.[23]

One particularly gruesome method which arose from operational considerations was the immolation of victims. The commanders of anti-partisan operations considered the burning of bodies expedient, as it used the destruction of the villages to meet sanitary guidelines regarding the disposal of corpses, as noted in a report from Operation Winterzauber, in March 1943. One unit commander ordered that where suspects could not be handed over to the security police for 'special treatment' – summary executions in the forest – his men should shoot their prisoners in houses and cover the bodies with straw to encourage their immolation once the buildings were set alight. This tactic literally enacted the type of cleansing purge discussed in operational after-action reports. Additionally, the purifying properties of fire were also well advocated in German medical circles, and this literature appears to have encouraged such methods, as well as the idea that the East was literally and figuratively ridden with deadly bacteria (i.e. its people), which had to be rooted out and completely destroyed in order to conquer the region and allow *Kultur* to take hold.[24]

Going one step further, many units burned their victims alive. Survivors recalled that soldiers often rushed into their homes and ordered them to lie on the floor, and in some cases their captors questioned them not only about local partisan activity but also about disease in the village or whether family members were sick. The buildings of those deemed guilty or a health risk were then set on fire, and anyone attempting to flee was shot. Barns in particular were considered good sites for these atrocities, because of their size and the ready supply of flammable material such as straw.[25]

Other motives must be taken into consideration alongside such 'rational' explanations as the disposal of bodies. The methods used by the Germans were also chosen to destroy their victims not only physically but also emotionally. For villagers across Eastern Europe, fire was viewed as a catastrophe; one survivor recalled that 'even the earth groaned' as her village was destroyed, underscoring the significance of this rupture in the intricate weaving of nature and society which comprised peasant cosmology.[26] Buildings constructed from wood and thatch were highly flammable, and even a small fire could destroy an entire community. Indeed, fire remained such an important collective concern that villagers often reserved their harshest punishments for members of the community who committed acts of arson.[27]

After the war, the anti-partisan operations were remembered as an apocalypse made worse by the fact that the majority of the victims were denied proper burial. In many cases German units did not record information regarding their executions, and the locations of many mass graves remain unknown. In other cases the victims became visible only after the spring thaw, when the snow and ice covering them melted. Once uncovered, some merged with the mud, becoming part of the horrific landscape imagined by the Germans. Other bodies lay exposed for weeks, often unrecognizable even to surviving family members. Likewise, those villagers who managed to escape returned to the smouldering ashes of their villages to find immolated corpses, which would disintegrate once they were moved, in some cases making the effort of recovering the body of a loved one a traumatizing act in itself. Burials after the atrocity broke with traditional practices, as they took place in secret locations, in the woods or swamps, unconsecrated spaces traditionally associated with corruption and evil.[28] A common theme in the post-war dreams of survivors was visitation by deceased family members, expressing their continued pain and anguish, a sign of the guilt felt by their relatives' inability to provide proper burials. Through their very form, these atrocities denied a sense of closure and continued to terrorize the victims for decades after the event.[29]

The violation of local custom caused by these crimes was likely known by the Germans. Many units garrisoned in the rear areas worked closely with local collaborators, and these militias often comprised the bulk of the manpower for anti-partisan operations. Additionally, due to the heavily forested terrain of Generalkommissariat Weissruthenia, troops in the region were often decentralized in small groups when not participating in large manoeuvres, spread out across a variety of strong points in areas considered to be less of a security risk. At these fortifications they trained local personnel and worked closely with the population in order to cultivate informers. Consequently, many must have been at least partially aware of local customs. For example, in one case German troops deliberately selected the village bathhouse as a site of execution for five suspected female partisans. This landmark served important village functions, and the murders desecrated this important social space, making it unusable. Thus even those locales spared from total destruction were environmentally and culturally affected by atrocity. Mass graves served an important, if unintentional, function in the Germans' scorched earth policy, as they poisoned groundwater, making villages and croplands unusable. They also attracted wild animals, creating yet another problem for survivors, while the killings also upended villagers' sense of cosmology, bringing the polluting forces of chaos and misfortune closer to their homes, angering local spirits, as allegedly evidenced by the earth moving as the graves shifted.[30]

If the Germans knew they were violating local norms, they also consciously violated their own. Cremation, for example, remained a contentious form of corpse disposal inside Germany, despite endorsements within the medical community, as graves, particularly individual ones, conveyed humanity. The dead were sacred and their proper care in specifically designated areas was considered a distinguished mark of a civilized people. If improperly cared for, the dead were an expression of disorder, and the growing tempo of the air war against the Reich posed serious challenges to the Nazi regime's legitimacy. As Monica Black has noted, the charred and mutilated bodies found in the streets of German cities after bombing raids were 'matter out of place', which threatened to undermine notions of social and cultural order. The regime struggled to cope with the challenges posed by the treatment of these corpses, and even the efforts to generate support for mass burials met considerable civilian resistance.[31]

As Mary Douglas famously remarked in her work on contamination, taboos protect 'the local consensus on how the world is organized', and the Germans' deliberate violation of their own sacred views on the treatment of corpses consequently cast the East as a dirty, chaotic space, a monstrous land of *Unkultur* populated by subhumans, as reflected in the unburied bodies exposed by spring thaws or hanging from trees along the streets of villages burnt to their foundations.[32] As Wilhelm B. remarked during his interrogation in 1975 by East German authorities regarding his participation in anti-partisan operations, 'The longer I stayed in the Soviet Union the more I hated the partisans'. Here 'the partisans' likely served as code for the civilian population at large. When asked about the motives behind the immolation of seventy villagers inside a barn near the village of Dmitrowo in 1943, he replied that his unit decided this was the most brutal and painful fashion in which to murder their victims, evidencing the hatred they felt towards them. Each act of violence and its physical aftermath enhanced pre-existing stereotypes, increased disgust and frustration at the apparent backwardness of the region, and encouraged new forms of brutality, allowing the corpses themselves to become a message conveying the hatred directed at the population.[33]

The anti-partisan operations of 1942–44 plunged the region into the type of catastrophic social and economic conditions the Germans expected to find during the invasion in June 1941. Enduring over 140 major sweeps and countless smaller actions, over 2 million of Generalkommissariat Weissruthenia died during the four-year occupation. The extent of the devastation is doubly reflected by the roughly 5,000 villages destroyed. At 629 of these locations, the entire population perished, further reflecting the magnitude of the damage done to the region's economic output, not to mention social and cultural life.[34]

This violence arose from, and was shaped by, the stereotypes of a 'Wild East', characterized by thick forests, murky swamps, and savage peoples closer to animals than human beings. A centrifugal dynamic emerged over the course of the occupation, as expectations of local behaviour called for the ruthless and pre-emptive application of punishment. These efforts in turn created physical conditions and civilian responses which then radicalized these perceptions, encouraging brutal new initiatives, whose scope constantly broadened, drawing in ever greater numbers of victims. Key elements in this process, and much overlooked, were the methods of execution and the treatment of the bodies of the victims. Breaking their own taboos concerning the treatment of corpses, the German occupiers created a land of *Unkultur*, a self-inflicted failure which hindered their attempts to reorder the landscape and bend its people to their colonial vision.

Notes

1 Generalkommissariat Weissruthenia was the German administrative designation for the area of what is now Belarus. Between 1941 and 1944 it was part of the larger Reichskommissariat Ostland, which encompassed the present-day Baltic states, in addition to Weissruthenia.
2 United States Holocaust Memorial Archive (USHMMA), RG 22.001, Fiche 3, Folder 21.1.
3 Ibid.

4 A. Confino, 'Fantasies about the Jews: cultural reflections on the Holocaust', *History and Memory*, special issue, *Histories and Memories of Twentieth Century Germany*, 17:1–2 (spring–winter 2005), 296–322, at pp. 301–2.
5 V. G. Liulevicius, *The German Myth of the East: 1800 to the Present* (Oxford: Oxford University Press, 2009), pp. 79, 137, 178. For an excellent discussion of such fantasies inside Germany during the interwar period, see A. Sammartino, *The Impossible Border: Germany and the East, 1914–1922* (Ithaca: Cornell University Press, 2010).
6 Quoted in C. Gerlach, *Kalkulierte Morde: Die deutsche Wirtschafts- und Vernichtnungspolitik in Weissrussland 1941 bis 1944* (Hamburg: HIS Verlag, 2000), pp. 874–5; H. R. Trevor-Roper, *Hitler's Table Talk: 1941–1944, His Private Conversations* (New York: Enigma Books, 2000), p. 621.
7 USHMMA, RG 14.015, Fiche 1671.5; T. Taylor, *International Military Tribunals, Case 11, 1948* (Nuremberg: Office of the Military Government, Germany, 1948), pp. 5, 19, 23; P. Lieb, 'A precursor of modern counter-insurgency operations? The German occupation of the Ukraine in 1918', in Alaric Searle (ed.), *Working Papers in Military and International History, No. 4* (Salford: University of Salford, 2007), pp. 2–32, at pp. 22, 25. On the Russian Civil War and its aftermath, see: P. Holquist, *Making War, Forging Revolution: Russia's Continuum of Crisis, 1914–1921* (Cambridge: Harvard University Press, 2002); A. Prusin, *Nationalizing a Borderland: War, Ethnicity, and Anti-Jewish Violence in East Galicia, 1914–1920* (Tuscaloosa: University of Alabama Press, 2005); D. Pohl, *Die Heerschaft der Wehrmacht: Deutsche Militärbesatzung und einheimische Bevölkerung in der Sowjetunion 1941–1944* (Munich: R. Oldenbourg Verlag, 2008).
8 Quoted in D. W. Oetting, *Kein Krieg wie im Westen: Wehrmacht und Sowjetarmee im Russland Krieg, 1941–1945* (Bonn: Osning Verlag, 2009), p. 54.
9 B. Musial, *Sowjetische Partisanen: Mythos und Wirklichkeit* (Munich: Ferdinand Schöningh, 2009), pp. 45–6, 55.
10 B. Waitmann, 'Calculus of complicity: the Wehrmacht, the anti-partisan war, and the Final Solution in White Russia, 1941–1942', *Central European History*, 44 (2011), 308–37, at pp. 318–24.
11 'The partisan's oath', USHMMA, RG 18.002, Reel 11, Fond R 83, Opis 1, Folder 122.7; RG 15.129, File 4379, 4–25.
12 USHMMA, RG 14.015, Fiche 2175.2; National Archives (NARA), T 175, Reel 74.2591694.
13 See J. Gumz, 'Wehrmacht perceptions of mass violence in Croatia, 1941–1942', *Historical Journal*, 44:4 (2001), 1015–38, at pp. 1028, 1032.
14 USHMMA, RG 18.001, Reel 8, Fond R 82, Opis 1, Folder 9, 2.
15 USHMMA, RG 53, Reel 11, Fond 370, Opis 1, Folder 386A.51; RG 53, Reel 5, Fond 655, Opis 1, File 3.2–3, 8, 60; RG 18.002, Reel 2, Fond R69, Opis 1A, Folder 6, 114. See also Paul Weindling, *Epidemics and Genocide in Eastern Europe, 1890–1945* (Oxford: Oxford University Press, 2000).

16 P. Blood, *Hitler's Bandit Hunters: The SS and the Nazi Occupation of Europe* (Dulles: Potomac Books, 2007), pp. 77–9; NARA, T175, Reel 140.2663246.
17 USHMMA, RG 14.015, Fiche 1671/3. 121; Gerlach, *Kalkulierte Morde*, pp. 884–5, 909.
18 USHMMA, RG 18.001, Reel 11, Fond R 83, Opis 1, Folder 122, 14–15; Gerlach, *Kalkulierte Morde*, pp. 889–90.
19 USHMMA, RG 18.001, Reel 8, Fond R 82, Opis 1, Folder 6.51, 72, 81.
20 USHMMA, RG 14.015.81, Fiche 3922.
21 USHMMA, RG 14.068, Box 29, Fiche 391.35.
22 USHMMA, RG 18.002, Reel 8, Fond R 82, Opis 1, Folder 6.4–6; RG 14.068, Box 29, Fiche 391, 101, Fiche 395.258.
23 USHMMA, RG 14.068, Box 29, Fiche 396; A. Adamovitch, Y. Bryl & V. Kolesnik, *Out of the Fire* (Moscow: Progress Publishing, 1980), p. 247; R. Wiegman, 'The anatomy of lynching', *Journal of the History of Sexuality*, 3:3 (January 1993), 445–67, at p. 446; USHMMA, RG 18.001, Reel 8, Fond R 82, Opis 1, Folder 9.63–4, Folder 10.15.
24 Weindling, *Epidemics and Genocide in Eastern Europe*, pp. 42–5; Liulevicius. *The German Myth of the East*, p. 166; USHMMA, RG 18.001, Reel 8, Fond R 82, Opis 7.25.
25 USHMMA, RG 14.068, Box 29, Fiche 396.28; Adamovitch *et al.*, *Out of the Fire*, pp. 96, 123, 132, 196.
26 Adamovitch *et al.*, *Out of the Fire*, p. 275; K. Brown, *A Biography of No Place: From Ethnic Borderland to Soviet Heartland* (Cambridge: Harvard University Press, 2004), pp. 67–9; O. S. Tian-Shanskaia & D. L. Ransel (trans., eds), *Village Life in Late Tsarist Russia* (Bloomington: Indiana University Press, 1993), p. 136.
27 Tian-Shanskaia & Ransel, *Village Life in Late Tsarist Russia*, pp. 116, 123.
28 Brown, *A Biography of No Place*, p. 68.
29 Adamovitch *et al.*, *Out of the Fire*, pp. 90–2.
30 USHMMA, RG 14.068, Box 29, Fiche 393, 112, 136; E. Haberer, 'The German gendarmerie and partisans in Belorussia, 1941–4', in B. Shepherd & J. Patterson (eds), *War in a Twilight World: Partisan and Anti-Partisan Warfare in Eastern Europe, 1939–45* (New York: Palgrave Macmillan, 2010), pp. 102–25, at pp. 107, 116–17; Brown, *A Biography of No Place*, p. 68; K. Stang, *Kollaboration und Massenmord: Die litauische Hilfspolizei, das Rollkommando Hamann und die Ermordung der litauischen Juden* (Frankfurt: Peter Lang, 1996), pp. 267–8.
31 M. Black, *Death in Berlin: From Weimar to Divided Germany* (Cambridge: Cambridge University Press, 2010), pp. 116–19, 132; Weindling, *Epidemics and Genocide in Eastern Europe*, p. 43.
32 M. Douglas, *Purity and Danger: An Analysis of the Concept of Pollution and Taboo* (New York: Routledge Classics, 2002), p. ix.
33 USHMMA, RG 14.068, Box 29, Fiche 392. 68, Fiche 394.203.
34 P. A. Rudling, 'The Khatyn massacre in Belorussia: a historical controversy revisited', *Holocaust and Genocide Studies*, 26 (spring 2012), 29–58, at pp. 29, 46–7.

Bibliography

Archives

National Archives (NARA), College Park, Maryland
United States Holocaust Memorial Archive (USHMMA), Washington, DC

Books, chapters, and articles

Adamovitch, A., Y. Bryl & V. Kolesnik, *Out of the Fire* (Moscow: Progress Publishing, 1980)
Black, M., *Death in Berlin: From Weimar to Divided Germany* (Cambridge: Cambridge University Press, 2010)
Blood, P., *Hitler's Bandit Hunters: The SS and the Nazi Occupation of Europe* (Dulles: Potomac Books, 2007)
Brown, K., *A Biography of No Place: From Ethnic Borderland to Soviet Heartland* (Cambridge: Harvard University Press, 2004)
Confino, A., 'Fantasies about the Jews: cultural reflections on the Holocaust', *History and Memory*, special issue, *Histories and Memories of Twentieth Century Germany*, 17:1–2 (spring–winter 2005), 296–322
Douglas, M., *Purity and Danger: An Analysis of the Concept of Pollution and Taboo* (New York: Routledge Classics, 2002)
Gerlach, C., *Kalkulierte Morde: Die deutsche Wirtschafts- und Vernichtnungspolitik in Weissrussland 1941 bis 1944* (Hamburg: HIS Verlag, 2000)
Gumz, J., 'Wehrmacht perceptions of mass violence in Croatia, 1941–1942', *Historical Journal*, 44:4 (2001), 1015–38
Haberer, E., 'The German gendarmerie and partisans in Belorussia, 1941–4', in B. Shepherd & J. Patterson (eds), *War in a Twilight World: Partisan and Anti-Partisan Warfare in Eastern Europe, 1939–45* (New York: Palgrave Macmillan, 2010), pp. 102–25
Holquist, P., *Making War, Forging Revolution: Russia's Continuum of Crisis, 1914–1921* (Cambridge: Harvard University Press, 2002)
Lieb, P., 'A precursor of modern counter-insurgency operations? The German occupation of the Ukraine in 1918', in A. Searle (ed.), *Working Papers in Military and International History, No. 4* (Salford: University of Salford, 2007), pp. 2–32
Liulevicius, V. G., *The German Myth of the East: 1800 to the Present* (Oxford: Oxford University Press, 2009)
Musial, B., *Sowjetische Partisanen: Mythos und Wirklichkeit* (Munich: Ferdinand Schöningh, 2009)
Oetting, D. W., *Kein Krieg wie im Westen: Wehrmacht und Sowjetarmee im Russland Krieg, 1941–1945* (Bonn: Osning Verlag, 2009)
Pohl, D., *Die Heerschaft der Wehrmacht: Deutsche Militärbesatzung und einheimische Bevölkerung in der Sowjetunion 1941–1944* (Munich: R. Oldenbourg Verlag, 2008)

Prusin, A., *Nationalizing a Borderland: War, Ethnicity, and Anti-Jewish Violence in East Galicia, 1914–1920* (Tuscaloosa: University of Alabama Press, 2005)

Rudling, P. A., 'The Khatyn massacre in Belorussia: a historical controversy revisited', *Holocaust and Genocide Studies*, 26:1 (spring 2012), 29–58

Sammartino, A., *The Impossible Border: Germany and the East, 1914–1922* (Ithaca: Cornell University Press, 2010)

Stang, K., *Kollaboration und Massenmord. Die litauische Hilfspolizei, das Rollkommando Hamann und die Ermordung der litauischen Juden* (Frankfurt: Peter Lang, 1996)

Taylor, T., *International Military Tribunals, Case 11, 1948* (Nuremberg: Office of the Military Government, Germany, 1948)

Tian-Shanskaia, O. S. & D. L. Ransel (trans, eds), *Village Life in Late Tsarist Russia* (Bloomington: Indiana University Press, 1993)

Trevor-Roper, H. R., *Hitler's Table Talk: 1941–1944, His Private Conversations* (New York: Enigma Books, 2002)

Waitmann, B., 'Calculus of complicity: the Wehrmacht, the anti-partisan war, and the Final Solution in White Russia, 1941–1942', *Central European History*, 44 (2011), 308–37

Weindling, P., *Epidemics and Genocide in Eastern Europe, 1890–1945* (Oxford: Oxford University Press, 2000)

Wiegman, R., 'The anatomy of lynching', *Journal of the History of Sexuality*, 3:3 (January 1993), 445–67

Part II: Practices

4

Earth, fire, water: or how to make the Armenian corpses disappear[1]

Raymond H. Kévorkian

In the planning of mass violence, the logistical aspects of the elimination of the corpses of victims have almost as important a place as the executions themselves. The mass violence committed by the Young Turk regime against the Ottoman Armenian population has sometimes hinted at improvisation, but works published in recent years have shown that the destruction of Armenians (and Syrians) had been organized with far more care than one might have imagined, including the logistics of eliminating the corpses.[2] As we shall see, the Young Turk authorities made every effort to enforce their directives on officials or paramilitaries reluctant to carry out these menial tasks or negligent in performing them. Weather and domestic or wild animals also played their part, as they brought to light a multitude of corpses sometimes buried several months earlier. The location of the massacres largely conditioned the method used to eliminate from public view the corpses of the victims, although the ideological dimension should not be downplayed, as the first priority for the Young Turks was to conceal all traces of their crimes as quickly as possible.

The first phase of the genocide

The first phase of the genocide, from April to September 1915, consisted of the forced deportation (the 'death marches') of the

Armenian and Syrian populations from the Ottoman Empire, in particular from six eastern provinces, where the majority had their historic roots. These are wild, mountainous regions, at average altitudes of 2,000 metres; the enclosed valleys – especially those of the Tigris and the Euphrates, but also of the Murat River – were used as traps, with their entries and exits controlled by the butchers of the regime's 'Special Organization'. The males, constituting the principal target of the Central Committee of Ittihad ve Terakki (Committee of Union and Progress), were systematically executed and tossed into the turbulent waters of the Tigris and the Euphrates.

The deportees were supposed to be 'relegated' to the deserts of Syria and Mesopotamia, to which they were transferred on foot. However, the first to arrive in these regions were the corpses of deportees floating on the Tigris and the Euphrates. By 10 June 1915, the German vice-consul at Mosul, Walter Holstein, wired his ambassador:

> Six hundred and fourteen Armenians (men, women, and children) expelled from Dyarbakir and conducted towards Mosul were all killed during the voyage by raft [on the Tigris]. The *keleks* [rafts] arrived empty yesterday. For several days now, corpses and human limbs have been floating down the river. Other convoys of Armenian 'settlers' are currently en route, and it is probable that the same fate awaits them, too.[3]

The situation was still worse on the Euphrates, as a report by the German consul at Aleppo, Walter Rössler, attested:

> The aforementioned presence of corpses in the Euphrates, which has been observed in Rumkale, Burecik, and Jerablus, continued for twenty-five days, as I was informed on 17 July. The bodies were all tied together in the same way, in pairs, back to back. This systematic arrangement shows that it is a question, not of random killings, but of a general extermination plan elaborated by the authorities.... The corpses have reappeared, after an interruption of several days, in ever greater numbers. This time, it is essentially a question of the bodies of woman and children.[4]

While the Euphrates made it possible to get rid of the corpses encumbering the northern provinces at small cost, they created problems for the local authorities in Syria and Mesopotamia. In confirming the information from the German diplomat, certain authenticated documents, mentioned during the trial of the Young Turks, show that this method was not to the taste of Ahmed Djemal Pasha, the commander of the Ottoman Fourth Army, who held authority over the entire region. In a telegram of 14 July 1915 (transcribed in the Gregorian calendar) addressed to the governor of Dyarbakir, Dr Mehmed Reshid, the navy minister, complained about the presence of corpses floating on the Euphrates. The governor then wired him two days later:

> The Euphrates has little relationship with our province. The floating corpses come probably from the side of the provinces of Erzerum and Harput. Those who fall dead here either are thrown into deep abandoned caves, or, as often happens, burned. There is rarely a place to bury them.[5]

One might also highlight a well documented case of 2,833 infants from the Bayburt district, who had passed the age limit accepted for 'adoption', who were drowned in the Euphrates at the level of the Kemah gorge.[6]

Not only the water courses, but also lakes, wells, and cisterns served to get rid of corpses. The extent of the crimes committed around Lake Geoljik/Gölcük in this regard is well documented in a report by the American consul in Harput, Leslie Davis. On 24 September 1915, the diplomat decided to take a ride on horseback towards this mountain lake, after a Turk had told him the place was covered in corpses.[7] Leaving at about four o'clock in the morning, in order to get away without being noticed, the consul and his Turkish guide were in the saddle for five hours towards Kurdemlik, finding all the way along the road hundreds of scarcely buried bodies, with arms or legs sticking out of the ground or partially eaten by dogs. Some of the bodies had been burned 'in order to find any gold which the people may have swallowed'.[8] After this, the consul decided to roam the cliff's north-eastern bank, intercut with 'deep valleys'. It seemed that the method most frequently used by the paramilitary bandits was to push the deportees over the top of the cliffs into these steep valleys, real traps whose sole exit was the lake. This doubtless explained why hundreds of bodies were floating on the banks of the lake. During this first part of the trek, Davis observed two valleys, one filled with at least 1,000 and another with more than 1,500 corpses, and many others less filled, but which he could not approach at that time as the stench was so great.[9]

Davis concluded the report of his second trek with an estimate of no fewer than 10,000 massacred and abandoned on the banks of Lake Gölcük. 'Few localities could be better suited to the fiendish purposes of the Turks in their plan to exterminate the Armenian population than this peaceful lake ... far removed from the sight of civilized man'.[10]

In the southern district of Nisibin, where Armenians, Jacobites, Chaldeans, Kurds, and some 600 Jews lived, the subgovernor, on 16 August 1915, organized a raid on Christian notables, including the Jacobite bishop, who were executed the same day outside the town's limits. Women and children were exterminated in the course of the following days and thrown into sixty-five pits that also received thousands of corpses of deportees coming from the north.[11] To the north of Nisibin, Dara was the scene of repeated massacres, which makes one think that the ruins of the ancient town were chosen as a slaughterhouse. For example, at Dara on 11 July 1915, some 7,000 deportees coming from Erzerum were thrown into the town's immense Byzantine underground cisterns.[12] Around the same time, a convoy of deportees from the north arrived at Argana Maden, where they saw on the banks of the Tigris a spectacle reminiscent of Dante: thousands of decomposing corpses.[13]

Several hundred kilometres downstream, during the winter of 1915–16, General Halil Kut, appointed in January 1916 by his nephew, the war minister Generalissimo Ismail Enver Pasha, as commander of the Sixth Army operating on the Iraq Front, gave the order to exterminate the 15,000 deportees 'residing' in Mosul and its surroundings. According to testimony collected by the Swiss historian S. Zurlinden, Halil had these 15,000 Armenians executed on two nights by Kurds and irregulars, by throwing them into the Tigris bound in batches of ten.[14]

All these elements show planning, the use of proven methods, and preparatory work by the executioners; they ensured that the victims did not escape drowning, by binding them in pairs or more, back to back, before tossing them into the water. This method, which was used only on male victims, seems to have come into widespread use with the removal of the Armenians from their homes over the months of May–June 1915. Its advantage was that it could be carried out quickly, but it also had the disadvantage of polluting waterways situated downstream, sometimes over a distance of several thousand kilometres.

The treatment of the bodies of women and children, who comprised the large majority of the convoys of deportees, was significantly different. During this first phase of the genocide, the hilly routes taken by the convoys, remote from any habitation, and the extreme conditions imposed by the escorts – the deportees were provided with neither food nor water – determined both the death of the deportees and the treatment of their corpses. A form of 'natural selection' occurred, with the weakest being simply left to die by the roadside or finished off with a gunshot. Survival was entirely dependent on the ability of the deportees to keep up with the convoy. In the eyes of the decision-makers, these 'natural' deaths corroborated the official description of the genocide as merely a 'population transfer'.

Among the countless sites chosen for the destruction of the deportees, the mountainous district of Kahta, situated to the south of Malatia, to the east of Adıyaman, was without doubt the most murderous. More than 500,000 deportees crossed by the Firincilar plain, about three hours to the south-east of Malatia, the arrival point for convoys of deportees coming from the north.[15] The site was littered with rotting corpses that emitted an extreme stench. An elderly Turk explained to one of the deportees that worse was to come next day, when he would embark on the 'death march' beyond the peaks of Malatya Dağları.[16] One witness reported seeing a battalion of 'gendarmerie' and a 'director' receiving orders by telephone.[17] It was in fact a command centre for the Special Organization, remote from everything but equipped with a field telephone, to coordinate the departure of the convoys for the 'death march'. The witness further noted that the 'gendarmes', with a certain courtesy, ordered the deportees to leave their belongings on the spot, by entrusting them to the commission responsible for the 'war tax' (*teklif-i harbiye*). He estimated that 80,000–100,000 deportees were then camping at the foot of the mountains.[18]

One by one, the convoys took the direction of the gorges opening beyond Firincilar, one of the killing fields regularly used by the Special Organization. It had been put under the supervision of the parliamentary deputy for Dersim, Haci Baloszâde Mehmed Nuri Bey, and his brother, Ali Pasha. They had two Kurdish chieftains of the Reşvan tribe, Zeynel Bey and Haci Bedri Aga, under their command, with their squadrons of bandits.[19] The deportees were suddenly confronted with an appalling sight: the gorge opening after Firincilar was filled with the corpses of people from earlier convoys.[20]

Once the convoy reached the gorge, Zeynel Bey directed operations from a height. He first had the few men still in the convoy separated from the other deportees and then put to death. The operation went on for a full hour and a half. According to Alphonse Arakelian, who was in this convoy, 3,600 people lost their lives, but around 100 men survived.[21] One of Arakelian's companions, Sarkis Manukian, later declared that 2,115 men were slain that day in the Kahta gorge.[22]

While isolated mountain passes, such as Kahta's, suited mass slaughter by relieving the killers of the need to get rid of the bodies, the mountain routes and sometimes the main roads the deportees had to follow presented problems from time to time. Tens of thousands of Armenians died en route, and were rarely buried, or only in haste. The increasing number of rotting corpses along the roads, as well as a typhus epidemic that spread rapidly within the local populations, could not fail to worry the governors and subgovernors, who were assailed with complaints on all sides. It was then essential that the ministry 'sanitize' the region, and take the necessary measures to put some order into the prevailing anarchy. Commander Djemal Pasha reported in his memoirs, 'I was furious when I learned that the exiled Armenians were to come to Bozanti on their way over the Taurus and Adana to Aleppo, for any interference with the line of communications might have the gravest consequences for the [Suez] Canal Expedition'.[23] In other words, epidemics caused by the rotting corpses threatened some crossing points essential to a switch from the Armenian plateau to the deserts of Syria and Mesopotamia, of major strategic importance for the commander of the Palestine Front.

As for the measures taken by the authorities to control these problems, the investigation files for the Young Turk criminals brought to trial in 1919 contain a series of exchanges between the governor-general of Mamuret ul-Aziz province, Sabit Bey, and the administrator of Malatia, Reshid Bey, and between the Minister of the Interior and Sabit Bey. The first telegram on this matter was addressed by Sabit to the Malatia administrator on 21 August 1915, or shortly after the passage of the main convoys of deportees from the northern and western regions in the department of Malatia. It tells us first that 'there are many corpses littering the roads' in the department, with 'the numerous inconveniences that engenders'. Sabit complains that the corpses were not buried with 'care' and says there should be no hesitation in punishing 'officials showing evidence of negligence'.[24] It seems, however, that the instructions were not always followed. On 10 September, Sabit renewed his complaints to Reshid. He wrote, 'We learn that there are rotting corpses on the boundary between [the departments] of Hüsni Mansur and Besni.... It is not appropriate, from the point of view of government and for reasons of hygiene, that one finds [corpses] in the open air, in a state of decomposition'.[25] In excuse for the administrator of Malatia, one must grant that the repeated passage of convoys demanded a regular renewal of road clearing by the gendarmes to whom, oddly, this task had been entrusted. These corpses rotting away betrayed rather too well the real purpose of the deportations.

Three months later, doubtless on the heels of complaints reaching Istanbul through diplomatic channels, the Minister of the Interior rebuked the governor-general of Mamuret ul-Aziz, on the grounds that 'one again finds exposed corpses ... or remains'.[26] It seems that these orders communicated to subgovernors and gendarmerie commanders, threatened with court martial,[27] did finally convince the latter 'to open trenches dug sufficiently deeply so that the dogs could not reach them'.[28]

These precautions lasted only a while. According to the official figures cited during what became known as the Yozgat trial, held some years after the events, before a military court, about 33,000 Armenians from the Yozgat department were deported, and the majority of them massacred in a valley near Keller, at Boğazkemin. Captain Şükrü, who served in the Yozgat gendarmerie, noted in his 'confessions' that the massacres were carried out under the order of the Minister of the Interior, and that the traces of these massacres 'were wiped out, at the end of October, by digging huge trenches into which the bodies were tipped, then burned, but the winter rains brought to light the rotted corpses or the bones'.[29]

Finally, one sees that during the first phase of the extermination of the Ottoman Armenians, the priority of the central authorities was the physical destruction of the deportees and the use of summary means to get rid of the bodies. The rivers flowing down from the Armenian plateau, principally the Tigris and the Euphrates, provided a low-cost means of doing so, although many of the bodies became stuck on the banks, where they took months to decompose. This method, in theory highly efficient, nonetheless therefore had unforeseen consequences: it was sometimes necessary to use explosives to clear what were quite literally dams formed by the mass of floating bodies, while the waters of these two legendary rivers remained polluted long afterwards, giving rise to epidemics among the Arab populations living downstream. This method was used exclusively on men, who were the first victims of the genocidal process. Some of the bodies drifted as far as the Syrian desert and the Persian Gulf, with lasting pollution to the feeder rivers, under the gaze of the local population and of other witnesses, especially Germans. Similarly, the land routes used for the deportation became littered with corpses, although attempts were certainly made by the local administrative services to clean them, but since the latter were reluctant to dig sufficiently deep trenches, the vagaries of the winter weather of 1915–16 and animals brought traces of these decomposed bodies to light, provoking the wrath of the Minister of the Interior.

The second phase of genocide and the network of concentration camps

The second phase of genocide, which stretched from autumn 1915 to autumn 1916, was in the context of Syria and Mesopotamia. These thinly populated desert regions afforded a very different treatment of bodies. Here, the deportees who survived the death marches were poured into a couple of dozen concentration camps. People there died a 'natural' death, from exhaustion, starvation, or epidemic disease.

The common lot of the several hundred thousand deportees in Syria or Mesopotamia was to clutter the makeshift concentration camps managed by the subdirectorate for deportees, created at Aleppo in the autumn of 1915. This quasi-official organ, which was attached to the directorate for the 'installation of tribes and migrants' (Iskân-ı Aşâyirîn ve Muhâcirîn Müdîriyeti, or IAMM) and dependent on the Ministry of the Interior, was entrusted with the task of organizing deportations, and of placing Armenian goods at the disposal of *muhacir* refugees (Muslim settlers), who were effectively being installed in place of the deportees. It was the coordinating body, for example, for relocating Roumeli Muslim emigrants or Circassians from Palestine and Asia Minor into the zones emptied of their Greek or Armenian populations.[30] Hence, the IAMM was the body charged with implementing the Ittihadist Central Committee's policy of 'demographic homogenization', or what now would be termed ethnic cleansing. Under its official remit, it was called upon to settle the displaced Muslims, but it was primarily charged with uprooting the Armenian populations and coordinating their deportation, and we now know what that means according to the location of the people targeted. When one observes the chronology of the movements of Muslim populations under its authoritarian orders, one sees a process almost parallel and synchronized with the cleansing of Armenians from the regions destined for the refugees displaced by the IAMM.[31] Its link with the Committee of Union and Progress is underlined by the very nature of its mission of 'Turkification' of the area, as well as by the choice of its director, Muftizâde Şükrü (Kaya) Bey, a Young Turk close to Mehmed Talât,³² who was delegated by the Committee of Union and Progress in the provinces of Adana and Aleppo in the summer of 1915,³³ like many of his Istanbul colleagues, when the situation demanded urgent intervention and the implementation of a policy determined by the Ittihadist centre.

If the first arrivals in the summer and the start of autumn 1915 had temporarily been established in the roadside inns of Aleppo, from November the governor-general, Mustafa Abdülhalik, forbade access to the town by the convoys, and they were systematically redirected along the Euphrates or the Baghdad Railway, towards Mosul. It was probably under his orders that the subdirectorate created a first transit camp, one hour to the east of the town, at Sibil, a vast plain heralding the deserts of Syria. The camp was supervised by Selanikli Eyub Bey, a bandit chief, and assistant to the director-general of deportations (*Sevkiyat müdüri*), and administered by the *Sevkiyat müdüri* himself, Cemil Hakim Bey.³⁴ Each day a convoy would arrive, as another left in the direction of Meskene and Der Zor (the modern Deir ez-Zor). Several thousand deportees were established there.

However, one establishment reserved for Armenians was maintained in the town: the vast roadside inn in the Achiol quarter, named Kasıldıh, in the court of which were ranged immense tents serving as a prison. The camp in fact was reserved for adult men still miraculously present in the convoys arriving at Aleppo, and for deportees who had hidden in the town whom the police or gendarmeries had caught during their countless night raids. The deceased there were so numerous that, as Walter Rössler wrote, 'towards mid-October, it was decided to set up a new cemetery outside the town. But before one could begin to bury the dead, one unloaded the corpses in piles there and they remained for several days in the open air.'³⁵

A second camp was put in place near a village situated on the northern periphery of the town, at Karlik, along the railway line. According to the American consul, Jesse B. Jackson, one would find there on average 500 tents, housing 2,000–3,000 deportees in appalling conditions, virtually without water. A hundred dead were taken away each day.³⁶

The humourist Yervant Odian, who was temporarily in another camp on the outskirts of Aleppo, witnessed terrible scenes.³⁷ He later wrote about a trench dug at the edge of the camp into which, every morning, were thrown the deceased of the night before, above all victims of the dysentery epidemic that raged there at the beginning of December 1915. He also observed how the Turks, Arabs, and Jews of Aleppo, without children, came to the camp to buy boys and girls from their parents. Cold weather and rain decimated especially those who had no tent; the lack of food did the rest. In this environment, ethical and moral standards are overthrown. Nonetheless, mothers often objected to these transactions, and would not always allow themselves to be convinced by the arguments of the buyers when the latter remarked that, in any case, the mothers would be going to their deaths, and so their child would be saved by being bought. Some mothers who had consented fell into madness or stupor soon after giving up their progeny. The most sought after were children of seven to ten years, above all girls. Thousands of boys and girls were thus sold by their parents.[38]

By October 1915, some 870,000 deportees had reached the border regions of Syria or Mesopotamia. The general strategy of the Turkish authorities was to leave them there to 'rot' in the temporary camps for a few weeks, then to set them on their way to another camp, and so on, until the convoys amounted to no more than a few moribund survivors. The Mamura camp, situated half an hour from Osmaniye, in a place called Kanlıgeçit, received during the months of August, September, and October 1915 around 80,000 Armenian deportees, who were then housed in makeshift tents on:

> a vast and muddy terrain stretching before the Mamura station. Every day, six to seven hundred would die.... The unfortunate, without roof, without clothing, without bread would like fall like dead leaves.... The unburied bodies of the dead piled up. The ground was covered with them. Under many tents, entire families would die of starvation and cold.[39]

The next stage of the deportation journey was to the Islahiye camp, situated on the eastern slope of the Amanus range, where the Baghdad Railway resumed its course. Islahiye was the first concentration camp in the province of Aleppo. A German missionary reported:

> The Islahiye camp is the saddest thing I have ever seen. Right at the entrance a heap of dead bodies lay unburied ... in the immediate neighbourhood of the tents of those who were down with virulent dysentery. The filth in and around these tents was something indescribable. On one single day, the burial committee buried as many as 580 people.[40]

Father Krikoris Balakian, who spent several months in the region and visited the camp in autumn 1915, reports that the subdirectorate for deportees, using the lack of militiamen and means of transportation as an excuse, deliberately let the convoys that arrived in quick succession crowd the camps, making it impossible to provide the deportees with the basic necessities and creating conditions that encouraged the spread of epidemics:

> People arrived by the thousands in Islahiye; only a few hundred were marched off.... There were days on which the deportees in the tens of thousands of tents died, not by the dozens, but by the hundreds, while no healthy people could be found to collect and bury the dead.... The victims were, first and foremost, Armenian children.... The area spread out before us looked like a battlefield. The plain just beyond Islahiye was covered with countless earthen mounds, large and small. These were the graves of Armenians, containing fifty or a hundred bodies each.... Some, unfortunately, were as high as hills.[41]

The camps in Rajo, Katma, and Azaz, located some 20 km south of Islahiye on the road to Aleppo, were in operation only briefly, in the autumn of 1915. In a telegram dated 18 October 1915, the interim German consul in Aleppo, Hermann Hoffmann, informed his ambassador that the director of political affairs in the province estimated that there were 40,000 deportees concentrated in the camps in Rajo and Katma, and that other convoys 'from western, central and northern Anatolia were on the way. Three hundred thousand people have to continue their route southward'.[42] The camp in Rajo lay approximately 1 km from the railway station. At this time of the year, it was a vast marshland, but nonetheless it was covered in tents. A deportee from Banderma reported:

> Corpses piled up in the tents. People who did not have tents had taken up quarters under the railroad bridge in order to protect themselves a little from the cold. A torrent caused by the rains suddenly inundated the spot and swept them off: they all drowned. There were bodies on all sides. Very few escaped with their lives.[43]

On 8 November the German consul, Dr Rössler, returning from Alexandretta, informed the Chancellor, Theobald von Bethmann-Hollweg, that 'the concentration camp in Katma is an indescribable sight'.[44] Within a few weeks, the number of deportees arriving at Katma had soared. According to the same deportee from Banderma, 40,000 tents were set up there in just over a month, housing nearly 200,000 people. Then the survivors 'were ultimately transferred, in the space of a few days, to Azaz, an hour's march away'. The concentration camp in Azaz remained in operation somewhat longer, until spring 1916, but with fewer deportees – those who had managed to bribe officials of the *Sevkiyat* to let them stay in the camp. In the account by the same witness:

> I may say that with the naked eye it was impossible to see from one end to the other of this gigantic tent camp.... Famine and lack of shelters caused great suffering to the population. Dysentery was omnipresent. Poverty was absolute. The dead past counting. [The system] of Armenian supervisors took shape here and was an additional appalling nightmare for the population.... The ground beneath the sagging tents, made of whatever was to hand, was strewn with the dead and dying. Many people were wasting away amid excrement, wracked by hunger. Odour and death reigned everywhere.... The gravediggers were unable even to remove all the bodies.... Every day a convoy was led away by force.

According to Aram Andonian, 60,000 deportees perished in these two camps, carried off by famine or typhus, in autumn 1915.[45]

Bab, the following stage, had a concentration camp set up half an hour from the city, on a clay plain that was transformed into a veritable lake whenever it rained. In October 1915, Bab acquired the status of transit camp and concentration camp. With the beginning of winter and the arrival of deportees from the camps of Islahiye and Katma-Azaz, typhus broke out in Bab. Each day, 400–500 people died there.[46]

Roughly 50,000–60,000 Armenians lost their lives in Bab between October 1915 and spring 1916, according to the evidence of Father Dajad Arslanian, who took it upon himself to bury the dead with as much respect as possible.[47] These figures are confirmed by the German consul and by the camp's chief gravedigger, an Armenian named Hagop, who counted 1,209 deaths in two days, 11 and 12 January 1916 (the gravediggers, recruited from the ranks of the deportees, were allowed to stay with their families until the camps were shut down). The consul, Rössler, stated in a report dated 9 February that 1,029 people died in two days in the same camp.[48]

Of the two main deportation routes on which the concentration camps were located, the first, Mosul–Baghdad, had the camp of Ras ul-Ayn, to the east of Urfa and to the south of Dyarbakir, on the borders of Syria and of Mesopotamia, in a particularly desert region. It had the advantage of being far from everything, screened from indiscreet observation. The first deportees to arrive there came in mid-July 1915; they were natives of Harput, Erzerum, and Bitlis.[49] In approximately the same period, the American consul in

Baghdad, Charles P. Brissel, noted in a report that the governor-general of Baghdad, when he had been the governor of the Mardin department, 'began at and near Mardin, persecutions against the Armenians and sent them to Ras ul-Ayn. There is a report in Baghdad that the Armenians sent to Ras ul-Ayn were massacred some time after their arrival at that place or en route to it'.[50]

Subsequently, many other convoys coming from Urfa, where the first and second deportation routes converged, reached Ras ul-Ayn. In his report of 13 August 1915, the German consul at Aleppo, Rössler, tells us that, thanks to the evidence of a Turkish-speaking Austrian engineer, Lismayer, who was working in the region on construction of the railway, he had been 'able to obtain precise information on another group that had left Adiyaman [to the north-west of Urfa]. Of the six hundred ninety-six people who set out, three hundred twenty-one arrived in Aleppo, two hundred six men and fifty-seven women were killed'.[51] Krikoris Balakian, who met this engineer some weeks later, reported:

> It was in the last days of October [1915], Lismayer had been busy constructing a narrow-gauge railway between Sormagha and Ras ul-Ayn, when he saw a large column coming from the north and slowly descending towards Ras ul-Ayn.... This mass of people moved slowly down the road, and only when it had drawn near did the Austrian realize that the army was made up, not of soldiers, but of an immense convoy of women guarded by gendarmes. On some estimates, there were as many as forty thousand women in the convoy.... There was not a single man among them.[52]

Another engineer working on the Baghdad railway, M. Graif, informed Dr Martin Niepage, a professor in Aleppo, 'that along the entire trajectory of the railroad leading to Tell Abiad and Ras ul-Ayn were piles of naked corpses of raped women', while the German consul in Mosul who had travelled on the road between Mosul and Aleppo 'had seen, in several places on the way, so many severed children's hands that the road could have been paved with them'.[53]

According to the evidence of the director of the concentration camp at Ras ul-Ayn, at the end of October 1915 it already contained 10,000 tents – housing about 50,000 Armenian deportees – ranged on a height ten minutes from the town.[54] A new subgovernor, Kerim Refif Bey, a committed Young Turk, took up his duties at the beginning of March and immediately got down to the task he had been given: extermination of the deportees from the camp at Ras ul-Ayn. The preparations were done from 17 to 21 March 1916, on which date began the operation aimed at the systematic liquidation of the 40,000 internees still there.[55]

The first information about the extermination of the deportees in the camp at Ras ul-Ayn did not reach Aleppo until the beginning of April. The first despatch of the consul, Rössler, is not until 6 April 1916, and alludes to a massacre by 'Circassians'.[56] The diplomat is more precise in his report of 27 April, drawing on the account of a reliably informed German who spent several days at Ras ul-Ayn and in the surrounding area:

> Every day or almost every day for a month 300 to 500 victims were taken from the camp and slain in a place about 10 kilometres from Ras ul-Ayn. The corpses were thrown into the river named Djirdjib el Hamar.... The Chechens established in the region of Ras ul-Ayn have served as executioners.[57]

One needs to draw on the evidence of some survivors to take the measure of the carnage. The camp director spells out:

> By 23 April only a few hundred people remained, the sick, the blind, the disabled and a few youngsters.... After each convoy was sent off, hundreds of dead were collected for whom large communal graves were dug.... A few days after the departure of the last convoy, the subgovernor made an announcement that the activities of the concentration camp were done with, [and] he ordered me to hand over the registers.[58]

Officially, the area around the Euphrates constituted the main region in which the Young Turk authorities chose to 'settle' the Armenian populations who had been 'displaced towards the interior'. By late September 1915, the number had risen to 23,300,[59] soaring to 310,000 by early February 1916.[60] These exiles were split up between Meskene and Der Zor. Throughout the period in question, this journey was synonymous with death for all the deportees. Strung out along the route was a succession of camps: Meskene, Dipsi, Abuhar, Hamam, Sebka/Rakka, and finally the camps of Der Zor/Marât. However, the number of those interned in them did not rise significantly until the winter of 1915–16, after the Constantinople authorities decided to purge northern Syria of its deportees. The camps of Mamura, Islahiye, Rajo, Katma, Azaz, Bab, Akhterim, Munbuc, and Mârra, all located in the outskirts of Aleppo, or at a relatively short distance from the town, were now shut down, one after the other, and the survivors of these camps were sent on, following the Euphrates.

The camp in Meskene was the first important way-station on the route leading to Zor; it lay at the point where the road from

Aleppo intersects the Euphrates. According to Hocazade Huseyin Avni Bey, who was appointed director of the camp in January 1916, barely 20,000 deportees were living there on his arrival. In the following weeks its population jumped to 100,000.[61] This camp was one of the most deadly on the Euphrates route. According to the testimony of Huseyin Avni Bey himself, the official estimate of the number of Armenians who died there in 1916, carried off by typhus, cholera, or other illnesses, or by hunger, was 80,000, although the real figure was much higher than is suggested by the well known *çeles* (sticks on which one made notches to record numbers) kept by the chief gravedigger (*mezarcı başı*). Since the chief gravedigger was illiterate, he contented himself with cutting a notch on one of his *çeles* for every body of which he took charge. Certain people learned from him that the number of bodies he counted – that had been buried – did not include those that had been thrown into the Euphrates: approximately 100,000, at the very least. There were only 2,100 internees left in the camp in Meskene by April 1916.[62]

In his report of 29 July 1916, the Greman consul, Rössler, confirmed that 'a Turkish army pharmacist who had been serving in Meskene for six months told him that 55,000 Armenians were buried in Meskene alone. A Turkish vice-commander had, moreover, cited the same figure'.[63] The American consul, Jesse B. Jackson, reported similar statistics in a despatch dated 10 September 1916:

> Information obtained on the spot permits me to state that nearly 60,000 Armenians are buried there, carried off by hunger, privations of all sorts, intestinal diseases and the typhus that results. As far as the eye can reach, mounds can be seen containing 200 to 300 corpses buried pell mell, women, children, and old people belonging to different families.[64]

The camp in Dipsi, located five hours from Meskene, was the next stage. The transfer from Meskene to Dipsi was customarily made in conditions that Krikor Ankut, a young Istanbul intellectual who spent more than a year in the region, describes:

> Mid-March [1916], we were transferred from Meskene to Dipsi. There were about a thousand persons on foot and fifty on wagons.... Along the route, we would meet at each step corpses, the dying or exhausted men and women who had no more strength to march and were waiting to die on the road, hungry and thirsty. On the stretch from Meskene to Dipsi, we met roving gravediggers who had the task of burying the dead. They were so ruthless that they would bury the dying with the dead to avoid a double task. We would ceaselessly find the corpses of people whose heads had had been chopped off. The dogs were

numerous and lived by devouring the corpses. All the unfortunates who had been displaced from Meskene on foot or on wagons were brought and abandoned in a place called the Hospital [*Hastahane*]. They remained there, naked, hungry, and thirsty, until death should come and harvest them. We would encounter corpses at every step, to such an extent that the gravediggers could not bury all the dead. Misery was absolute in this place and had reached its peak. Day after day, the number of tents at the Hospital was increasing, with the arrival of people from Meskene. Dipsi was in effect the Meskene death ward where the most seriously ill deportees were sent. The camp operated for only six months, from November 1915 to April 1916, but 30,000 people gave up the ghost there.[65]

On the Der Zor route, across the Syrian desert, lay the camps of Abuharar, nine hours' march from Meskene, Hamam, requiring another nine hours' march from Abuharar, and Sebka, opposite the locality of Rakka, on the left bank of the Euphrates, which was the last stop before reaching what the deportees regarded as the supreme hell, Der Zor.

With the camps of Der Zor and its periphery, we approach in some ways the final chapter of the massacres of 1915–16. Zor was, in effect, the end of the road for the survivors reaching it from across the desert. Despite the gradual elimination of the deportees all along the route following the Euphrates, from camp to camp, tens of thousands reached Zor. According to a German witness who gave an account to Rössler of his journey to Zor, by the beginning of November 1915 there were already about 15,000 Armenians in this corner of the Syrian desert, where '150 to 200 people die each day. Moreover it explains how the town can absorb the deportees who continue to arrive in thousands'.[66] As a result of the killings, but also of famine and epidemics, Zor largely respected the orders to maintain a 'reasonable' proportion of Armenians in the area. When the norms were exceeded, the local authorities' solution to the problem was to send small convoys to Mosul, to restore the balance. This situation lasted for as long as the influx of new arrivals was compensated for, as it were, by the fairly temporary placement of deportees in the concentration camps in the Aleppo and Ras ul-Ayn regions.

The decision to rake out the Armenian deportees from the entire region of Aleppo and its surroundings, taken in February 1916, as is confirmed in a telegram from the Minister of the Interior, dated 9/22 February 1916,[67] gave rise during February, March, April, and above all in May and June 1916, to a real obstruction of the Euphrates route. The route was overrun with survivors from the convoys from the camps in the north. The Ottoman archives count the arrival in Zor of 4,620 deportees, for 7, 8, 11, and 12 February 1916. These figures give some indication of the rate of despatch from Zor.[68]

According to information gathered from a Turkish officer by Rössler, towards the middle of April Zor had no more than about 20,000 deportees.[69] The consul in Mosul communicated to his colleague Hoffmann, interim consul in Aleppo, that of two convoys leaving Zor on 15 April 1916 by two different routes, only 2,500 people reached Mosul on 22 May and that later not a single convoy arrived there,[70] although twenty-one groups had in fact left in that direction during the summer of 1916.

At the end of June 1916, the last cleansing operations in the region of Aleppo and on the Euphrates route caused an exceptional increase in the number of convoys arriving one after the other, following an order from Talât addressed to the governorate of Aleppo, on 16 June, demanding the expulsion of the last Armenians towards Zor.[71] The Minister of the Interior appointed Salih Zeki as the new governor of Zor, probably to handle these deportees, then estimated at some 200,000.[72] Zeki's bloody exploits at Everek were known to everyone. The machine ground into action. Customarily, when some 10,000 deportees were concentrated on the other bank of the bridge in Zor, Zeki would organize their dispatch towards Marât, a camp situated five hours to the south, some way from the Euphrates. Generally, the gendarmes delivered their 'protégés' to the Chechens, recruited by Zeki, who took on the task of selecting the folk who still had some financial resources: they were methodically stripped of their last goods and killed on the spot, to avoid the risk of leaving the benefit of this significant revenue stream to the Bedouins who were entrusted with the final extermination of the convoys deeper in the desert. Marât was a 'decantation' camp. The big convoys were sectioned into groups of 2,000–5,000 people, who were gradually sent to Suvar, in the Khabour valley, two days' march by the desert route. There came the task of definitively separating the last male survivors – to be executed in the surrounding area – from the women and children. Then, in a continuing method of splitting, people were regrouped according to their region of origin.[73] After a stay – on rations – of some ten days in these desert places, women and children were sent on their way to Sheddadiye, where they were customarily exterminated behind the mountain overlooking the Arab village.

There was a total of twenty-one convoys, six large and fifteen more modest. The first left the camp at the Zor bridge (on the other bank) about 15 July 1916, with some 18,000 people, in the direction of Marât. A group of women, however, escaped the fate of the others and were finally taken to Haseke, some hours to the north of Sheddadiye, where they were given to the local tribes, who shared them out.[74]

To recruit enough people to exterminate the tens of thousands of remaining deportees, as there were insufficient numbers of Chechens available, Zeki turned to the nomad tribes in the region stretching from Marât to Sheddadiye, especially the Baggara tribe, established between Zor–Marât and Suvar, the Ageydid, who lived nomadically between Suvar and Sheddadiye, and the Ceburi, located at Sheddadiye and its surroundings, whom he could dazzle with the prospect of pillage.[75]

In a despatch dated 29 July 1916, the German consul, Rössler, confirmed that Zeki had moved swiftly into action. He wrote:

> Just received communication from Der Zor, dated 16 July, informing us that the Armenians have received orders to quit the town. On 17 July, all the ecclesiastics and the notables were thrown into prison.... Now those who remained will be exterminated in their turn. It is possible that this measure is directly bound up with the arrival of a new pitiless governor.[76]

Late in August, the interim consul, Hoffmann, reported that:

> On the official version of events, they were conducted to Mosul (a route on which only a small minority has any chance of arriving at the destination); the general view, however, is that they were murdered in the little valley lying southwest of Der Zor, near the spot where the Khabour flows into the Euphrates. Gradually, all the Armenians are being evacuated in groups of a few hundred people each and massacred by Circassian bands recruited especially for that purpose. A [German] officer received confirmation of this information from an Arab eyewitness who had only recently been present at a scene of this sort.[77]

These despatches, however, present no more than bits and pieces of what actually happened. Only first-hand accounts by survivors can give a true picture of the events.

Zeki left to last the extermination of 1,500 orphans kept in Zor in appalling conditions and a few hundred others gathered on the Meskene–Zor line by Hakki Bey, a creature of Zeki. A witness reported the fate of these children:

> They walked about, for the most part, bare-footed and naked, the burden of fatigue on their shoulders.... The arms and legs, as well as the reddened shoulders of many of them, were covered with untold

wounds that had become horrible sores. Since the wounds had not been treated, these sores were devoured by worms that the poor little children pulled out with their fingers.... In a company of eight hundred orphans of Der-Zor, they endured, for a while, a great many hardships in this hell that had been christened an orphanage, and were then, on a freezing December day, packed off in carts and put on the road.[78]

Some of them were blown up with dynamite in their carts, in an uninhabited spot in the desert. Others were put in natural cavities in the ground, sprinkled with kerosene, and burned alive. Zeki Bey found a pretext for sending them off. He had the *müdir* of Zor write a report that, given the increase in the orphans' numbers, there was a danger that they would spread contagious diseases. Only two children survived this massacre.[79]

Investigations conducted after the Moudros armistice revealed that it was the police chief, Mustafa Sidki, who supervised the slaughter of these children from the orphanage in Zor on 9 October 1916, followed on 24 October by that of some 2,000 more orphans, whom Hakki had rounded up in the camps to the north. Here they had been tied together in pairs and thrown into the Euphrates.[80]

According to information gathered by Aram Andonian, 192,750 people were victims to the massacres in Zor in the five months (July–December 1916) that Salih Zeki took to cleanse the region.[81] The indictment of the Young Turk leaders, read out at the first session of their trial on 27 April 1919, states that 195,750 people were murdered in Zor in 1916,[82] of whom 82,000 were liquidated between Marât, Markade, and Sheddadiye, and another 20,000 were liquidated at the fort of Rav, near Ana, under the supervision of Lieutenant Türki Mahmud.[83]

In having these nearly 200,000 victims slain in the remotest corners of the Syrian desert, far from traffic routes, the Young Turk authorities dispensed with a mammoth task: their burial. Public health issues, along with the question of potential witnesses, were thus removed from the equation, the bodies being simply left beneath the sun. The corpses rotted naturally there. In 1974, when this author went to the sites, notably at Markade, the bones of the deportees were still visible over considerable areas.

Conclusion

The bodies of the deportees generally underwent two forms of treatment: in the concentration camps, the deceased – most of whom died by 'natural' causes – were buried by the deportees themselves, sometimes by the families, but most often by the brigades of diggers recruited among the internees, as was highlighted above; in the uninhabited zones of the desert, where the deportees had been most often actively slain, nature took care of making all but the bones of the corpses disappear.

A measure of rationality, an evident pragmatism, was not lacking in the Young Turk authorities seeking to eliminate the traces of their abuses. The Tigris and the Euphrates, then the Syrian deserts, were the instruments most frequently employed. Clearly, after giving priority to physical destruction of the Armenian populations, the local authorities were short of personnel or were reluctant to bury the bodies, even in summary fashion. Only under orders from Istanbul, whose aim was to conceal the crimes and avoid epidemics reaching the army and the local non-Armenian populations, did they bend to the task, sometimes several months after the events. Scavengers may well have played a part too in the sanitization of the public realm.

These few comments complete our understanding of the prevailing ideology within the Young Turk Central Committee, which was steeped in social Darwinism and had as its priority the planning of the speediest possible elimination of Armenians. Even rudimentary means, such as earth, fiery sun and water, would be used to bring about the disappearance of the 'internal enemy', these 'microbes polluting the social fabric'.

On the left bank of the Euphrates, across from the modern town of Deir ez-Zor, some dozens of metres from the bridge, a vast meadow of several hectares was still a score of years ago left without buildings or cultivation: it more or less matched the bounds of the Zor concentration camp. The local population was keeping the remembrance of the place where the Armenians had been massacred, and regarded it as a sacred site that must be left to rest.

A memorial was built in Zor in the 1980s, including a genocide memorial church and victims' remains, where there gather, every year on 24 April, Armenians from all over the world, local authorities, heads of Bedouin tribes, and descendants of the Arabized deportees of the Khabour valley.

Based on evidence gathered on the ground, the observations presented in this short study allow us to draw some conclusions of a general nature. It will first be noted that some of these methods of killing involved the simultaneous destruction of the bodies or, in some cases, their physical transportation to less populated areas.

This was the case in particular with rivers such as the Tigris and the Euphrates, which guaranteed both death by drowning and removal of the corpses to Syria and Mesopotamia.

The death marches, which killed most of the women and children forced into the convoys, gave rise to significant pollution over a vast area. The cursory burial given to the resulting heaps of bodies – the Ministry of the Interior complained bitterly that the local authorities had not dug pits deep enough to guard against the attentions of scavengers – is evidence of a certain repugnance on the part of the local employees as regards disposing of these bodies, and even of gross negligence in respect of this task.

The siting of the concentration camps in the middle of the Syrian desert was much more effective in this respect, insofar as daily burials were carried out by the deportees themselves, sometimes with the assistance of a priest. The gradual shutting down of the camps, which began in April 1916, nevertheless forced the Young Turk authorities to liquidate the 200,000 or so surviving deportees whom they held by slitting their throats in the Kabur valley. These are the traces that survive to this day. They reveal the successive ways in which the Young Turk leaders adapted their methods of dealing with bodies.

Notes

1 The text of this chapter was translated from the author's French by Cadenza Academic Translations.
2 Notably R. Kévorkian, *Le Génocide des Arméniens* (Paris: Odile Jacob, 2006); and see R. Kévorkian, *The Armenian Genocide: A Complete History* (London: I. B. Tauris, 2011); T. Akçam, *Un acte honteux: le génocide arménien et la question de la responsabilité turque* (Paris: Denoël, 2008), available in translation as T. Akçam, *A Shameful Act: The Armenian Genocide and the Question of Turkish Responsibility* (trans. P. Bessemer) (New York: Henry Holt, 2006).
3 A. A. Türkei, '183/376, K169, 48', in J. Lepsius, *Archives du génocide des Arméniens* (Paris: Fayard, 1986), p. 93.
4 Ibid., A23991, pp. 112–13.
5 French translation of the indictment in the trial of the Unionists published in M. Fisch, *Justicier du génocide arménien, le procès de Tehlirian* (Paris: Éditions Diasporas, 1981), p. 266, in which this telegram is cited.
6 A. Krieger, *Yozghadi hayasbanoutian vaverakragan badmutiune* (in Armenian) (*Documentary History of the Massacre of Yozgat Armenians*) (New York: publisher unknown, 1980), p. 10.
7 The precise date of this ride is given in T. Atkinson, '*The German, the Turk and the Devil Made a Triple Alliance*': *Harpoot Diaries, 1908–*

1917 (Princeton: Gomidas Institute, 2000), p. 55; Report of L. Davis to the State Department, 9 February 1918, reproduced in L. A. Davis, *La Province de la mort: archives américaines concernant le génocide des Arméniens (1915)* (trans. Anne Earth) (Brussels: Complexe, 1994), p. 166; L. A. Davis, *The Slaughterhouse Province: An American Diplomat's Report on the Armenian Genocide of 1915-1917* (trans. A. Terre & Y. Ternon) (New York: Aristide D. Caratzas, 1988).
8 Davis, *The Slaughterhouse Province*, p. 167. Davis indicates he thought at first that this had been done as a 'sanitary measure', but was soon made aware of the practices of the assassins.
9 Ibid., pp. 168-9.
10 Ibid., pp. 175-7. The precise date of departure of the two men is given in Atkinson, *The German, the Turk*, p. 58.
11 Y. Ternon, 'Mardin 1915: anatomie pathologique d'une destruction', *Revue d'Histoire Arménienne Contemporaine*, 5 (2002), 182-4; H. Simon, *Mardine, la ville héroïque: autel et tombeau de l'Arménie durant les massacres de 1915* (Lebanon: Jounieh, n.d.), p. 12.
12 Simon, *Mardine*, p. 86.
13 Bibliothèque Nubar (Nubar Library, Paris, hereafter BNu), Fonds A. Andonian, P.J.1/3, Bundle 39, Tchemchgadzak, ff. 2-3.
14 S. Zurlinden, *Der Weltkrieg* (Zurich: Art Institut Orell Rissli, 1918), vol. 2, p. 707, cited by V. N. Dadrian, 'Documentation of the Armenian genocide in Turkish sources', in I. W. Charny (ed.), *Genocide: A Critical Bibliographic Review* (London: Mansell Publishing, 1991), vol. 2, pp. 116-17.
15 BNu, Fonds A. Andonian, P.J.1/3, Bundle 10, Arapkir, fo. 11r-v, evidence of Kaloust Kaloyan.
16 Ibid., fo. 12.
17 Ibid., fo. 12v.
18 Ibid. Their escort left for Arapkir.
19 BNu, Fonds A. Andonian, P.J.1/3, Bundle 10, Arapkir, ff. 1-4. This source contains the evidence of three female survivors of the Arapkir convoy who arrived at Urfa, then Aleppo, after having crossed the Kahta gorge.
20 BNu, Fonds A. Andonian, P.J.1/3, Bundle 59, Erzerum, fo. 4v, evidence of Alphonse Arakélian. The convoys of deportees from the regions of Erzerum, Sıvas, Bitlis, and Harput nearly all passed through the Kahta gorge and were decimated there by these same squadrons.
21 Ibid. See also Archives of the Patriarchate of Constantinople/Archives of the Patiarchate of Jerusalem, Patriarchate of Constantinople Information Bureau (hereafter APC/APJ, PCI Bureau), T 358-60 and T 723-6, Faits et documents, doc. no. 29, 'Les déportations des Arméniens d'Erzerum'.
22 H. Kaiser, '"A Scene from the Inferno": the Armenians of Erzerum and the genocide, 1915-1916', in H.-L. Kieser & D. J. Schaller (eds), *Der Völkermord an den Armeniern und die Shoah* (Zürich: Chronos Verlag, 2002), p. 157, n. 152, citing a report addressed by the Aleppo consul Rössler to Bethmann-Hollweg, on 30 November 1915.

23 D. Pasha, *Memoirs of a Turkish Statesman, 1913-1919* (London: Hutchinson, 1922), p. 277.
24 APC/APJ, PCI Bureau, File XXIX, T 578, certified copy of decoded telegram, and T 578/3, copy of encrypted telegram from the *vali* of Mamuret ul-Aziz, Sabit Bey, to the *mutesarif* of Malatia, dated 21 August 1915, at Mezreh.
25 APC/APJ, PCI Bureau, File XXIX, T 579/3, copy of encrypted telegram from the *vali* of Mamuret ul-Aziz, Sabit Bey, to the *mutesarif* of Malatia, dated 10/23 September 1915, at Mezreh. (Translator's note: such alternative dates reflect Turkey's continued use of the Julian calendar in this period, when many Western countries had long before moved to the Gregorian calendar.)
26 APC/APJ, PCI Bureau, File XXIX, T 578, certified copy of decoded telegram, and T578/4, copy of encrypted telegram from the Minister of the Interior, Talât, to the *vali* of Mamuret ul-Aziz, Sabit Bey, dated 19 December 1915.
27 APC/APJ, PCI Bureau, File XXIX, T 578, certified copy of decoded telegram, T 578/2 copy of encrypted telegram from the *mutesarif* of Malatia to the gendarmerie captains assigned to the regions and to the *müdir*, dated 20 December 1915.
28 APC/APJ, PCI Bureau, T 578, certified copy of decoded telegram, T 578/5, copy of encrypted telegram from the *vali* of Mamuret ul-Aziz, Sabit Bey, to the *mutesarif* of Malatia, dated 20 December 1915, at Mezreh.
29 SHAT, Service Historique de la Marine, Service de Renseignements de la Marine, Turquie, 1BB7, 231, doc. no. 259, Constantinople, 7 February 1919, 'rapport sur les atrocités de Yozgat, dressé par un fonctionnaire turc', dated 30 December 1918. See also Confessions de Şükrü, gendarmerie captain at Yozgat, collected in K. Balakian, *1915 ou le Golgotha arménien* (Paris: publisher unknown, 1984), pp. 221-30, which is an unpublished French translation from the Armenian original published in 1922, but see also K. Balakian, *Le Golgotha arménien: Berlin-Deir es-Zor* (trans. H. Bedrossian) (Chamigny: Le cercle d'écrits caucasiens, 2004).
30 F. Dündar, *Ittihat ve Terakki'nin Müslümanları Iskân Politikası (1913-1918)* (Istanbul: Baski Temmuz, 2001), notably pp. 92-174 and the map on p. 93.
31 Ibid., pp. 201-25; APC/APJ, PCI Bureau, x 370, 'Musulmans qui ont émigré pendant la guerre balkanique et la guerre générale', gives the following breakdown: province of Andrinople 132,500; province of Adana 9,059; province of Angora 10,000; province of Aydın 145,868; province of Aleppo 10,504; province of Brousse 20,853; province of Sıvas 10,806; province of Konya 8,512, etc., for a total of 413,922 people.
32 British Foreign Office file FO 371/6500, personal dossiers on the main Turkish war criminals and notably Şükrü Bey, published in V. Yeghiayan (ed.), *British Foreign Office Dossiers on Turkish War Criminals* (Pasadena: Doctorian Production, 1991), pp. 143-6. Şükrü Bey would become Minister of the Interior in the Kemalist era.

33 APC/APJ, PCI Bureau, T 125-8, 129-30.
34 BNu, Fonds A. Andonian, Materials for the history of genocide, P.J.1/3, Bundle 14, Konya, which presents the evidence of people originating from Akşehir, drafted at Aleppo on 23 February 1919, fo. 2v.
35 Report dated 8 November 1915, cited in Lepsius, *Archives du génocide*, p. 164.
36 US National Archives, State Department, Record Group 59, 867.4016/373, report of 4 March 1918, published in A. Sarafian (ed.), *United States Official Documents on the Armenian Genocide* (Princeton: Gomidas Institute, 2004), vol. 1, p. 146.
37 Yervant Odian was a humourist and journalist well known in Istanbul. He just escaped the raid on the Armenian élite on 24 April 1915. Finally arrested and deported to Syria in July that year, he survived thanks to the intervention of secret Armenian mutual aid networks, and to his language skills, by becoming a translator for a German officer who was unable to communicate with his Turkish colleagues.
38 Y. Odian, *The Cursed Years, 1914-1919: Personal Memories* (published as a series in the *Jamanag* newspaper, Istanbul, starting from 6 February 1919), n. 51. On the fate of the children taken away or sold, see R. Kévorkian, L. Nordiguian & V. Tachijan, *Les Arméniens, la quête d'un refuge, 1917-1939* (Beirut: Presses de l'Université Saint-Joseph, 2008).
39 Balakian, *1915 ou le Golgotha arménien*, pp. 332-4. Balakian's information is matched by the evidence of Alèksan Tarpinian, who made the journey from Osmaniye to Mamura at the beginning of September, and already counted there 37,000 Armenian deportees. See R. Kévorkian, 'L'Extermination des déportés arméniens ottomans dans les camps de concentration de Syrie et de Mésopotamie 1915-1916', *Revue d'Histoire Arménienne Contemporaine*, 2 (1998), 68-74.
40 Report of visit to the camp in Mamura, dated 26 November 1915, of Béatrice Röhner, in V. Bryce & A. J. Toynbee (eds), *The Treatment of Armenians in the Ottoman Empire 1915-16: Documents Presented to Viscount Grey of Fallodon, Secretary of State for Foreign Affairs* (London: H. M. Stationery Office, 1916), pp. 391-2; see also Report of the visit of Paula Schafer to the camp in Mamura, dated 1 December 1915, ibid. Both original documents, with the name of the missionaries, are in the Public Record Office, Kew, FO 867.4016/260.
41 Balakian, *1915 ou le Golgotha arménien*, p. 253.
42 Lepsius, *Archives du génocide*, pp. 160-1.
43 Kévorkian, 'L'Extermination des déportés'.
44 Lepsius, *Archives du génocide*, p. 164.
45 Kévorkian, 'L'Extermination des déportés', pp. 73-4.
46 Ibid., p. 79, evidence of Aram Andonian.
47 Ibid., pp. 87-8, evidence of Father Dajad Arslanian.
48 Ibid.; see also Lepsius, *Archives du génocide*, p. 199.
49 Türkei, '183/38, A23991', in Lepsius, *Archives du génocide*, p. 114.
50 US National Archives, State Department, Record Group 59, 867.4016/191, no. 372, report of 29 August 1915 addressed to ambassador Henry

How to make the Armenian corpses disappear 113

Morgenthau, published in Sarafian, *United States Official Documents*, vol. 1, pp. 127-8.
51 Lepsius, *Archives du génocide*, pp. 130-3.
52 Balakian, *1915 ou le Golgotha arménien*, p. 294.
53 Kévorkian, 'L'Extermination des déportés', note 86, evidence of Martin Niepage.
54 Ibid., pp. 110-14, evidence of J. Khéroyan.
55 Ibid., text of Aram Andonian, Ras ul-Ayn/1,106. See also below.
56 Andonian's propositions are matched by the report of Rössler in Lepsius, *Archives du génocide*, pp. 200-1. It was in fact a case of Chechens, as is made clear in later reports, settled at Ras ul-Ayn at the end of the nineteenth century by Sultan Abdul Hamid II, when a station was built there on the Baghdad railway.
57 Türkei, '183/38, A27200', in Lepsius, *Archives du génocide*, pp. 203-5. This information is matched by the overall report drafted by the American consul J. B. Jackson: US National Archives, State Department, Record Group 59, 867.4016/373, report of 4 March 1918, published in Sarafian, *United States Official Documents*, vol. 1, pp. 148-9. The information is completed by the evidence of Garabèd K. Mouradian, published in Kévorkian, 'L'Extermination des déportés', pp. 119-20.
58 Kévorkian, 'L'Extermination des déportés', pp. 113-14, camp director's evidence.
59 US National Archives, State Department, Record Group 59, 867.4016/219, letter and annex from the consul, Jackson, to Henry Morgenthau, both dated 29 September 1915, published in Sarafian, *United States Official Documents*, vol. 1, pp. 100-1.
60 US National Archives, State Department, Record Group 59, 867.48/271, letter and annex of 8 and 3 February 1916, published in Sarafian, *United States Official Documents*, vol. 1, pp. 112-13.
61 Kévorkian, 'L'Extermination des déportés', evidence of Aram Andonian, pp. 128-9.
62 Ibid., evidence of Aram Andonian, pp. 124-5.
63 Lepsius, *Archives du génocide*, p. 219.
64 US National Archives, State Department, Record Group 59, 867.4016/302, published in Sarafian, *United States Official Documents*, vol. 1, p. 131.
65 Kévorkian, 'L'Extermination des déportés', evidence of Krikor Ankout, p. 144.
66 Lepsius, *Archives du génocide*, p. 182.
67 T. C. Başbakanlık Arşivi (Turkish Republic Prime Minister's Office Archives), 18Z1333, 27 October 1915 (Şfr 57/135), EUM, order from Talât to the prefectures, doc. no. 146; 'Aram Andoniani hradaragadz tourk basdonagan vaverakrerou vaveraganoutioune', 1915-65, in *Houchamadian medz Yegherni* (trans. Krikor Gergerian) (Beirut: 1965), p. 241. See also Y. Ternon, *Enquête sur la négation d'un génocide* (Marseille: Editions Parenthèses, 1989), p. 122.
68 T. C. Başbakanlık Arşivi, 2R1334, 3R1334, 6R1334, 7R1334, dated 7,

8, 11 and 12 February 1916, DN, telegrams from Ali Suad, DH. EUM, 2.Ş.69/6, 7, 8, 9, doc. nos 158, 159, 160, 161.
69 Lepsius, *Archives du génocide*, p. 203.
70 Ibid., report of 5 September 1916, p. 227.
71 T. C. Başbakanlik Arşivi, 16Ş1334, 16 June 1916; IAMM, Talât to the prefecture of Aleppo, Şfr 65/32-1, document no. 187.
72 The figure is given in the indictment during the first session of the trial of the Unionists, 27 April 1919, *Takvim-ı Vakayi* (official bulletin of the Ottaman state, Istanbul), no. 3540, dated 5 May 1919.
73 Kévorkian, 'L'Extermination des déportés', p. 176, evidence of Aram Andonian.
74 Ibid., p. 177.
75 Ibid., p. 185.
76 Lepsius, *Archives du génocide*, p. 219.
77 Ibid., despatch of 29 August 1916, pp. 223-4. A report from Auguste Bernau, sent to the American consul, Jackson, on 10 September 1916, says nothing different.
78 Kévorkian, 'L'Extermination des déportés', p. 186, evidence of Aram Andonian.
79 Ibid., pp. 188-9.
80 APC/APJ, PCI Bureau, T 301-9, Memorandum on the judicial process against Mustafa Sidki, one of those responsible for the Zor massacre, before Court Martial No. 1. This document mentions the names of the survivor witnesses, who came from Rodosto, Geyve, Erzincan, and Adabazar, along with the names of the Ottoman officers who served in the region.
81 Kévorkian, 'L'Extermination des déportés', p. 190, evidence of A. Andonian and of M. Aghazarian, p. 224. This information was probably gathered from the source mentioned in note 82, but with a misprint in the figure.
82 *Takvim-ı Vakayi*, no. 3540, dated 5 May 1919.
83 APC/APJ, PCI Bureau, T 304-9, Memorandum against Mustafa Sidki. The figures of massacres between Marât and Sheddadiye were communicated by the head of the statistics bureau in Zor, Urfali Mahmud Bey.

Bibliography

Archives

Archives of the Patriarchate of Constantinople/Archives of the Patiarchate of Jerusalem, Patriarchate of Constantinople Information Bureau (APC/APJ, PCI Bureau)
Bibliothèque Nubar (Nubar Library), Paris (BNu)
Public Record Office, Kew, London, UK, Foreign Office papers (FO)

SHAT, Service Historique de la Marine, Service de Renseignements de la Marine, Turquie, Vincennes, Paris
T. C. Başbakanlik Arşivi (Turkish Republic Prime Minister's Office Archives), Istanbul
US National Archives, State Department, Washington, DC

Books, chapters, and articles

Akçam, T., *A Shameful Act: The Armenian Genocide and the Question of Turkish Responsibility* (trans. P. Bessemer) (New York: Henry Holt, 2006)
Akçam, T., *Un acte honteux: le génocide arménien et la question de la responsabilité turque* (Paris: Denoël, 2008)
Atkinson, T., *'The German, the Turk and the Devil Made a Triple Alliance': Harpoot Diaries, 1908-1917* (Princeton: Gomidas Institute, 2000)
Balakian, K., *1915 ou le Golgotha arménien* (Paris: publisher unknown, 1984)
Balakian, K., *Le Golgotha arménien: Berlin-Deir es-Zor* (trans. H. Bedrossian) (Chamigny: Le cercle d'écrits caucasiens, 2004)
Bryce, V. & A. J. Toynbee (eds), *The Treatment of Armenians in the Ottoman Empire 1915-16: Documents Presented to Viscount Grey of Fallodon, Secretary of State for Foreign Affairs* (London: H. M. Stationery Office, 1916)
Dadrian, V. N., 'Documentation of the Armenian genocide in Turkish sources', in I. W. Charny (ed.), *Genocide: A Critical Bibliographic Review* (London: Mansell Publishing, 1991), vol. 2, pp. 86-138
Davis, L. A., *La Province de la mort: archives américaines concernant le génocide des Arméniens (1915)* (trans. A. Earth) (Brussells: Complexe, 1994)
Davis, L. A., *The Slaughterhouse Province: An American Diplomat's Report on the Armenian Genocide of 1915-1917* (trans. A. Terre & Y. Ternon) (New York: Aristide D. Caratzas, 1988)
Dündar, F., *Ittihat ve Terakki'nin Müslümanları Iskân Politikası (1913-1918)* (Istanbul: Baski Temmuz, 2001)
Fisch, M., *Justicier du génocide arménien, le procès de Tehlirian* (Paris: Éditions Diasporas, 1981)
Houchamadian medz Yegherni (trans. Krikor Gergerian) (Beirut, 1965)
Kaiser, H., '"A scene from the Inferno", the Armenians of Erzerum and the genocide, 1915-1916', in H.-L. Kieser & D. J. Schaller (eds), *Der Völkermord an den Armeniern und die Shoah* (Zürich: Chronos Verlag, 2002), pp. 129-86
Kévorkian, R., *Le Génocide des Arméniens* (Paris: Odile Jacob, 2006)
Kévorkian, R., 'L'Extermination des déportés arméniens ottomans dans les camps de concentration de Syrie et de Mésopotamie 1915-1916', *Revue d'Histoire Arménienne Contemporaine*, 2 (1998), 68-74
Kévorkian, R., *The Armenian Genocide: A Complete History* (London: I. B. Tauris, 2011)

Kévorkian, R., L. Nordiguian & V. Tachijan, *Les Arméniens, la quête d'un refuge, 1917–1939* (Beirut: Presses de l'Université Saint-Joseph, 2008)

Krieger, A., *Yozghadi hayasbanoutian vaverakragan badmutiune* (New York: publisher unknown, 1980)

Lepsius, I. (ed.), *Archives du génocide des Arméniens* (Paris: Fayard, 1986)

Odian, Y., *The Cursed Years, 1914–1919: Personal Memories* (published as a series in the *Jamanag* newspaper, Istanbul, starting from 6 February 1919)

Pasha, D., *Memoirs of a Turkish Statesman, 1913–1919* (London: Hutchinson, 1922)

Sarafian, A. (ed.), *United States Official Documents on the Armenian Genocide* (Princeton: Gomidas Institute, 2004)

Simon, H., *Mardine, la ville héroïque: autel et tombeau de l'Arménie durant les massacres de 1915* (Lebanon:, Jounieh, n.d.)

Takvim-ı Vakayi (official bulletin of the Ottaman state, Istanbul), no. 3540, 5 May 1919

Ternon, Y., *Enquête sur la négation d'un génocide* (Marseille: Editions Parenthèses, 1989)

Ternon, Y., 'Mardin 1915: anatomie pathologique d'une destruction', *Revue d'Histoire Arménienne Contemporaine*, 5 (2002), 182–4

Türkei, A. A., '183/376, K169, 48', '183/38, A23991', '183/38, A27200', in J. Lepsius, *Archives du génocide des Arméniens* (Paris: Fayard, 1986)

Yeghiayan, V. (ed.), *British Foreign Office Dossiers on Turkish War Criminals* (Pasadena: Doctorian Production, 1991)

Zurlinden, S., *Der Weltkrieg* (Zurich: Art Institut Orell Rissli, 1918), vol. 2

5

Sinnreich erdacht: machines of mass incineration in fact, fiction, and forensics

Robert Jan van Pelt[1]

On burning people, and corpses

On 10 May 1933, students at the University of Berlin threw 25,000 books on a large pyre located in the square in front of the university. In the days that followed, gleeful students mounted book burnings at all the major universities in Germany. Newspapers from as far afield as China and Japan printed photographic and descriptive images of this violence. The world sensed that some kind of terrible rupture of civilization was taking place in the country of *Dichter und Denker* (poets and philosophers). Not a few journalists remembered the poet Heinrich Heine's prediction a century earlier: 'Where one burns books, one soon will burn people'.[2]

Twelve years later it appeared that Heine's prophecy had been realized: the Nazis and their allies had killed 6 million European Jews, and driven another million into exile overseas. I use the word 'appeared' because, in fact, only very, very few of those victims were burned alive. Over 3 million Jews were killed in gas chambers, while bullets killed some 2 million, and almost all the rest died as the result of starvation and disease. To be sure, there are testimonies of living Jewish babies thrown on pyres in Auschwitz-Birkenau in the summer of 1944.[3] There are also reports of some Jewish *Sonderkommandos* having been put alive in the ovens, but the setting on fire of live human beings was exceptional.

Yet *burning* has become the central icon of the event that, significantly, has become known first in English and later in many other languages as the Holocaust, derived from a Greek word that means 'something wholly burnt'.[4] Often people refer loosely to the 'gas ovens' of Auschwitz, collapsing the gas chambers and crematoria ovens into one spurious umbrella concept that equates killing and burning. One of the first memoirs of Auschwitz, written by Sonia Landau and published under the Polish-Christian name she had adopted after her escape from the Warsaw ghetto, Krystyna Zywulska, systematically conflated the killing and burning. Indeed, while 99.99 per cent of the bodies that were burned were the corpses of people killed by other means (mostly by gas), most authors who refer to the Holocaust choose to emphasize the importance of the act of burning within that genocide. There are various reasons for this. First of all there is the traditional association of the death camps, where half of the Jews were killed, with hell. Sonia Landau recalled that when she arrived in Auschwitz-Birkenau, her friend Zosha remarked, 'We've arrived in hell', adding the question 'do you think we'll roast?' For the Polish-Catholic Zosha, who had been raised within the sacred topography of Christianity, the identification of Birkenau with hell was obvious. Landau quickly internalized the Christian view. Later in her memoir she described the nighttime scene during the Hungarian Action, when the crematoria ovens were overloaded and bodies were also burnt on large pyres, in terms that literally evoke the traditional iconography of the infernal part of the afterlife. The association with the medieval image of hell was direct:

> Every chimney was disgorging flames. Smoke burst from the holes and the ditches, swirling, swaying, and coiling above our heads. Sparks and cinders blinded us. Through the screened fence of the second crematory we could see figures with pitchforks moving against the background of flames.... I felt, as if at any moment, the earth would open and swallow us with this hell.[5]

The comparison became routine. In 1971 the Jewish critic and philosopher George Steiner noted that the death camps 'are the transference of Hell from below the earth to its surface.... In the camps, the millenary pornography of fear and vengeance, cultivated in the Western mind by Christian doctrines of damnation, was realized'.[6] The comparison was, of course, not that appropriate: hell has always been associated with the fires that burn the wicked. In the case of the camps, the fires burned the corpses of the innocent.

The prominence of fire – the fires of hell – in the Holocaust narrative is also the result of the fact that the gas chambers are unimaginable. Indeed, their very architecture suggests so. They were enclosed spaces, and those who died in there died invisibly to the world. There is a fundamental contradiction between the act of witnessing and death in a gas chamber. Only a few writers and visual artists have tried to imagine death in such a place, and mostly they have not been successful. Camp survivor Jorge Semprun reflected on this some years ago. 'There are of course survivors of Auschwitz', he noted, and he immediately added:

> but there are no survivors of the gas chambers.... We have the proofs, but not the testimonies. In Humanity's collective memory, legendary or historical, fable or document, there will always be this ontological vacuum, this lack of being, this appalling emptiness, this infected and poisonous wound: no one could ever tell us that he has been there.[7]

The burning of the corpses in the crematorium and on the open pyres, and the smoke darkening the skies fill this vacuum.

Furthermore, it is important to note that destruction by fire carries long associations with Jewish martyrdom. Beginning in Roman times, Jews like Rabbi Akiva, Rabbi Shimon ben Gamliel, and Rabbi Hanina ben Teradion had suffered martyrs' deaths on the pyre – the last, as the Mishna records, wrapped in a Torah scroll.

Finally, the image of the crematorium makes it a specific symbol of the catastrophic interaction of the German and Jewish worlds in the mid-twentieth century. From the end of the nineteenth century, Germany was the industrialized economy par excellence. The label 'Made in Germany' may have been imposed on German products by the British Merchandise Act of 1887 because they were considered of inferior quality and reliability, but by 1900 German manufacturers stamped the label proudly on their products, as it had come to mean the ingeniously devised perfection of German engineering and industrial production, which had become firmly anchored in a culture of research and invention guarded by the Kaiserliche Patentamt (Imperial Patent Office), renamed in 1919 the Reichspatentamt (Reich Patent Office), located in its monumental headquarters in the Kreuzberg district of Berlin.

At the same time as Germany was rising as an economic power, Jewish religious authorities proclaimed an explicit injunction against cremation when it acquired increasing popularity in the late nineteenth century. From rabbinical times onwards, rabbis had tried to establish which acts of non-observance of religious law led to a separation between an individual and the Jewish community. These discussions acquired greater urgency in the Age of Emancipation, when it became possible for a Jew to fully participate in civil society without having to take the radical step of conversion. Nevertheless, the question arose of whether there was a boundary short of conversion that those born as Jews should not cross if they were to remain acknowledged as Jews by orthodox Jewry. In the early twentieth century, the act of cremation became, in the words of religious scholar Adam S. Ferziger, 'an especially potent boundary marker, in part because it was a relatively new deviation against which a broad-based Jewish consensus could be built'.[8] One of the key reasons was the centrality of burial within the Jewish tradition. Ultimately, the community that existed in the Jewish burial ground represented the totality of a Jewish congregation at peace with itself. Cremation implied a wilful severance from the community. The concentration camp crematoria, therefore, can be interpreted as a symbol of the particularity of the *German* assault on the *Jews*. The German-Jewish poet Nelly Sachs clearly expressed this in one of the most famous lines to come out of the Holocaust: 'O die Schornsteine / Auf den sinnreich erdachten Wohnungen des Todes, / Als Israel's Leib zog aufgelöst in Rauch / Durch die Luft – ' ('O the chimneys / On the ingeniously devised habitations of death / When Israel's body drifted as smoke / Through the air – ').[9]

A patent application

Sinnreich erdacht (ingeniously devised): we know that if the Germans did not exactly plan the deaths through disease and starvation in the ghettos, they at least welcomed the high mortality. We know that they carefully prepared the massacres by means of shootings. And it took some planning to design and construct the gas chambers in Belzec, Sobibor, Treblinka, and the original gas chambers, those in Auschwitz (the improvised gas chamber of Block 11 and crematorium 1) and Auschwitz-Birkenau (bunkers 1 and 2, which were originally peasant cottages). But real technical ingenuity and advanced engineering skills became important when the SS commissioned the firm of Topf & Söhne to supply ovens for four modern crematoria in Auschwitz-Birkenau (there were no crematoria in Belzec, Sobibor, and Treblinka, and the other concentration camps where crematoria were built, such as Dachau, Buchenwald, and Sachsenhausen, did not play an important part in the German genocide of the Jews).[10] The crematoria in Auschwitz were necessary to allow the camp to operate both as an extermination camp and as a supply of labour to industries both

Machines of mass incineration   121

in Auschwitz and, in 1944, elsewhere in the Reich. Belzec, Sobibor, and Treblinka were isolated places, and the environmental mess that came with the mass burials or the burning of bodies on open pyres did not impede industrial production or attract unwanted attention. Auschwitz was located in the midst of a densely populated and intensely developed area, and rapid and final disposal of the remains of the murdered was the only way it could operate as a factory of death. Each of the four crematoria built in Auschwitz-Birkenau was equipped with a gas chamber. But the gas chambers were, so to speak, the simple and straightforward part of those buildings. The ovens were the technological cores, as the speed of cremation was the rate-limiting step in the killing operation. On 9 April 1946, the American psychiatrist Gustave Gilbert visited former Auschwitz commandant Rudolf Höss in the Nuremberg jail, where he was kept as a defence witness in the trial against Ernst Kaltenbrunner. Gilbert recorded in his diary Höss's dispassionate discussion of the extermination process. 'The killing itself took the least time', Höss told him. 'You could dispose of 2,000 head in a half-hour, but it was the burning that took all the time.'[11]

It did not only take all the time, but also required much thought. In order to accommodate the daily massacres in the gas chambers, each muffle in the furnaces designed and built for the crematoria in Auschwitz-Birkenau was to have the enormous capacity of ninety-six corpses per twenty-four hours (with fifteen muffles in crematoria 2 and 3 each, and eight muffles in crematoria 4 and 5 each, this resulted in a total daily cremation capacity in Auschwitz-Birkenau of 4,416 corpses per day). In order for the massacres to continue, day after day, week after week, month after month, the ovens, the flues, and the chimneys had to be extraordinarily resilient to cremate thousands of corpses between the massacre of one transport and the arrival, generally twenty-four hours later, of the next train with deportees. In addition, they had to be economical. When civilian crematoria incinerate a body, they do not have to be concerned about the availability of the fuel to heat the oven, and they can easily recoup the costs of the fuel through the usually substantial fee they charge the client for the service. But in the death camps, fuel was a big concern. Not only was it strictly rationed within the context of the war economy, but also the expense could not be charged to a third party: it came out of the general operation budget. Indeed, fuel economy was one of the reasons for the firm of Topf & Söhne being so successful in its business relations with the SS. In the history of cremation, there was no precedent for either the cremation capacity or the economies achieved in Auschwitz-Birkenau.

The development of the ovens in Auschwitz had been the result of an evolutionary process that can be reconstructed on the basis of archival evidence. Each muffle of the original ovens designed and installed in crematorium 1 had a daily capacity of some fifty-seven corpses, but within a year Topf & Söhne had been able to increase the productivity of each muffle by almost 70 per cent. Yet this remarkable story of technical betterment was meant to remain unknown. If history had unfolded as SS Chief Heinrich Himmler imagined it in the war years, the camp ought to have disappeared not only from the earth, but also from the record of history. In a speech given in Posen (Poznan) in October 1943, Himmler discussed the responsibility of the SS for the genocide of Europe's Jews, and he reminded the assembled that 'in our history, this is an unwritten and never-to-be-written page of glory'.[12] This secrecy did not serve the commercial interests of Topf & Söhne. In developing the Auschwitz ovens, the company had broken new ground in thermo-mechanical engineering, and under normal circumstances it would have sought publication in the relevant trade journals. Such avenues were closed to the company – and not only because it was participating in genocide. The ovens themselves broke German law because they were based on multi-corpse incineration, which made the identification of ashes impossible, and because they brought the corpse into direct contact with the flame. The German cremation law of 1934 stipulated that the body should be incinerated through the application of hot air, and that only one corpse at a time could be cremated in a muffle: these ashes, this name. Yet, in order to safeguard its commercial interests, Topf & Söhne did something that broke the confidentiality agreement with the SS: it applied in November 1942 for a patent for a *Kontinuierliche arbeitender Leichen-Verbrennungsofen für Massenbetrieb* (Continuous Operation Corpse Incineration Furnace for Intensive Use). This patent application is very important as it explicitly refers to the high mortality in 'the gathering camps in the occupied territories in the East' and the impossibility of burying 'the great number of deceased inmates'. It goes on:

> A number of multi-muffle ovens were installed in some of those camps, which according to their design are loaded and operated periodically. Because of this, these ovens do not fully satisfy, because the burning does not proceed quickly enough to dispose of in the shortest possible time the great number of corpses that are constantly presented. The last

can only be done in ovens which are fed continuously and hence also work continuously.[13]

Fritz Sander, the engineer who developed the design to be patented, confessed in March 1946, during an interrogation by Soviet officials, that this new installation 'was to be built on the conveyor belt principle. That is to say, the corpses must be brought to the incineration furnaces continuously. When the corpses were pushed into the furnaces, they would fall onto a grate, then slide into the furnace and be incinerated. The corpses would serve at the same time as fuel for heating the furnaces.' When challenged why he had volunteered to design such ovens when he knew they were to serve a genocide, Sander responded: 'I was a German engineer and key member of the Topf works, and I saw it as my duty to apply my specialist knowledge in this way to help Germany win the war, just as in wartime an aircraft construction engineer builds airplanes, which also kill human beings'.[14] Obviously Sander did not realize the elemental distinction between a weapon to be used in an armed conflict and a tool designed to kill unarmed and powerless prisoners.

The patent application describes the continuous-cremation furnace as a structure in which the corpses are inserted at the top, and as they slowly slide down a system of inclined grids they are quickly reduced to ashes. It does not provide data on the capacity of the furnace, but in 1985 Rolf Decker, manager of incinerator production at the Ruppmann company in Stuttgart, made an engineering assessment of Topf's continuous-cremation furnace.[15] He assumed that the furnace could be initially loaded with fifty corpses, and in the upper part of the furnace the bodies would dry out through evaporation; after falling into the second part, these corpses would be burned, while the first part would be reloaded. After falling into the third part of the furnace, the remains would be completely reduced to ashes. 'On the basis of the plan one may only theoretically calculate the capacity and duration, because exact data can only be determined through practical trials…. With continuous operation one could arrive at an incineration capacity of around 4,800 corpses per 24 hours.' The most important achievement was not only in capacity (which could be easily expanded to 7,200 corpses per day), but also in economy:

> Pre-heating of such an oven should take at least two days. After this preheating the oven will not need any more fuel due to the heat produced by the corpses. It will be able to maintain its necessary high

temperature through self-heating. But to allow it to maintain a constant temperature, it would have become necessary to introduce at the same time so-called well-fed and so-called emaciated corpses, because one can only guarantee continuous high temperatures through the emission of human fat. When only emaciated corpses are incinerated, it will be necessary to add heat continuously.[16]

The question, of course, was where one would find a supply of 'well-fed' corpses in Auschwitz in 1942. It is important to note that, when he wrote his assessment of the mass-incineration oven, Decker did not know yet of Sander's statement, given in 1946, that the corpses were to serve also as fuel for heating the furnaces. Sander's interrogations were to be unearthed in the Osobyi (Special) Archive in Moscow only in the early 1990s.[17]

In his classic study *Modernity and the Holocaust*, philosopher Zygmunt Bauman postulated that the key to the success of the Nazis was their insight that one must make the victims 'part of that social arrangement that was to destroy them'.[18] In the same way that the rationality of the Final Solution turned human nature against itself, the principle of recuperative heat utilization by the combustion of body fats, which structured the Topf mass incinerators, transformed the very substance in the body that protected and sustained life into a tool to eradicate the final physical trace of that life.

With the Topf patent application, the Holocaust linked not only back to the core principles of the rationality of the Final Solution, but also to the 'normal', everyday world defined by the ideals of progress and the desire for achievement, and the experience of compromise, disappointment, and defeat. When he was interviewed by Claude Lanzmann for the movie *Shoah*, Holocaust historian Raul Hilberg observed that most of the persecution of the Jews that unfolded from 1933 to 1941 was *not* original. The Nazis invented very little: earlier persecutions inspired them. But they had to become inventive when they began to kill Jews en masse. 'That was their great invention, and that is what made this entire process different from all others that had preceded the event. In this respect, what transpired when the "final solution" was adopted – or, to be more precise, bureaucracy moved into it – was a turning point in history.' Lanzmann follows Hilberg's reflections on the Holocaust being the result of a series of absolutely original inventions with eyewitness testimonies on the use of the gas vans in Chelmno, the first of the death camps. The sequence ends with Lanzmann reading a document dated 5 June 1942, detailing technical changes to the gas vans to improve their efficiency. They involve reduction of the load space to improve the gas vans' stability, better protection of the lights, and the provision in the floor of a drain 'with a slanting trap, so that fluid liquids can drain off during the operation'.[19] Images of the Ruhr accompany the reading of the document, a bleak landscape crowned with cooling towers and factory chimneys – symbols of German industrial power.

Yet the Final Solution was an invention that did appear different from all the other inventions that energize the modern world: it was one without an official patent, understood as a publicly issued government licence (the noun 'patent' derives from the Latin verb *patere*, which means 'to lay open', which in this case means to make available for public inspection), conferring on the inventor for a limited time the sole right to manufacture, sell, or deal in the process or product that results from the invention *in exchange for the publication of a description of that invention*. The gas vans that were the object of the improvements mentioned in the document of 5 June 1942 were not patented, nor were the gas chambers built in the Operation Reinhard camps. The Topf patent application is the only such patent application that preserved in a regular, official form the inventiveness that turned 'ordinary' persecution into an unprecedented Holocaust. Hence it marks an important moment in the history of the Holocaust. It is significant, however, that the Reichspatentamt refused to issue the patent during the war. 'This patent could not then be approved … because of its secrecy classification', Sander explained to his interrogators in 1946. 'The project file is registered in the Patent Office but the invention could not be patented in wartime.'[20] Did he have hopes that, in 1946, the prospects looked better?

The patent and Cold War politics

In 1953 the West German patent office issued patent no. 861731 to the firm of Topf & Söhne in Wiesbaden for 'a treatment and processing for the burning of corpses, cadavers, and parts thereof'.[21] Initially, patent no. 861731 did not attract attention. Yet in the late 1950s the real or perceived continuity of the Federal Republic of Germany (FRG) with the Third Reich became a matter of public debate. From 1956 onwards, officials of the communist German Democratic Republic (GDR) had begun to look for documents that would incriminate the West German elites as former Nazis. In 1957 they began with a campaign against 'Hitler's blood judges who serve the Adenauer regime'. This campaign against judges and public prosecutors inspired socialist students in West Germany to research and mount an exhibition of the Nazi-era personal files of current judges, and copies of death sentences they had imposed. For the next couple of decades the West German justice system operated under a cloud. In 1959 the GDR began to focus on senior politicians and civil servants. The Federal Minister for Expellees, Theodor Oberländer, was forced to resign and was subjected to a show war crime trial in absentia in East Berlin, and the most senior and powerful civil servant in the FRG, Hans Maria Globke, came under attack for having written a lengthy commentary on the Nuremberg Laws of 1935 and for having authored other anti-Semitic legislation. Because Globke was Adenauer's most trusted advisor, being considered the puppet-master who controlled the politicians, the attack on Globke equalled an attack on Adenauer.[22]

The Austrian-Jewish author Robert Neumann supported the outing of the West German elites and was disgusted by the general opinion that the documents that had been presented were all forgeries created by the East German secret service.[23] A native of Vienna, Neumann had become a bestselling author in Germany in the late 1920s. In May 1933 his books had been burned on the pyres created by Germany's students. In a novel that appeared a few years later, Neumann recalled the event. His alter ego, the Jewish writer Werner Marcus, has done his best to ignore the Nazis. When on 10 May he hears that students will burn his books, he decides to attend the event. 'It would interest him, Werner Marcus, to watch it in person at close range, just for the sake of amusement, from the angle of pathological psychology.' And thus he leaves his house to see the bonfire, telling his mistress that he will be back at nine. He returns at ten.

> He was in no way disarrayed. On the contrary, if that signified anything, he was even more correctly dressed than usual; his hat was on straight, his tie straight, his gloves spotless, not a speck of dust on his coat. Only he was rather pale when one looked closer, with a corpse-like pallor that was terrifying at first sight. He rang for his valet. 'Pack the bags,' he said in a flat voice.[24]

Neumann knew there was no future for him in either Nazi Germany or clerico-fascist Austria, and moved to England in 1934. He returned to the continent only in 1959, settling in Switzerland. His arrival coincided with the outing of the judges, Minister Oberländer, and Secretary of State Globke. At the same time, Neumann only met Germans who all sang the tired refrain that 'wir haben es nicht gewusst' and who proclaimed their great love for the Jewish people and their great respect for the Jewish contribution to civilization in general, and German civilization in particular. In January and February 1960 Neumann hosted a series of four radio programmes in which he read documents that testified to the deep involvement of German civil society in the Holocaust. At the beginning of the third programme, having read twenty documents, he observed that 'we have now moved beyond ascribing the responsibility for the atrocities simply to the men at the top, or them and their closest co-conspirators, the killer simply formations of the SD and the SS'. By the beginning of the fourth programme he told his listeners that he had read enough documents. 'Every single one, I say, stands for a hundred, is proven a hundred times, with copies, with legally valid attestations of their authenticity, with sworn statements by witnesses, bystanders, murderers, and in a few cases by the murdered themselves.'[25] These documents he published in late 1960 under the title *Ausflüchte unseres Gewissens* (*Excuses of Our Conscience*). That same year he published *Hitler: Aufstieg und Untergang des dritten Reiches* (published in English in a radically shortened version as *The Pictorial History of the Third Reich*). It is a picture book that begins with the childhood pictures of Hitler, his rise to power, and then leads to a fifty-page documentation of the killing of the camps and the Holocaust of the Jews – including a long passage from Sonia Landau's (Krystyna Zywulska's) *I Came Back*. Neumann noted how few SS men had been brought to trial, and how they had good times at their reunions. The main text ends with an afterword with photographic reproductions of key documents that trace the involvement of bureaucrats, lawyers, physicians, and industrialists in the persecution and destruction of the Jews. The final section, 'The shared guilt of the industrialists', begins with the reproduction of a letter in which the director of I. G. Farben, Otto Ambros, reports on 'the new friendship' with the Auschwitz SS and the nice dinner hosted by the leadership of the Auschwitz concentration camp, a bill for 459,844.30 reichsmark to be paid by I. G. Farben to the Auschwitz SS for prisoner labour done in December 1943, and a list of Ambros's leading positions in the West German business world. The next spread is devoted to Topf & Söhne. Neumann included reproductions of the first page of the Topf patent application of 1942, the first page of patent no. 861731 issued in 1953, a letter written by the chief architect of Auschwitz to his boss in Berlin, reporting on the progress in the construction of crematorium 2 and its Topf ovens, and a letter on Topf letterhead dealing with the cracks in the ovens of crematorium 4. The caption that accompanies the first three documents states that 'the experiences with the Continuous Operation Corpse Incineration Furnace for Intensive Use' in Auschwitz, which are substantiated by letters of 26 October 1942 and 29 January 1943 (reproduced on page 250), resulted on 5 January 1953 in a new patent for the firm J. A. Topf & Söhne in the Federal Republic.[26] The caption that accompanies the letter on the cracks of crematorium 4 was a quote from Krystyna Zywulska's memoir – one that Neumann has also printed earlier in the book:

> About an hour later the chimney of the fourth crematorium, which was just behind our dormitory barrack, began to gush flames.... At first a thin grey ribbon appeared, then thick billows, growing heavier until they spread like a cloud veiling the sky over that part of the camp.... The smoke carried the smell of burning flesh.[27]

The American edition did not include the documentary section – to have done so would not have made much sense, as most Americans did not read German. Instead, Neumann provided a narrative summary of the argument. After mentioning the continuous employment of Nazi 'hanging judges and prosecutors' in the West German courts, the cases of Oberländer and Globke, the text stated that 'the Ruhr corporation that built the cremation ovens, asked for a new mass cremation oven patent in the Federal Republic in 1953 – and got it'.[28] Neumann did not think that more was needed to bring the point home that Germans, and especially German youth, should be watchful.

Neumann's outing of Topf & Söhne through the publication of the patent application of 1942 and the 1953 patent did not have much effect on the two companies that could be burdened with the Topf legacy. In East Germany the 'people-owned' Erfurter Mälzerei und Speicherbau (Erfurt Malting Equipment and Granary Construction), which continued the Topf business on the old site but without the furnace business, was safely ensconced within the communist state; the West German branch, established in 1950 by Ernst Wolfgang Topf, had effectively ceased to exist by 1960 and was to be formally closed in 1963. And it did not have any effect on the historiography of the Holocaust for the next quarter of a century: more detailed questions concerning the crematoria and their incineration capacity were to become a focus of research only in the mid-1980s.[29] But the patent application of 1942 and the patent of 1953 did speak to the poetic imaginations of two men born in the Netherlands: the novelist, essayist, and journalist Harry Mulisch, and the Israeli engineer, businessman, film producer, and playwright Wim van Leer.

Criminal case 40/61 and DRP 861731

On 30 September 1961, Harry Mulisch visited the Auschwitz museum. It was in some ways a very personal visit: Mulisch was half Jewish. His Jewish mother, Alice Schwarz, had been targeted for deportation to Auschwitz. His Austrian-born non-Jewish father, Karl Victor Mulisch, had played a key role in the despoliation of the Dutch Jews, and had been imprisoned after the war as a Nazi collaborator. The son of a perpetrator and a victim, Harry believed that he embodied the whole of the Holocaust in his person. From early April 1961 he had attended the Eichmann trial in Jerusalem as a correspondent for *Elseviers* magazine, and in his despatches he had developed a theory that Eichmann was the prototype of a new kind of man, a man who is a machine. 'If I called Eichmann a "medium without hypnosis" earlier, then that is the definition of a machine', Mulisch had written on 18 June 1961.

> A machine is a rational tool set up to execute any command whatsoever, without comment.... He personifies the perfectly ordinary man, the 'Massentier', the 'Gewohnheitstier' with the mechanical order receptor.... He is precisely the opposite of a man who wants to be bad. He is a machine that is good for anything.... This is why I called Eichmann 'the symbol of progress'. This living dead person is the prototype of modern man, who created the machine in his own likeness.

Yet in his despatches 'the machine' had remained a metaphor. At the end of the trial Mulisch decided to visit the main site of the crime for which Eichmann was tried: Auschwitz. There the machine had been a reality, embodied in a site, a physical infrastructure, and the crematoria. First he visited the exhibitions in the *Stammlager*, and then he moved on to Auschwitz-Birkenau, 'The loneliest spot on Earth, describable only through silence'. The crematoria, he erroneously stated, had a daily capacity of 60,000 corpses. It is unclear if he wrote the last despatch from the trial while in Birkenau, or after his return to Amsterdam. What is clear is that he had Neumann's recently published *Hitler: Aufstieg und Untergang des dritten Reiches* on his desk when he tried to write it. Not burdened by a university-formed super-ego concerned with academic convention, Mulisch lifted, without giving proper credit, significant pieces of Sonia Landau's testimony from Neumann's book.

Mulisch had gone to Auschwitz because he had great difficulty bringing his reportage to closure. How does one close a journey into an abyss? He decided to use Landau's quotes about the arrivals' confusion about the purpose of the crematoria, in a collage of fragments that included SS doctor Johann Kremer's diary entries on the meals he ate and the wines he drank after attending the killings, and commandant Höss's recollections of what one could see through the peephole when the Zyklon B was thrown into the gas chamber. The end began with the observation that the Zyklon B was delivered 'by the companies of Degesch and Testa, of the I. G. Farben Konzern' and that 'the crematoriums were supplied by the company of Topf & Söhne in Wiesbaden. On January 5, 1953, this company obtained patent no. 861731 for a treatment and processing for the burning of corpses, cadavers, and parts thereof. And in the white mist the sun of Birkenau is hanging. In the distance the locomotives are still steadily blowing their whistles.'[30] It is as good or bad an ending as one can make. As a collage, with its somewhat anomalous juxtapositions, it uses the surrealistic technique to defeat the traditional narrative sequence that makes sense of the world, and gives it meaning. In Auschwitz everything is disjointed and fractured. The world is in pieces. It is a world as wasteland.

Mulisch's articles on the Eichmann trial were bundled into *De Zaak 40/61: Een Reportage* (*Criminal Case 40/61: A Report*). As a result, by the end of 1961 the Topf patent figured at the conclusion of two books. It attracted the attention of the Dutch-born Israeli man of many talents Wim van Leer. Born in the Netherlands in 1913, van Leer had apprenticed in the metal industry, and spent the war manufacturing ammunition in Britain. After the war he moved to Israel, set up the country's crop-spraying industry, established factories to produce plastics and steel barrels, and was instrumental in creating a native film culture through the production of films and the establishment, with his wife Lia, of the Jerusalem Cinemathèque.[31] Van Leer knew patents. His father had become very wealthy on the royalties of a patent to seal oil barrels, and he owned a few patents himself. The ending of Mulisch's book, with the reference to patent no. 861731 issued by the West German Patent Office in 1953 to the firm of Topf & Söhne,[32] motivated van Leer to do some research. He contacted the Wiener Library in

London, which was in the early 1960s the primary collection of Nazi-era books and documents. It provided him with a copy of the 1953 patent and the patent application of 1942. Van Leer erroneously assumed that patent no. 861731, which mentioned Martin Klettner as its inventor, was a reworked version of the Sander design of 1942, and he was enraged by the chutzpah of the post-war Topf & Söhne management and the West German Patent Office.

Van Leer had also ambitions as a playwright, and in the early 1960s plays that raised issues related to the camps were popular: Max Frisch's *Andorra* was a critical success, and Rolf Hochhuth's *Der Stellvertreter* (*The Deputy*) had made an unknown author famous and wealthy overnight. When van Leer saw during a visit to the Wiener Library a photocopy of the Topf patent application, he not only understood the technical and the moral issues, but also realized that it had a great dramatic potential, and that it would allow him to tackle an issue that had not yet been addressed: the motivation of those involved. The Eichmann trial had shown that the simple explanation of anti-Semitism did not hold. 'The Holocaust is the best documented crime in history, and what is more, documented in the handwriting of the perpetrator', van Leer wrote in a letter to a Canadian advertising executive in March 1967, 'yet about the motivations of this crime there is little or nothing known.... Chana [Hannah] Arendt was certainly right when she spoke of the banality of the war criminal, but is it really as simple as that?'[33]

Van Leer believed that a play that focused on the circumstances surrounding the creation of the Topf patent application would allow him to raise the question of motivation, and to show the complexity of Arendt's 'banality of evil', by which term she referred to evil deeds committed by people who have neither a wicked heart nor a criminal temperament, but who are essentially 'thoughtless'.[34] He therefore wrote a three-act play that focused on the fictive firm Troeltsch & Sons, which produced large automatic bread-baking ovens, and that by 1942 had fallen on hard times – the concept that crematorium ovens in concentration camps were modified bread ovens went back to a *New York Times* article on the liberation of Buchenwald which noted that 'in the crematory itself were two batteries of three ovens, each prominently marked with the makers' name – J. A. Topf & Söhne, Erfurt. This concern customarily manufactured baking ovens'; the claim was repeated in the narration of the movie *Nazi Concentration Camps* shown on 29 November 1945 during the Nuremberg Trials.[35] By reviving the erroneous assumption that Topf & Söhne had been suddenly jolted into the construction of incineration ovens, van Leer could introduce an element of decision which was largely absent in the slippery-slope history of the historical Topf firm, as it had moved from the construction from civilian crematoria to 'regular' concentration camp crematoria to the 'special' concentration camp crematoria with gas chambers and a very high incineration capacity.

The play, which in its original Hebrew version sported the title *DRP 861731*,[36] and which in its English version appeared under the titles *Final Solution* and *Patent Pending*, is set in the office of the bomb-damaged Troeltsch & Sons bakery oven plant. The main protagonists are the company's owner, the elderly Edgar Troeltsch, the chief engineer, who has just returned from a stint as an army officer on the Eastern Front, Wilhelm Baumann, and the Mephistophelean SS-Obersturmbannführer Dr Hamlin. 'Gentlemen, the problem I'm placing before you concerns the cremation of human corpses on a – how shall I put it? – unusually large scale', Hamlin tells the industrialist and his engineer. 'Cremation?' Troeltsch asks. 'Yes, my dear Troeltsch', Hamlin responds, 'either cremation or incineration or any other method you can invent which will reduce the human body, after death of course, to the smallest amount of substance in the shortest possible time. Have I made myself clear? And when I say on a large scale, I mean sometimes in the order of thirty to forty thousand per day.' Hamlin tells Troeltsch that crematorium oven-builders only offer incineration installations of up to thirty-six corpses per day. 'At that rate I'd need over a thousand furnaces. They have no idea of automation. It is the *scale* of the operation that presents the difficulty.' Hamlin proceeds to present Troeltsch and Baumann with some relevant facts. 'Take the human body, weighing about seventy kilos, which is a fair average. It contains twelve kilos of carbon, two kilos of hydrogen, half a kilo of phosphorus and the rest – fifty-five and a half kilos of water. It has a calorific value of 160,000 thermal units.' The technical problem, Hamlin argues, is to achieve the simultaneous 'evaporation of body fluids, water in fact, and the incineration of solid matter'. With a down payment of 50,000 marks, and a guarantee that the workers will not be drafted, Troeltsch agrees to undertake the work. Yet Baumann sees some extra problems, such as 'the effect of clothing, uniforms – the physical dimensions, the disposal of the ashes or whatever it is that remains'. Hamlin responds with a cryptic remark: 'If it'll help you, I can let you have a few samples, dead or alive'.[37]

Baumann begins doing calculations for the ovens, and realizes quickly that the fuel requirement is immense: 3,500 corpses per day will require 260 tons of fuel every twenty-four hours. This is not available. 'If we could only in some way separate the fats contained in the human body, in some way break up the hydro-carbon and nitrogen bonds, we would incinerate the bodies with their own fat', he tells Troeltsch. Yet this requires a temperature that far exceeds that achieved in bread ovens. He also realizes that the units cannot be mobile. When Hamlin tells him that he can design a stationary oven, Baumann is somewhat surprised, as he had assumed the installation would be used to incinerate the remains of soldiers, and a stationary installation would not make much sense in the dynamic circumstances of the Front. And he is puzzled when an SS man brings Hermann Israel Bernstein, a Jewish concentration camp prisoner. Baumann gets to know Bernstein, who tells him about the killings in the camps. Baumann begins to realize new things. 'I know that there are concentration camps, who doesn't?' he tells Bernstein. 'It is one of the Führer's secret weapons. Not so secret either. What I didn't know … I suppose I could have known if I had thought about it, but who does think these days? It doesn't bear thinking about.' Baumann begins to realize that he is involved in the construction of a death factory. 'What's happening out there in these camps? … What we're doing? … The real purpose of these experiments?' Troeltsch tries to calm Baumann. 'There is nothing we can do about it. We'd be very unwise to stick our noses into matters like that.' Yet Baumann reminds him that they are already in the middle. 'With all due respect Sir, can't you put two and two together? They can collect them, strip them, gas them but they can't dispose of them without any traces, that's where we come in, Troeltsch and Sons, purveyors to the bakery industry.' While Troeltsch defines their job as producing an automated crematorium, Baumann corrects him: it is 'the last stage in a human slaughter-house'. Troeltsch responds that if it is true, it is a ghastly business, but they are not involved with the dirty work. 'All we do is clean up after them.'[38]

Finally, Baumann confronts Hamlin, who suggests that he does not know enough 'to question decisions taken at the highest level'. He threatens the arrest of Baumann's wife and children if he does not cooperate. Baumann surrenders. In the last scene, he has stopped thinking about the moral issues, and has retreated into the narrow world defined by the engineering problem that Baumann now spells out in great detail.

BAUMANN: In the ideal system we have a furnace which, once heated by oil to say 1,200 degrees and continuously fed with combustion material....
TROELTSCH: You mean fuel oil?
BAUMANN: No Herr Troeltsch, not fuel oil. Corpses, in other words body-fats. That's the whole idea, don't you see. The corpses themselves supply the fuel.
TROELTSCH: Oh, I see. Carry on Baumann, this is fascinating.
BAUMANN: If you look here at Station A, the hopper containing some 250 corpses feeds onto a conveyer-belt. We have an advantage – and here the particular construction of the body comes to our aid – that the head and limbs are dehydrated first, being of relatively small dimensions. They now separate from the body, and drop off into this funnel-shaped duct onto grid B. Since all circulating air passes through this grid, the limbs burn fiercely in the draft.
TROELTSCH: And the body itself?
BAUMANN: When the dehydration phase is over, which takes longer because of its larger volume, it will disintegrate in the same way.
TROELTSCH: So you have to light the furnaces only once a day.
BAUMANN: Yes, for an hour or so until she is at 1,200 degrees. Then you can switch off, and the corpses keep the furnace going. It is a tremendous fuel saving.[39]

After Baumann confirms the originality of his design, Troeltsch calls in his secretary, and dictates to her a letter to the Reichspatentamt in Berlin. As he dictates the text of the original Topf patent application of November 1942, the curtain closes, and on a descending screen is projected the first page of the (other) patent as it was issued in 1953.[40]

On 3 November 1964 *The Final Solution* debuted in Wimbledon. Later that month the production ran in Edinburgh, and Wolverhampton, and in June 1965 it had a few performances in London under the title *Patent Pending*. It had a final hurrah in April 1967, when, again under the title *The Final Solution*, it had a few performances in Toronto.[41]

The Six Day War occurred two months after the last performance of *The Final Solution*. When van Leer wrote his play, he did so in a vacuum. 'The world is still trying to fit the Holocaust into its framework of thinking; is trying to give some meaning to the figure of 6 million dead which now hangs over us meaningless like the distance to the moon or the American National Debt',[42] he had written in March 1967. But the fear so many Jews felt in May and June 1967 – the fear that the Arab armies were to finish the Nazi Final Solution – mobilized the collective memory of the Jewish people. The Six Day War initiated a new perspective on the genocide of the 6 million. The great trials of the perpetrators had come to an end. And the fundamental values of society rapidly changed as we became collectively more open to the psychological needs of others, and as we began to appreciate the variety of human society, with its implication that each single person, irrespective of gender, race, religion, sexual orientation, or health has his or her place and purpose. Television also changed the way we negotiate the relationship between the public, the private, and the intimate. As it began to bring us heart-rending testimonies of victims as our daily fare, it suggested that listening to testimonies of traumatized people and identification with their psychological needs were an important moral duty. Thus we came to live in what Annette Wieviorka labelled *l'ère du témoin*, the era of the witness.[43] Therefore the men and women who became after 1967 the focus of attention, and who through their testimonies, memoirs, and works of the creative imagination have defined the way we think about the Holocaust as one of the greatest catastrophes in human history, were not real German engineers and industrialists like Fritz Sander and Ludwig Topf, or imagined ones like Walther Baumann and Edgar Troeltsch, but Jewish survivors like Rudi Vrba and Alfred Wetzler, who in 1944 risked all to tell the world about Auschwitz and its crematoria, or artists like Primo Levi and Imre Kertész, whose *If This Is a Man* and *Fatelessness* are the cornerstones of a new and imperishable library built from letters that took wing on the pyres of Treblinka and in the ovens of Auschwitz, and the many, many survivors who, up to today, bear witness to the lives and deaths of their fathers and mothers, uncles and aunts, brothers and sisters, and children, who were murdered, and who have given them, in the words of Isaiah, 'a place and a name that shall not be cut off'.[44]

High Court of Justice, Queen's Bench Division, 1996-I-1113

In the era of the witness, the mass-incineration ovens, embodied in the Topf patent application, did, indeed, cease to have significance as a means to understand the Holocaust. Yet, despite this, the application regained centre stage one more time. The stage this time was not located in a theatre built for entertainment, but in a courtroom in the Royal Courts of Justice in London. The year was 2000, and the case the libel action brought by David Irving against Deborah Lipstadt, author of *Denying the Holocaust: The Growing*

Assault on Truth and Memory, and her British publisher, Penguin Books.[45] The origin of this case was the endorsement by Irving, a well known writer of popular histories of the Second World War, of hard-core Holocaust denial after he read in 1988 a forensic report, commissioned by Holocaust deniers Robert Faurisson and Ernst Zündel, and written by American engineer Fred Leuchter. In this report Leuchter came to the conclusion that Auschwitz had not been an extermination camp because he found only negligible traces of cyanide in the walls of the 'alleged' gas chambers, and because the ovens would not have been able to incinerate the 'alleged' number of corpses. Following the method of denial developed by Faurisson in the 1970s, Leuchter had totally ignored eyewitness testimony concerning the operation and technique of the crematoria. Irving had identified the Leuchter report as a major breakthrough in the historiography of the Second World War, and he lent his name and reputation as a researcher of the Third Reich to the proposition that the German murder of 6 million Jews was a hoax perpetrated by Allied secret services as atrocity propaganda, and that it had been kept alive by Zionists to swindle the Palestinians out of their homeland, and by Jewish financiers to swindle the Germans out of billions of marks.

Irving's endorsement of the allegation that the Holocaust was a hoax had rattled Lipstadt, and she consequently identified him in her book on Holocaust denial as a particularly dangerous denier because, unlike Faurisson, Zündel, Leuchter, and others, he had actually done substantial archival research on the Second World War. When Lipstadt's condemnation caused a publisher to cancel a contract with Irving, leading to substantial financial loss, the latter decided to sue in the High Court of England and Wales. In accordance with the applicable law, Irving needed only to make the complaint; it was up to Lipstadt and her publisher to prove that she had been right.

Having worked in the Auschwitz Zentralbauleitung archives, and having published a book and a number of other pieces that focused on the construction history of the camp, I was hired as an expert witness by the lawyers of Lipstadt and Penguin.[46] My brief was to prepare an expert report that focused on Auschwitz. I was to assemble and discuss the evidence that, indeed, more than a million people, mostly Jews, had been killed at Auschwitz, mostly in gas chambers, and that their bodies had been disposed of in crematoria and by means burning on open pyres. (If mass graves still existed, a forensic investigation of their contents would have provided a straightforward method of establishing at least the number of victims.) In addition, I was to review the arguments concerning Auschwitz proposed by Holocaust deniers, and show that they were without value. All of this was to demonstrate that, in his quick and unequivocal endorsement of the Leuchter report, Irving had not acted as an unbiased, objective, and conscientious historian would have acted. Or, in other words, I was to aid the general case to be presented in court that Irving had not treated sources with appropriate reservation, that he had dismissed counter-evidence to his hypotheses without proper scholarly consideration, that he had been 'cherry-picking' the evidence to suit his purposes, and so on.[47]

In my expert report, which was to run to more than 700 pages, I reviewed the evidence about the killings at Auschwitz.[48] I showed, again and again, how eyewitness evidence provided by both former camp personnel and camp survivors, and material evidence such as German documents and the remains of the crematoria, converged to give a clear record of the use of the camp as a place of extermination of human beings, mainly Jews. I also showed that none of the arguments proposed by deniers survived a critical examination of either the evidence they called on to make their case, or the logic they employed. In my attack on the Leuchter report, I paid special attention to his assertion that the daily incineration capacity of crematorium 1 had been eighteen corpses, of crematoria 2 and 3 had been forty-five corpses each, and of crematoria 4 and 5 had been twenty-four corpses each, leading to a total daily incineration capacity in Auschwitz of 156 corpses – which would have provided over the lifespan of the crematoria a total cremation capacity of 85,000 corpses. I had, however, a German document from the Zentralbauleitung archive, dated 28 June 1943, which reported the incineration capacity to Berlin. This letter stated that crematorium 1 had a daily incineration capacity of 340 corpses, crematoria 2 and 3 had a daily incineration capacity of 1,440 corpses each, and crematoria 4 and 5 of 768 corpses each, leading to a total daily incineration capacity of 4,756 corpses. If Leuchter's number suggested a camp with 'normal' mortality, the German document suggested that the crematoria were built to serve a genocide. I noted that the information given in the letter of 28 June 1943 converged with the testimony provided in May 1945 by Henryk Tauber, a former *Sonderkommando* (a prisoner forced to work in the camp), who had worked first in crematorium 1, and who had noted that bodies of thin people 'burned very slowly' and that 'bodies of fat people burn very much faster. The process of incineration is accelerated by the combustion of human fat which thus produces additional heat'.⁴⁹ In crematorium 2 he and his fellow *Sonderkommandos* proved able to reach a high level of fuel efficiency. When dealing with the corpses of victims who had arrived in Auschwitz that very same day, and who were not emaciated, 'we used the coke only to light the fire of the furnace initially, for fatty corpses burned of their own accord thanks to the combustion of the body fat. On occasion, when coke was in short supply, we would put some straw and wood in the ash bins under the muffles, and once the fat of the corpse began to burn the other corpses would catch light themselves'.⁵⁰ I also invoked a statement by Topf engineer Kurt Prüfer on the capacity of the ovens, and, finally, the Topf patent application of 1942. After a lengthy discussion of the patent, I concluded: 'both the text of the patent application and the design of the incinerator make the incineration process described in Tauber's testimony not merely plausible, but indeed probable'.⁵¹

I finished the report in June 1999. In January 2000 I had to defend it in court under cross-examination by Irving, who represented himself. During my cross-examination, the issue of the coke consumption of the crematoria became a point of contention. It was important for two reasons: first of all, Tauber had claimed that, once the ovens were heated and going, hardly any coke had to be added, as the corpses themselves began to act as fuel. For Holocaust deniers, Tauber's statement is proof that he had lied, as this is 'impossible'. Furthermore, Holocaust deniers, taking the situation in a civilian crematorium as their standard, postulate that it 'always' takes 20–30 kg of coke to incinerate a body, and as a result the coke supplies to Auschwitz, which were recorded for 1943, were sufficient to incinerate only one-tenth of the alleged number of corpses. Or, in other words, the bills for the coke supply were to prove that it is 'impossible' that the crematoria had been involved in a genocidal operation. This argument has been fully developed by Holocaust denier Carlo Mattogno in his *Auschwitz: fine di una leggenda* (1994).

Irving challenged me on the coke use on the first day of my cross-examination, after I had discussed the projected incineration capacity in Auschwitz indicated by the letter of 28 June 1943.⁵² In my reply I noted that it appeared that the Auschwitz crematoria had been very efficient, using only 3.5 kg of coke per body. I quoted a number of documents that supported my allegation, including the Topf patent application.

MR JUSTICE GRAY: I am afraid I have completely forgotten what is supposed to be the significance of the patent application one way or the other.
MR RAMPTON: I could tell your Lordship but then I would be giving evidence and I cannot do that.
MR JUSTICE GRAY: I am simply asking what case is sought to be made, but perhaps it is better elicited from Professor van Pelt.
MR RAMPTON: The case sought to be made is that it explains how it was that they were able to incinerate as many corpses as they could, and also how they managed to use as little fuel as these were able to do.[53]

I quoted the relevant sentences of the report, those on the patent, where it stated that after preheating the oven for two days it would not need any extra fuel, due to the heat produced by the corpses, and noted that it went back to the experience made with multi-muffle ovens in crematorium 1. Key was the comment that one should use a combination of fat corpses and emaciated corpses to obtain the desired result. Rampton then asked me if this chimed with descriptions given by eyewitnesses. I suggested that Tauber described the problem in his testimony given in 1945.[54] The patent application thus became a key document in confirming the reliability of the witness, Tauber.[55]

It convinced Mr Justice Gray. In his judgement he came back to the report on various occasions.[56] After reviewing all the evidence, including the patent, Mr Justice Gray stated: 'I accept that the evidence of van Pelt, which was based on contemporaneous documents…, that, if the incinerators were operated continuously and many corpses were burnt together so themselves providing fuel, no more than 3.5 kg of coke would have been required per corpse'.[57] Thus the convergence of the evidence provided by Tauber and Höss, and that provided by documents such as the Topf patent application of 1942, led Mr Justice Gray to conclude:

> having considered the various arguments advanced by Irving to assail the effect of the convergent evidence relied on by the Defendants, it is my conclusion that no objective, fair-minded historian would have serious cause to doubt that there were gas chambers at Auschwitz and that they were operated on a substantial scale to kill hundreds of thousands of Jews.[58]

Conclusion

The ovens that Topf & Söhne built in Auschwitz have done much harm to humankind. Without the massive daily incineration capacity that they provided from March 1943 onwards, the camp could not have killed and burned the more than 400,000 Hungarian Jews in the spring of 1944. However, Fritz Sander's patent application from 1942, based on the experience of multi-corpse incineration, did in the end do little damage to the prospects of humanity. In fact, within the context of a lengthy and costly trial, it proved to be a key piece of evidence that confirmed the validity of eyewitness evidence provided in 1945 by a survivor of the Auschwitz *Sonderkommando* and, through that, the factual truth of the commonly accepted historical record concerning the most deadly of German death camps.

Notes

1 With my thanks to Élisabeth Anstett, Jean-Marc Dreyfus, Robert Rozett, Miriam Zagiel, Lia van Leer, and Miriam Greenbaum. This work was supported by a grant from the Netherlands Institute for Advanced Study in the Humanities and Social Sciences (NIAS).
2 The quote is from Heinrich Heine, *Almansor*, available on the web through the freie digitale Bibliothek (Dig.Bib) at www.digbib.org/Heinrich_Heine_1797/Almansor. For an analysis of the use and abuse of Heine's quote, see Theodor Verweyen, *Bücherverbrennungen: Eine Vorlesung aus Anlass des 65. Jahrestages der 'Action wider den undeutschen Geist'* (Heidelberg: Universitätsverlag Winter, 2000), pp. 1ff.
3 International Military Tribunal, *Trials of the Major War Criminals*, 41 vols (Nuremberg: Secretariat of the Tribunal, 1947–49), vol. 8, p. 319.
4 Zev Garber & Bruce Zuckerman, 'Why do we call the Holocaust "the Holocaust?" An inquiry into the psychology of labels', *Modern Judaism*, 9:2 (May 1989), 197–211.
5 Krystyna Zywulska, *I Came Back* (trans. Krystyna Cenkalska) (New York: Roy Publishers, 1951), pp. 16, 179–80.
6 George Steiner, *In Bluebeard's Castle: Some Notes Towards the Re-definition of Culture* (London: Faber & Faber, 1971), pp. 46ff.
7 Jorge Semprun, 'Une petite lampe s'est allumée dans la baraque des contagieux…', in Ariana Kalfa & Michaël de Saint Cheron (eds), *Élie Wiesel en Hommage* (Paris: Les Editions du Cerf, 1998), pp. 60–1; as quoted in Caroline Fournet, *The Crime of Destruction and the Law of Genocide: Their Impact on Collective Memory* (Aldershot: Ashgate, 2007), p. 32.
8 Adam S. Ferziger, 'Ashes to outcasts: cremation, Jewish law, and identity in early twentieth-century Germany', *AJS Review*, 36 (2012), 71–102, p. 73.
9 Nelly Sachs, *O the Chimneys: Selected Poems, Including the Verse Play, Eli* (trans. Michael Hamburger) (New York: Farrar, Straus & Giroux, 1967), pp. 2–3.

10 See Jean-Claude Pressac, *Auschwitz: Technique and Operation of the Gas Chambers* (New York: Beate Klarsfeld Foundation, 1989); Debórah Dwork & Robert Jan van Pelt, *Auschwitz: 1270 to the Present* (New York: Norton, 1996); Annegret Schüle, *Industrie und Holocaust: Topf & Söhne – Die Ofenbauer von Auschwitz* (Göttingen: Wallstein, 2010).
11 Gustave M. Gilbert, *Nuremberg Diary* (New York: Da Capo Press, 1995), pp. 249–50.
12 As quoted in Lucy S. Dawidowicz (ed.), *A Holocaust Reader* (New York: Behrman House, 1976), pp. 132–3.
13 J. A. Topf & Söhne Erfurt, Patent application, 'Kontinuierliche arbeitender Leichen-Verbrennungsofen für Massenbetrieb', Archive Auschwitz-Birkenau State Museum, Oswiecim, BW 30/44, 1f.
14 For the transcript of the interrogation see File 1/9 Topf & Söhne, in Gerald Fleming, *Hitler and the Final Solution*, augmented edition (Berkeley: University of California Press, 1984, 1994), pp. 204–5.
15 Decker was commissioned by the Berlin publisher Klaus Kunz, who was preparing a book on the future of a Nazi-ruled Europe based on the counterfactual assumption that Germany had won the Second World War. See Ralph Giordano, *Wenn Hitler den Krieg gewonnen hätte: Die Pläne der Nazis nach dem Endsieg* (Hamburg: Rasch & Röhring Verlag, 1989), pp. 277–9.
16 Report by Rolf Decker, 25 April 1985, on patent application T 58240 Kl. 24 for a 'Kontinuierliche arbeitender Leichen-Verbrennungsofen für Massenbetrieb', Auschwitz-Birkenau State Museum, Oswiecim, ms. BW 30/44.
17 The collections of the Osobyi Archive are now part of the Russian State Military Archive. Significant parts, including the interrogations of Sander and other Topf engineers, are available in microfilm at the archive of the United States Holocaust Memorial Museum.
18 Zygmunt Bauman, *Modernity and the Holocaust* (Ithaca: Cornell University Press, 1989), p. 122.
19 Claude Lanzmann, *Shoah: An Oral History of the Holocaust* (New York: Pantheon, 1985), pp. 71, 104.
20 Fleming, *Hitler and the Final Solution*, p. 204.
21 See Schüle, *Industrie und Holocaust*, pp. 327ff.
22 See Annette Weinke, *Die Verfolgung von NS-Tätern im Geteilten Deutschland* (Paderborn: Ferdinand Schöningh, 2002), pp. 76–160.
23 See Robert Neumann, *Ein Leichtes Leben* (Vienna: Kurt Desch, 1963), pp. 528–35.
24 Robert Neumann, *By the Waters of Babylon* (New York: Simon & Schuster, 1940), pp. 237–8.
25 Robert Neumann, *Ausflüchte unseres Gewissens: Dokumente zu Hitlers 'Endlösung der Judenfrage' mit Kommentar und Bilanz der politischen Situation* (Hannover: Verlag für Literatur und Zeitgeschehen, 1960), pp. 19, 45.
26 Robert Neumann with Helga Koppel, *Hitler: Aufstieg und Untergang des dritten Reiches* (Munich: Kurt Degesch, 1961), pp. 166–9, 178–9, 250–1.

27 Zywulska, *I Came Back*, p. 165.
28 Robert Neumann with Helga Koppel, *The Pictorial History of the Third Reich* (New York: Bantam, 1962), p. xxix.
29 One of the first major studies that considered the technical aspects of the Auschwitz crematoria is Jean-Claude Pressac, 'Étude et realization des Krematorien IV et V d'Auschwitz-Birkenau', in Francois Furet (ed.), *L'Allemagne nazie et le genocide juif* (Paris: Gallimard & Le Seuil, 1985), pp. 539–86.
30 Harry Mulisch, *Criminal Case 40/61, the Trial of Adolf Eichmann: An Eyewitness Account* (trans. Robert Naborn) (Philadelphia: University of Pennsylvania Press, 2005), p. 171. Comparison of the texts of Mulisch's and Neumann's book proves beyond reasonable doubt that Mulisch took his information from Neumann. Interestingly, Mulisch did not acknowledge his debt to *Hitler: Aufstieg und Untergang des dritten Reiches*.
31 See Wim van Leer, *Time of My Life* (Jerusalem: Carta, 1984).
32 See Schüle, *Industrie und Holocaust*, pp. 327ff.
33 Letter from Wim van Leer to Harry J. Pollock, 3 March 1967, in the van Leer family archive, Jerusalem.
34 See Hannah Arendt, 'Thinking and moral considerations', in *Responsibility and Judgment* (New York: Schocken, 2003), pp. 159ff.
35 'Nazi death factory shocks Germans on a forced tour', *New York Times*, 18 April 1945, p. 8; US Army Signal Corps, *Nazi Concentration Camps*, James B. Donovan, E. Ray Kellogg & George C. Stevens, Nuremberg prosecution exhibit 230, RG-60.2629, Tape 2322, Archive at United States Holocaust Memorial Museum, Washington, DC (available at http://resources.ushmm.org/film/display/detail.php?file_num=219, accessed 27 May 2012).
36 DRP stands for *Deutsches Reichspatent*. This was the designation of a patent issued by the Reichspatentamt between 1919 and 1945. The number 861731 referred to the patent issued by the West German Patent Office in 1953, and hence the title is *formally* erroneous: it should have been DP 861731. In addition, the title is also *historically* erroneous, because DP 861731 was not based on the patent application of 1942.
37 Wim van Leer, *Patent Pending: A Play in Three Acts*, mimeographed typescript, Library Yad Vashem, Jerusalem, inventory no. 66-0545, pp. 23–5, 27.
38 Ibid., pp. 30, 58, 60–4.
39 Ibid., pp. 81, 88, 91–2.
40 Ibid., p. 93.
41 A German translation was commissioned by Felix Bloch Erben publishers in Berlin, and made by the German journalist and scriptwriter Eckart Heinze (writing under the pseudonym Michael Mansfeld). The translation, entitled *Sonderbehandlung* (*Special Treatment*), contained many changes, and van Leer was very unhappy with the result. It was never performed. A copy of *Sonderbehandlung* is in the van Leer family archive.
42 Letter from Wim van Leer to Harry J. Pollock, 3 March 1967.

43 Richard Sennett, *The Fall of Public Man* (New York: Knopf, 1977), p. 259; Annette Wieviorka, *L'Ère du témoin* (Paris: Plon, 1998).
44 Isaiah 56:5.
45 On this trial, see Deborah E. Lipstadt, *History on Trial: My Day in Court with David Irving* (New York: Ecco, 2005).
46 See Robert Jan van Pelt, *The Case for Auschwitz: Evidence from the Irving Trial* (Bloomington: Indiana University Press, 2002).
47 See Wendie Ellen Schneider, 'Past imperfect: *Irving v. Penguin Books Ltd*, No. 1996-I-1113, 2000 WL 362478 (Q. B. Apr. 11), appeal denied (Dec. 18, 2000)', *Yale Law Journal*, 110 (2001), 1535.
48 Robert Jan van Pelt, 'Expert opinion written by Robert Jan van Pelt, D.Lit., Professor of Architecture at the University of Waterloo, Canada, on instructions of Davenport Lyons and Mishcon de Reya, Solicitors, for the purpose of assisting the Queen's Bench Division in the High Court in London in the case between David John Cawdell Irving, plaintiff, and Penguin Books Limited and Deborah E. Lipstadt, defendants'. An electronic version of this report is available at www.hdot.org/en/trial/defense/van (accessed 13 June 2013).
49 Van Pelt, 'Expert opinion', p. 534. For the electronic edition see http://hdot.org/en/trial/defense/van/ix (accessed 13 June 1013).
50 Ibid., p. 535.
51 Ibid., pp. 540–1.
52 High Court of Justice, Queen's Bench Division, 1996-I-1113, *Irving* v. *Penguin and Lipstadt* transcripts, day 9 (25 January 2000), pp. 139–43. For the electronic edition see www.hdot.org/en/trial/transcripts/day 09/pages136-140 and www.hdot.org/en/trial/transcripts/day09/pages 141-145 (accessed 13 June 2013).
53 Ibid., transcripts, day 11 (28 January 2000), p. 161. For the electronic edition see www.hdot.org/en/trial/transcripts/day11/pages161-165 (accessed 13 June 2013).
54 Ibid., transcripts, day 11 (28 January 2000), p. 163. For the electronic edition see www.hdot.org/en/trial/transcripts/day11/pages161-165 (accessed 13 June 2013).
55 Ibid., transcripts, day 11 (28 January 2000), p. 166. For the electronic edition see www.hdot.org/en/trial/transcripts/day11/pages166-170 (accessed 13 June 2013).
56 The judgement was published in book form: Charles Gray, *The Irving Judgement: David Irving v. Penguin Books and Professor Deborah Lipstadt* (Harmondsworth: Penguin Books, 2000). An electronic edition is available at www.hdot.org/en/trial/judgement (accessed 13 June 2013).
57 Gray, *The Irving Judgement*, p. 323. For the electronic edition see www.hdot.org/en/trial/judgement/13.40 (accessed 13 June 2013).
58 Ibid.

Bibliography

Archives

Archive Auschwitz-Birkenau State Museum, Oswiecim, Poland
Library Yad Vashem, Jerusalem
Osobyi Archive, now part of the Russian State Military Archive, Moscow
United States Holocaust Memorial Museum, Washington, DC
van Leer family archive, Jerusalem

Books, chapters, and articles

Arendt, H., 'Thinking and moral considerations', in *Responsibility and Judgment* (New York: Schocken, 2003), pp. 159–89
Bauman, Z., *Modernity and the Holocaust* (Ithaca: Cornell University Press, 1989)
Dawidowicz, L. S. (ed.), *A Holocaust Reader* (New York: Behrman House, 1976)
Dwork, D. & R. J. van Pelt, *Auschwitz: 1270 to the Present* (New York: Norton, 1996)
Ferziger, A. S., 'Ashes to outcasts: cremation, Jewish law, and identity in early twentieth-century Germany', *AJS Review*, 36 (2012), 71–102
Fleming, G., *Hitler and the Final Solution*, augmented edition (Berkeley: University of California Press, 1984, 1994)
Fournet, C., *The Crime of Destruction and the Law of Genocide: Their Impact on Collective Memory* (Aldershot: Ashgate, 2007)
Garber, Z. & B. Zuckerman, 'Why do we call the Holocaust "the Holocaust?" An inquiry into the psychology of labels', *Modern Judaism*, 9:2 (May 1989), 197–211
Gilbert, G. M., *Nuremberg Diary* (New York: Da Capo Press, 1995)
Giordano, R., *Wenn Hitler den Krieg gewonnen hätte: Die Pläne der Nazis nach dem Endsieg* (Hamburg: Rasch & Röhring Verlag, 1989)
Gray, C., *The Irving Judgement: David Irving v. Penguin Books and Professor Deborah Lipstadt* (Harmondsworth: Penguin Books, 2000)
International Military Tribunal, *Trials of the Major War Criminals*, 41 vols (Nuremberg: Secretariat of the Tribunal, 1947–49)
Lanzmann, C., *Shoah: An Oral History of the Holocaust* (New York: Pantheon, 1985)
Lipstadt, D. E., *History on Trial: My Day in Court with David Irving* (New York: Ecco, 2005)
Mulisch, H., *Criminal Case 40/61, the Trial of Adolf Eichmann: An Eye-witness Account* (trans. R. Naborn) (Philadelphia: University of Pennsylvania Press, 2005)
'Nazi death factory shocks Germans on a forced tour', *New York Times*, 18 April 1945, p. 8
Neumann, R., *Ausflüchte unseres Gewissens: Dokumente zu Hitlers 'Endlösung der Judenfrage' mit Kommentar und Bilanz der politischen Situation* (Hannover: Verlag für Literatur und Zeitgeschehen, 1960)

Neumann, R., *By the Waters of Babylon* (New York: Simon & Schuster, 1940)
Neumann, R., *Ein Leichtes Leben* (Vienna: Kurt Desch, 1963)
Neumann, R., with H. Koppel, *Hitler: Aufstieg und Untergang des dritten Reiches* (Munich: Kurt Degesch, 1961)
Neumann, R., with H. Koppel, *The Pictorial History of the Third Reich* (New York: Bantam, 1962)
Pressac, J.-C., *Auschwitz: Technique and Operation of the Gas Chambers* (New York: Beate Klarsfeld Foundation, 1989)
Pressac, J.-C., 'Étude et realization des Krematorien IV et V d'Auschwitz-Birkenau', in F. Furet (ed.), *L'Allemagne nazie et le genocide juif* (Paris: Gallimard & Le Seuil, 1985), pp. 539–86
Sachs, N., *O The Chimneys: Selected Poems, Including the Verse Play, Eli* (trans. M. Hamburger) (New York: Farrar, Straus & Giroux, 1967)
Schneider, W. E., 'Past imperfect: *Irving v. Penguin Books Ltd*, No. 1996-I-1113, 2000 WL 362478 (Q. B. Apr. 11), appeal denied (Dec. 18, 2000)', *Yale Law Journal*, 110 (2001), 1531–45
Schüle, A., *Industrie und Holocaust: Topf & Söhne – Die Ofenbauer von Auschwitz* (Göttingen: Wallstein, 2010)
Semprun, J., 'Une petite lampe s'est allumée dans la baraque des contagieux...', in A. Kalfa & M. de Saint Cheron (eds), *Élie Wiesel en Hommage* (Paris: Les Editions du Cerf, 1998), pp. 53–61
Sennett, R., *The Fall of Public Man* (New York: Knopf, 1977)
Steiner, G., *In Bluebeard's Castle: Some Notes Towards the Re-definition of Culture* (London: Faber & Faber, 1971)
van Leer, W., *Time of My Life* (Jerusalem: Carta, 1984)
van Leer, W., *Patent Pending: A Play in Three Acts*, mimeographed typescript, Library Yad Vashem, Jerusalem
van Pelt, R. J., 'Expert opinion written by Robert Jan van Pelt, D.Lit., Professor of Architecture at the University of Waterloo, Canada, on instructions of Davenport Lyons and Mishcon de Reya, Solicitors, for the purpose of assisting the Queen's Bench Division in the High Court in London in the CASE between David John Cawdell Irving, plaintiff, and Penguin Books Limited and Deborah E. Lipstadt, defendants', available at www.hdot.org/en/trial/defense/van (accessed 13 June 2013)
van Pelt, R. J., *The Case for Auschwitz: Evidence from the Irving Trial* (Bloomington: Indiana University Press, 2002)
Verweyen, T., *Bücherverbrennungen: Eine Vorlesung aus Anlass des 65. Jahrestages der 'Action wider den undeutschen Geist'* (Heidelberg: Universitätsverlag Winter, 2000)
Weinke, A., *Die Verfolgung von NS-Tätern im Geteilten Deutschland* (Paderborn: Ferdinand Schöningh, 2002)
Wieviorka, A., *L'Ère du témoin* (Paris: Plon, 1998)
Zywulska, K., *I Came Back* (trans. Krystyna Cenkalska) (New York: Roy Publishers, 1951)

6

When death is not the end: towards a typology of the treatment of corpses of 'disappeared detainees'[1] in Argentina from 1975 to 1983[2]

Mario Ranalletti
(with the collaboration of Esteban Pontoriero)

On 24 March 1976, the Argentine armed forces, with extensive civilian support, carried out a new military coup against President Isabel Perón, claiming the need to combat guerrilla groups. In order to achieve this goal, task forces and clandestine detention centres were created, which launched an intense campaign of repression, reaching far beyond the confines of the guerrilla organizations. For decades, a negative conception of otherness had been constructed in military social circles and training settings – one that threatened Argentina's Catholic essence. According to this conception, the guerrilla was only the 'tip of the iceberg' of a broader and heterogeneous group, referred to as 'the subversion'. Within this interpretative framework, state repression focused on the guerrilla, but included a much wider population. The personnel assigned to carry out repressive acts and the facilities used for the purpose belonged to the Argentine state in most known cases. Soldiers, members of the security forces (police officers, gendarmes, municipal prison staff, and National Prison Service personnel), and civilians were organized to kidnap, torture, murder, and pillage, and to destroy and/or hide the corpses of an as yet indeterminate number of people accused of belonging to 'the subversion'. In the terminology used at the time, this was the 'war on subversion'.

The military junta remained in power until 1983, when democratic elections were held. Between 1984 and 1985, an investigation undertaken by a special presidential commission managed to identify about 9,000 cases of 'forced disappearance' at the hands of the aforementioned groups. It also confirmed the heterogeneity[3] of the population that had been annihilated, identified a considerable part of the state structure deployed in the massacre, and documented thousands of murders committed with extreme and indiscriminate violence within the framework of the campaign of repression. The testimonies of survivors and witnesses, and the work of forensic anthropologists, confirm that the people who were targeted for destruction were mostly civilians, and that at the time when this phase of mass violence was initiated these people were defenceless against the Argentine state's deployment of repression.

We understand that this violence on the part of the state represented a massacre of different (peaceful or violent) challengers,[4] elites, and egalitarian and reformist social movements that sought to establish a real democracy, or a social revolution, and/or to reduce social inequalities in Argentina. This heterogeneous set of actors and political practices was, for the perpetrators and their civilian allies, a negative otherness[5] that was labelled 'subversion', whose aim was to change the 'Western and Christian' lifestyle and essence of Argentina.

Given what happened in Argentina, it is valid to ask how a professional of war (a soldier) or a security professional (a police officer or gendarme) becomes a perpetrator of mass murder and can exercise extreme violence against a largely civilian population that is unarmed and unable to resist or defend itself. To put it another way, what are the mechanisms that allow the breach of the cultural boundary that prohibits consciously and deliberately inflicting harm on another human being who has no chance to defend himself or herself against this violence?

Through research conducted on the ideological and moral training received by Argentine army officers in the period preceding the coup, we identified – adopting the analysis of massacres proposed by Jacques Sémelin[6] – within this training the constituent elements of an *imaginaire* of destruction, in which was constructed the aforementioned negative otherness, to be targeted for destruction as a way of saving the threatened nation. In this chapter we attempt to show how the technical processes in the treatment (destruction or concealment) of the bodies of the people targeted were based on the representations and interpretations that made up this *imaginaire*. From this we propose a typology of the treatment of the corpses during and after the outbreak of mass violence. In developing this preliminary typology, we worked with two types of sources.

The typology was constructed from an analysis of a selection of cases of destruction and/or concealment of corpses reported by the National Commission on the Disappearance of Persons (Comisión Nacional sobre la Desaparición de Personas, henceforth CONADEP)[7] or investigated by the criminal justice system, based on the work of the Argentine Forensic Anthropology Team (Equipo Argentino de Antropología Forense, henceforth EAAF).[8] With regard to this chapter, the following cases were examined:

1. *Avellaneda Cemetery, Sector 134*. At the beginning of 1983, the mayor of the town of Avellaneda (to the south of Buenos Aires city) initiated an administrative inquiry to establish whether clandestine burials had been made in the municipal cemetery. This investigation established that, from May 1976, the number of bodies buried as 'unidentified' grew exponentially, and identified a notable characteristic relating to them: the majority of bodies labelled as 'unidentified' were those of young people – the average age was twenty-five years – who had died from gunshot wounds. This contradicted historical trends relating to the burial of unidentified bodies. The same inquiry found that this anomaly ended in 1978, when the pattern returned to normal (a few unidentified burials, of elderly people).
2. *The cemetery of the village of Santa Teresita*. Here, a total of thirty-seven unidentified bodies had been buried, according to a complaint made by the mayor of General Lavalle district (in the south of the province of Buenos Aires) in court no. 1 of the Dolores Judicial Department. The bodies had been found on the beach, from mid-1976 onwards. According to witnesses, they were in a terrible state and bore the marks of extreme violence.[9]
3. *The Fátima massacre*. On 19–20 August 1976, about thirty missing 'disappeared detainees' in the custody of the federal police were murdered. These individuals were taken to a field at kilometre 62 of National Highway 8 (in the town of Fátima, in the district of Pilar, province of Buenos Aires). They were killed by gunshots to the head before their bodies were blown up.[10]
4. *Clandestine burials in the San Vicente cemetery (Córdoba)*. The burial of at least seventy unidentified bodies with signs of extreme violence that were brought to the Córdoba judicial morgue by military personnel was investigated, following a complaint made by Juan Caro, an employee of the morgue. Caro told Córdoba Federal Court No. 1 (in the 'Menéndez' case) that between 1976 and 1977 he remembered receiving a large

quantity of corpses from military personnel, and in some cases he counted up to eighty gunshot wounds on a single body.[11]

In addition, we used information relating to the fate of the bodies that was collected by CONADEP and published in the 1991 edition of its report *Nunca más* (first published in 1984).[12] We also analysed reports on the exhumation of clandestine graves and the work of identifying human remains produced by the EAAF as part of different trials for crimes against humanity brought against civilian and military figures and the so-called 'truth trials'. We have drawn on investigations by judges as they passed sentences during different trials for crimes against humanity brought against their perpetrators. We have also used research into court cases conducted by María José Oliveira Sarrabayrouse[13] and Gabriela Águila.[14]

This chapter is organized into three parts. In the first, we provide a basic introduction of the configuration of the *imaginaire* of destruction that preceded the phase of mass violence. In the second part, we present the basic features of the spatial deployment of extreme violence and its use on the bodies of the 'disappeared detainees'. Finally, we present an outline of a preliminary typology of the treatment of the corpses.

The *imaginaire* of destruction

Indoctrination: the preparatory *imaginaire* for the massacre

Alongside their strictly professional training, Argentine soldiers[15] received political and moral indoctrination[16] – disguised as a pseudo-religious education – from lay and religious figures belonging to the domestic extreme right and the intransigent domestic form of Catholicism. Constituted as an informal network that had firm roots in the military sector and a prolonged presence in it through talks, courses, conferences, sermons in church, publications, and spiritual retreats, the indoctrinators drummed a work of fiction into the Argentine military mentality: a Catholic Argentina was threatened by 'international communism' through external agents and their local allies, who formed a complex grouping called 'the subversion'.[17] This indoctrination was based on a series of inventions that structured an interpretation of social conflict emanating from two areas: the existence of an 'internal enemy' hidden within the civilian population, and the idea of a 'third world war' that was already underway. In the mid-1950s, the notion of an 'internal enemy', historically part of the Argentine military mentality, was updated and adapted to the bipolar logic of the Cold War, but still subsumed within the idea of 'subversion'. This process is important, as this was the era when the leaders of the military coup of 1976 received their training, and they in turn would be responsible for the training of many of the perpetrators of the slaughter.

The central pillar of this indoctrination was the subordination of the notion of war to religious principles. Intransigent Catholicism functioned, as part of this indoctrination, as a pre-existing cultural model – in line with Hinton's analysis of genocide in Cambodia[18] – that belonged to the nineteenth century, but was successfully adapted to the context of the Cold War in Argentina. The Argentine military sphere was a social space in which Catholicism had a significance of its own,[19] which went beyond its own particular domain[20] (namely a belief in the supernatural). For the Argentine military, religion upheld a sense of social and political order, and created a historical teleology. Thanks to the persistent and prolonged work of the indoctrinators, the Argentine military took the Catholic religion as the principle for ordering Argentine society. This type of Catholicism therefore became a cultural model. Cultural models neither produce genocidal behaviour nor cause the use of extreme violence, but they do combine with social changes which, in the case of twentieth-century Argentina, took the form of the redistribution of wealth implemented by Peronism between 1946 and 1955, the social modernization of the 1950s, and the emergence of young people as political actors. Faced with these changes, this form of Catholicism turned into a violent ideology, a precondition for slaughter to take place. From the outlook of this *imaginaire*, attacking the Catholic essence of Argentina was considered the worst crime possible, and accordingly a punishment commensurate with such a crime was likewise imagined.

Crossing the threshold of tolerable violence: the notion of subversion

The adoption of the concept of subversion to define Argentina's main enemy during the Cold War was not just a semantic change. This category allowed a much broader and more imprecise definition of the enemy, one that went beyond ideologies and methodologies of collective action. Rather, the indoctrinators designated any form of protest that sought to diminish social inequalities as the action of an enemy to be destroyed. Social protest, struggles for equality, and the actions of guerrilla groups were defined by the indoctrinators as interlinked parts of a single process, the ultimate goal of which was to establish communism in the country and take away its status as a 'Catholic nation'. While these were disparate social movements,[21] to the Argentine military there was no doubt about them belonging to a process with a worldwide reach that was against 'Western Christian civilization', as part of a 'third world war' of a 'revolutionary' nature. Thus, for the Argentine military, a questioning of established authority, sympathy for egalitarian projects, labour-union demands, and student agitation were all considered to be of the same nature as a terrorist attack on the state.

These changes to the definition of the 'internal enemy' took place within an ideological framework that combined different referents: the doctrine of the French revolutionary war, intransigent Catholicism, domestic right-wing extremism, and the USA's national-security doctrine.[22] The idea that Argentina was under attack from 'international communism' was in fact incorporated into laws[23] and military regulations[24] that effectively established legal guarantees for those committing mass murder.

From the imagined to the real: the beginning of the phase of mass violence

Following decades of indoctrination, the return to power of democracy, Peronism, and challengers – above all guerrilla forces – in May 1973[25] sent indoctrinators and indoctrinated into a state of paroxysm. Public speeches from those years show an important radicalization regarding what immediate courses of action were seen as required to confront 'subversion'. For example, one member of the network of indoctrinators, Dr Carlos Sacheri, president of the Argentine section of the lay group 'La Ciudad católica', argued that it was time for a heroic struggle to save civilization from the clutches of the Marxist forces that had just been installed in government. Speaking to a university audience, Sacheri stated that Argentina needed a 'bloodbath' in which it would 'purify' itself. He also declared that 'without blood there will be no redemption'. This text and *Verbo*, the magazine that Sacheri ran, were freely distributed in barracks and military schools.[26]

The phase of mass violence broke out in 1975, when the government ordered the armed forces to take charge of repressing the activities of a guerrilla detachment that had settled in an inhospitable region of the province of Tucumán in northern Argentina. The constitutional government gave sweeping powers to the armed forces to 'annihilate' guerrilla activities, at first only in that area of Tucumán, but then, shortly after, throughout the country. This is demonstrated by one of the provisions enacted to this effect in October 1975:

> The strategy [is to] ... give free rein for the deployment of these measures in 'hot spots' ... [and the] intervention of the security and armed forces.
> 1) Given the offensive position that has been taken, the forces will have the broadest free rein to intervene in all situations in which there appear to be links to subversion.[27]

Following the death of General Perón on 1 July 1974, a wave of parastatal violence, which would precede the state's own terrorism, was unleashed. In charge of operations against the guerrilla detachment in Tucumán, the army created the first clandestine detention centres (henceforth CDCs) in the province and resorted to extreme violence in carrying out its intelligence and repression activities.[28] This was accompanied by an internal confrontation between different sectors of Peronism that were disputing the Peronist leadership following the death of its leader. Perón had returned to Argentina on 20 June 1973 as an old man in a deteriorating state of health. Since his return, Peronism faced internal clashes to decide which sector would control the movement, imagining that soon Perón might no longer be able to act as its leader. Broadly speaking, Peronism was divided between two wings, one comprising 'orthodox', politically integrated groups such as the large labour unions, which hoped to return to 'classic' Peronism, and self-described 'revolutionaries', such as the movement's student group, which had the support of the 'Montoneros' guerrillas.[29] For their part, the guerrilla forces launched a series of armed offensives against officers and barracks.

The spatial deployment of extreme violence

Sliding into extreme violence, or the 'war' that was not a war

By the time of the coup, the perpetrators had not only psychologically conceived the possibility of slaughter as a solution to the problem of 'subversion', but they had also suffered numerous attacks and losses at the hands of the guerrillas. Moreover, they had put the basic structure of state terrorism to the test in the province of Tucumán between February and December 1975. The argument of avenging the dead, an issue that deserves investigation in the search for a deeper understanding of the slaughter that ensued, was added to the received indoctrination. From 24 March 1976 the armed forces and their civilian allies embarked on a campaign of repression against the 'subversion' that was unprecedented in terms of its breadth, intensity, and methodology. To the classic measures taken by military governments in twentieth-century Argentina[30] – suspension of liberties, banning political parties, control of the judiciary, and control of the economy – something new was added that represented a departure from previous military interventions: the creation of a clandestine apparatus within the state to carry out what the perpetrators called the 'war against subversion'. More than 300 CDCs were created nationwide, which, in most cases, were installed on state premises (for example, barracks, police stations, schools, and hospitals), albeit in hidden places or ones without free access, while the rest of the premises functioned 'normally'. There were also CDCs on private property. Task forces that were made up of civilians, soldiers, gendarmes, and police officers operated within these CDCs, dealing with intelligence activities, kidnapping, torture, and the clandestine detention of those designated 'subversives'. Research indicates that those who enacted violence against the disappeared detainees represented a small proportion of the security and armed forces.[31]

The detainment of victims in CDCs followed a sequence of five basic steps: (1) abduction; (2) torture; (3) continued clandestine detention; (4) murder or release; (5) concealment of the remains of those killed. This sequence took place within a context of an absolute disparity of forces that favoured the perpetrators;[32] this asymmetry was reinforced at each successive stage of the sequence, by the systematic use of torture in intelligence work and the clandestine holding of detainees. CONADEP's report[33] made it clear that the majority of people held in CDCs were apprehended at night, in their homes, that very few of them had weapons with which to defend themselves, and that abductions were carried out through the deployment of task forces, and even in some cases with aerial support. This invalidates the perpetrators' claim that their actions were justified by the country being in a state of war.[34] Rather than waging a war, the security forces were hunting people who were trying to remain hidden, who were devoid of support networks, and who were fleeing from the colossal repressive apparatus that had been set up by the Argentine state. From the moment they were captured, the victims immediately lost their humanity, being subjected to senseless violence and being broken down over an indefinite period within the CDCs, a clandestine space that was cut off from the outside and completely controlled by the perpetrators. The perpetrators then repeated this sequence with further torture and mistreatment.

Argentine state terrorism: exceptionalism, 'normality', and CDC operational autonomy

The spatial structure of the repressive state apparatus exhibited the particular feature of combining the clandestine with 'normality'. The institutions where many of the CDCs were located did not significantly alter their own operations. Rather, it was a case of there being a section reserved for perpetrating slaughter while the remaining space operated normally, open to the public and continuing with its usual activities. For example, in 1977 it was common for elementary school students to visit the School of Naval Mechanics to find out more about it, with a possible view to continuing their secondary education there. At the same time, within certain parts of the same institution dozens of people were held captive, many of whom were being tortured. Here, Argentine state terrorism led to a convergence, in both space and time, of the hidden and abused bodies of the 'disappeared detainees' with children having a day of fun and careers guidance.[35] In our opinion, this duality facilitated the slaughter, by giving its perpetrators operational autonomy.

Through the reconstructions carried out during the course of some of the trials and the work of forensic anthropologists, it can be seen that the perpetrators adapted the chain of command to the power relations that grew internally within the CDCs, rather than following set schemata. The perpetrators held the lives and property of the disappeared in their hands; these spoils proved to be very large and difficult to manage appropriately, owing to the extremely corrupt morals and professionalism of those who operated in the CDCs.[36] The perpetrators' substantial operational autonomy made them more like a gang than a task force within a regular army.

The operational methods of the task forces appear to reflect a principle of Argentine army troop management, that operations are centrally overseen, but that their execution is decentralized.[37] Army regulations were also explicit in their authorization of the use of maximum levels of violence against 'subversives':

> Apply combat force and maximum violence to annihilate subversive criminals, wherever they may be.... Military action is always violent and bloody, but it must have its justification and the support of psychological operations. It is the role of the security forces and police to determine levels of violence. The guiding concept will be that a subversive criminal wielding weapons must be destroyed, because when the Armed Forces undertake operations against these criminals they should neither break off from combat nor accept their surrender.[38]

In our view, the pronounced gap between the oversight and execution of repressive actions led to the increasing operational autonomy of the perpetrators, which was made more potent by their clandestine nature and the indoctrination they had received. One year on from the coup, when the mass violence was at a peak, it seems likely that even members of the army themselves noticed that the violence being deployed was so extreme that it could have negative consequences for the forces of repression. In an attempt to establish basic rules to mitigate the possible negative effects of repressive activities, the army set a series of guidelines that seem to have been an attempt to organize the execution of the 'disappeared detainees'. In June 1977, the Commander of the First Army Corps issued 'Operations Order No. 9/77 (Continuation of the offensive against the subversion during the period 1977)'. Although this was limited in its geographical application to the city of Buenos Aires and the surrounding area, it can also be understood as the manifestation of a desire to regulate exceptionalist state terrorism. A judicial inquiry noted of this legislation:

> with every case of excess, abuse, or outrage carried out on behalf of the Force or 'joint forces', damage was done to the National Reorganization Process,[39] and having gained experience of ethical considerations being neglected during military and security operations by the taskforce members who carried them out, it was decided that henceforth, in order that these operations should be carried out with a modicum of guarantees and reliability and with the aim of improving the situation, responsibility for oversight would fall on the senior personnel of Zone 1 Command.[40]

Under the same order, the military authorities also established the procedures for returning corpses to families:

Likewise, it was stipulated that when an opponent had been killed, the sub-area involved would be in charge of the corpse until it was received by relatives or given a burial. To that end, the body would be sent to the judicial morgue following the involvement of the relevant police authority, and following identification, Zone 1 Command, Department III – Operations – Planning Division would be notified to then pass on the information. Upon certification of the relationship to the deceased, the bereaved relatives would be allowed to take the body from the judicial morgue.

Alternatively, after the passage of thirty days without the body being claimed, administrative steps would be taken for burial.[41]

Some attempts to create an alternative reality about the circumstances and method of murder of the 'disappeared detainee' were extremely crude, something that in our view should be considered a demonstration, firstly, of the extreme levels of violence exercised and, secondly, of the dysfunctional relationship between the perpetrators charged with the torture and murder of detainees ('decentralized execution' is referred to in Order 9/77) and their hierarchical command, charged with the strategic management of state terror. The murder of Miguel Ángel Ceballos provides an example of this:

> Frida Angélica Cappatto de Ceballos, the wife of Miguel Ángel Ceballos, said that after finding out about the death of her husband, who was kept in the UP1, and after looking for the body, having been told he had been killed while attempting to escape, found it in the morgue of San Roque hospital, among a pile of corpses. He had been gagged and had numerous gunshot wounds, including one to the chin, by which she knew he could not have died while attempting to escape, with the cause of death (gunshot wound) being recorded on the death certificate.[42]

The treatment of the bodies: extreme violence and suffering beyond murder

It is known, principally from the investigations carried out by the judicial system, journalists, and human-rights organizations between June 1982 and December 1983, that most of the people who went through the CDCs were held in clandestine captivity for a prolonged period and were killed after being tortured. As Frank Graziano has noted, the bodies of the 'disappeared detainees' were the 'battlefield' on which a totally uneven war was waged between good and evil.[43]

The combination of 'normality' and exceptionalism that shaped the implementation of state terrorism in Argentina seems to have had a counterpart in the treatment of the bodies. Making them disappear, by destroying, hiding, or returning them to the legal domain as if the death had been 'normal' (discussed in the next section), was meant to erase the crime.[44] A study of the sources shows that the death of the disappeared detainees was not the perpetrators' only objective. Before that happened, they seem to have prized the infliction of a great, great deal of pain on them. Observing this, one judge noted:

> The exertion of violence on the bodies of these detainees was visible from the number of inflicted shots: five shots for young Irazusta and fourteen for Chiavarini, who were already in a severely damaged physical state as a result of the brutality of the near-fatal torture inflicted on them. All this corroborates the opinion put forward by the crime lab's Doctor Chalub at that time that the excessive number of shots found on the bodies that he had to examine as a result of these alleged clashes revealed a hostility that was about more than killing.[45]

In spite of the attempts at organization mentioned above, the exercise of extreme violence to destroy people labelled as 'subversives' could not be controlled or regulated. Operational freedom in the CDCs appears to have prevailed over the chain of command and any planning. The torture room became the theatre in which the perpetrators chose to fight 'their' war. The catalogue of the acts of violence carried out in the CDCs was extremely varied and shows a degree of cruelty which matched that under colonialism and in the civil war that followed Argentine independence. The common forms of violence within the CDCs included: rape; torture of pregnant women; humiliation (both physical and psychological) of children as a form of torturing their parents; the electrocution of genitals; blackmailing relatives when the disappeared detainee had already been killed; and the destruction, desecration, or concealment of the bodies of those killed.

From the moment they were abducted, and preceding their murder, the bodies of the disappeared detainees underwent a severe process of decline. Prolonged captivity in inhumane conditions, a lack of medical care, the terror caused by repeated torture, and poor diet were also part of the 'punishment' that was, in the perpetrators' view, deemed appropriate for the 'subversives'. Similarities can be identified here that recall the conditions experienced by the victims of the Holocaust and concentration camps,[46] or the psychological abuse of prisoners in the Soviet gulags.[47]

The fate of the dead: removing any traces and normalizing exceptionalism by reintroducing the body into the legal domain

The treatment of the corpses indicates an intention to dismiss the story of state terrorism that might arise from the condition of the tortured bodies. When perpetrators disposed of the bodies without destroying them, they delegated the responsibility for delivering the body to the relatives to the police or the judiciary. When corpses were thus reintroduced into the legal domain, the causes of death, evident from the bodies themselves, were not recorded on the relevant documents. The perpetrators had to put a lot of effort into ensuring that this was achieved. Their desire for denial was absurd, as the terrible autopsy descriptions contained in the sources demonstrate. However, combinations of different forensic, police, and judicial proceedings were set in train, as though this glut of procedures would hide the truth forever. Among one of many possible examples is the kidnapping, torture, and murder of Eduardo Ruibal. In his case, the way in which different military and judicial authorities (the army, the judicial morgue, and the police) were involved in creating a large number of documents can be seen. On the one hand the records gave a fictional account of a death that resulted from an armed clash with a task force, while on the other hand they provided important information about the truth of Ruibal's death.[48] The delegation of CONADEP for the city of Bahía Blanca noted the use of the same procedure in the south of Buenos Aires province.[49]

Research conducted by María José Oliveira Sarrabayrouse corroborates this information, and provides an analysis of a criminal and administrative trial regarding operational irregularities at the judicial morgue of the city of Buenos Aires in relation to bodies sent there by military authorities during the dictatorship.[50] In this case, it was the judicial branch of the military dictatorship itself that highlighted the attempts made to transform the 'exceptionalism' of state terrorism into bureaucratically and procedurally regulated normality.

A case study: the Buenos Aires city judicial morgue

Recounting an episode that was subject to a criminal investigation – and reconstructed in Oliveira Sarrabayrouse's work – is revealing, as it gives a sense of how the perpetrators began using the Buenos

Aires city judicial morgue to dispose of the bodies of the disappeared detainees who were murdered.

During the night of 29 September 1976, a group of soldiers appeared at the morgue, bringing with them six bodies to be given an appropriate autopsy before being handed over to the relatives. The perpetrators, who were in uniform but who refused to give their names, informed the morgue official that six 'subversives' had been killed during a clash that had occurred that day. They did not have a court order of any kind. The morgue official who was on duty, and then his immediate superior, refused to take the bodies without an appropriate court order issued by a judge. In response to this refusal, the perpetrators threatened to just leave the bodies there. The morgue official eventually agreed to take the bodies following a promise from the perpetrators to bring the missing documents. A few hours later, the perpetrators brought a note signed by the deputy head of the Central Military Hospital, in which the official asked the morgue to take the bodies, which in the meantime had been left in the morgue's courtyard.

The morgue took charge of the bodies, carried out the autopsies, and delivered them to the families. The morgue officials had not permitted the military to disrupt established bureaucratic and procedural practice, and had resisted taking the corpses without a court order. This is an interesting detail, especially because, as Sarrabayrouse indicates, the military dictatorship did not make changes to the roster of judges, but instead retained the existing one, except in the case of the highest courts (the national and provincial supreme courts).[51]

The incident caused the morgue officials to demand specific instructions in writing, firstly from the head of the institution and then from the top judicial body, the National Criminal and Correctional Appeals Court, over the actions arising in this situation, which were irregular from a procedural point of view. Moreover, the morgue sent similar requests to the highest military authority of the city of Buenos Aires, which at this time was the Commander-in-Chief of the First Army Corps, General Guillermo Suárez Mason. Extremely perturbed by this request, Suárez Mason sent the deputy chief of the Corps, Colonel Roberto Roualdés, to meet with the head of the morgue, Dr Mario H. Pena. On 20 December 1976, Roualdés went to the morgue, along with some armed soldiers, and demanded to speak with Pena, without having previously made a request to meet him. The two spoke, and from that date there were no further problems with bodies sent by military authorities.[52]

For their part, both junior and senior morgue officials sought to incorporate into established bureaucratic practice the irregularities of the military authorities sending corpses that showed signs of having been tortured. When interviewed by Sarrabayrouse, some of the officials from that time reported that what bothered them was, at a basic level, the bureaucratic disruption – since the sending of the corpses by the military authorities violated the prevailing principle that this was something a judge should do – and the fact that the autopsy report was sent to a military commander.[53] In these testimonies at least, it was not the sudden influx of corpses exhibiting clear signs of torture per se that seems to have disturbed the morgue officials.

Further examples

A comparable situation occurred in different cases investigated in Córdoba province. In one instance, three bodies were deposited in the morgue of the San Roque Hospital in the city of Córdoba (in the centre of the country) by a military and police task force. The medical examiners proceeded to carry out autopsies, completed death certificates, and released the bodies to the families. They recorded in the documentation that the deaths had occurred through clashes with the police and army, but failed to note that the bodies showed signs of torture and numerous close-range shots.[54] Ignoring these obvious signs of extreme violence became particularly common in the early, more repressive days of the dictatorship (especially 1976–79). Morgue officials avoided starting official investigations by recording 'no name' in the paperwork and sending the bodies to different graveyards.

The morgue became a key point in the procedure of reintegrating bodies of the 'disappeared' into the legal domain and, ultimately, returning them to society. The Córdoba delegation of CONADEP[55] found a similar pattern, but for a different group: prisoners housed in a regular prison. Many years later, with the so-called Menéndez case, the Argentine justice system resumed the investigation initiated by CONADEP. This verified the investigation into the case of Prison Unit No. 1 of the city of Córdoba. Several 'special prisoners' (i.e. members of guerrilla forces, or individuals accused of being so) who had been jailed during the period of constitutional government between 1973 and 1976 were held here. Investigations related to the Menéndez case show that a number of detainees in the prison unit were removed from it, taken to a CDC to be tortured, sent back to jail, and then eventually murdered at the CDC and sent to either the morgue of the Córdoba Central Hospital, or the city's judicial morgue, to be handed over to the relatives.[56] As in the cases discussed above, the autopsy reports are incomplete – in general they do not record the marks of torture and mistreatment – and state the circumstances of death as a fabricated clash with police forces, resisting arrest or an identity check, or even an attempt to escape from their place of detention.[57]

There are some cases in which bodies were returned to families without information of any sort. This is something that – if such a thing were possible – increased the horror. Various testimonies indicate that some bodies were returned to their families with the expressed instruction not to open the coffin at any point. The inhumanity inflicted during captivity was extended with the contempt displayed for the corpse and the family. This can be seen in the case of the abduction and murder of Cecilio Kamenetzky, carried out by a police task force – in this instance from the Police Information Department (DIP) of Santiago del Estero – in the province of Santiago del Estero (northern Argentina). Kamenetzky's relatives, who knew his whereabouts, were informed that the death had occurred in an escape attempt. It is worth noting that Santiago del Estero is a poor province with a small population and subtropical climate. In the understanding of the judge handling the case,

> Cecilio Kamenetzky had been monitored since June 1975 by members of the DIP. He was taken from his home by Miguel Tomás Garbi without a warrant on 9 August 1976. He was transferred to the DIP, where he was detained under the authority of Musa Azar, Garbi, and López Veloso. He was tortured for 20 days until the start of a court case against him. He was then transferred to the men's prison, from where at various times he was taken back to the DIP to be interrogated again. Finally, on 13 November Cecilio Kamenetzky was killed at the headquarters of the DIP by shots fired by López Veloso and Corbalán that entered his back at close range, which it was argued resulted from him fleeing. There was no inquiry in the case filed against him to determine why he was at the DIP and not at the men's prison to which his transfer had been ordered during his indictment. His body was not autopsied.
> … It was extremely hot at that time of year but the morgue of the Independence Hospital was unrefrigerated, and Cecilio's body was destroyed and in a state of decomposition. His father was later told that he had been summoned to the Federal Court, and the court records show that a death certificate was issued by order of Federal Judge Dr Liendo Roca, without the cause of death or anything else being specified.[58]

In the case of the operations of the Buenos Aires morgue and that of the Rosario region's communal cemetery, this procedure of reintroducing the corpse into the 'legal' domain also demonstrated a certain level of collaboration by civil society – whether it was wished for or carried out with repugnance under obligation – in the mass murder that was taking place. In the case of the Buenos Aires morgue, when asked about how it operated under the military dictatorship, an official from those years said, during a criminal case, that his work was undertaken

> according to standard practice, i.e., in the usual environment, with the appropriate protocols, the usual staff of medical examiners, assistants and cleaning staff, photographers, radiology technicians etc. Furthermore, the fact the bodies found their way onto the autopsy table with their corresponding protocols signified that they had passed all the prior and accompanying administrative safeguards for the admission of bodies.[59]

Outlining a typology

Five methods for the disposal of corpses can be identified. All the procedures used display the strength of the desire to create a fictitious account of the circumstances surrounding the murders:

1. Bringing the bodies into normal bureaucratic and forensic channels. This course of action was used after a murder in a CDC, and took one of several forms:
   a. The registration and burial of the corpse in an official cemetery. The sources consulted indicate this took place in Buenos Aires province, in municipal cemeteries in Quilmes, La Plata, Moreno, Rafael Calzada, San Martin, Grand Bourg, and Avellaneda.[60] However, it should be noted that some burials in cemeteries were in fact done clandestinely, and sometimes using mass graves, as happened in San Vicente Cemetery (Córdoba), the training grounds of the Third Army Corps Command (Córdoba), and La Piedad cemetery (La Piedad is the area surrounding the city of Rosario, in Santa Fe province).[61]
   b. The referral of the body to a morgue, with the agreement of the authorities, and the body being labelled 'unidentified' following an autopsy and/or visual examination by one of the morgue's medical examiners.

The treatment of corpses in Argentina   163

    c. Passing off the murder as having resulted from combat between the security forces and guerrilla forces, or a prisoner attempting to escape. In fact, an ad hoc military authority (i.e. under army jurisdiction) was created, supposedly to investigate such cases, in the form of a 'court-martial'.[62]

    d. In addition, there are recorded cases of bodies being left in the street, which were then collected by the police as a result of complaints being made by local residents.[63]

2. Throwing corpses or people still alive into the sea or waterways[64] from aeroplanes or helicopters. CONADEP's report identified the existence of these 'death flights' from the army's Campo de Mayo base[65] and the School of Naval Mechanics.[66] This method, according to the EAAF's work on identifying bodies, took place later, in 1978, than the phase of mass violence.[67]

3. Destruction of corpses.

    a. Burning bodies in the CDCs or in the vicinity. It has been verified that this procedure took place in the following CDCs: El Banco (San Justo, Buenos Aires province);[68] the School of Naval Mechanics (Buenos Aires city), in the sports field; 'Pozo de Arana' (La Plata, Buenos Aires province);[69] 'Vesuvius' (La Tablada, Buenos Aires province);[70] and 'Arsenal Miguel de Azcuénaga' (Tucumán province).[71] The crematorium of the largest cemetery in Buenos Aires city was also used to dispose of the corpses of the disappeared detainees.[72] Four bodies that were burned in Escobar (Buenos Aires province) were sent to the morgue,[73] after a judge intervened to have the charred bodies identified.

    b. Using explosives (the 'Fátima massacre', Pilar, Buenos Aires province).[74]

    c. Clandestine burials. Anthropologists have established that there was a large increase in 'unidentified' burials in Buenos Aires province during the period 1976–78. There is a positive correlation between this increase and the proximity of the cemetery to a CDC, as well as a very significant growth in the burial of 'unidentified' people whose cause of death was head trauma and/or gunshot wounds.[75] In its study of Sector 134 of Avellanada Municipal Cemetery, the EAAF reached identical conclusions, in both quantitative and chronological terms.[76]

4. Placing corpses in concrete-filled barrels and throwing them into rivers.[77]

5. Burying bodies in mass graves, either within the CDCs or in adjoining areas.[78]

The sources cited reveal that after a murder occurred, the body was passed into the hands of a second type of perpetrator, who became involved by making the remains either disappear or re-enter the legal domain. A division of labour within the CDC in relation to the corpses can be noted, with those responsible for torturing and murdering being different people from those who took charge of the corpses after the murder.

All this amounts to a preliminary typology, which will surely be modified by new and more in-depth investigations. It should be noted that in many sources combinations of these five methods appear, suggesting new lines of research that could delve into the motivations of the perpetrators in relation to specific cases. We believe that this outline, which is preliminary and subject to revision, allows an appreciation, based on work with forensic and judicial sources, of the complexity and scale of the deployment of extreme violence and its spatio-temporal structuring in Argentine state terrorism.

Conclusion

Much more remains to be uncovered concerning the treatment of the corpses of disappeared detainees in Argentina. Based on the work conducted so far, it is possible to make some concluding comments. It is our understanding that Argentine state terrorism was rooted in the moral and ideological training imparted in the military sector from 1954. The indoctrination received by the perpetrators during their professional training stated that enemies were hiding among civilians, that they sought to conceal their status as a mortal enemy by assuming the guise of a private citizen, and that they had an unwavering desire to put an end to Catholicism in Argentina. Thus the perpetrators of state violence became convinced that the extermination of the enemy was the only appropriate action, that such action was just, and that any means could be employed to achieve this objective. The indoctrinators presented extreme violence against the disappeared detainees as an act of defending a God and country that were under threat, and therefore also as a deserved punishment for the offence committed by the subversives. This indoctrination maintained that the enemy would stop at nothing to achieve their goals. Between 1954 and 1975, this indoctrination progressively erased the line between war and atrocity, and therefore the line between a soldier and a murderer.[79] In our view, this indoctrination was a determining factor in the social construction of the cruelty displayed by the perpetrators during the phase of mass violence. Its main function was to ensure that extreme violence was exercised in response to different challengers, who were understood to be participants in a global offensive against Catholicism. The indoctrination turned to traditional knowledge and standards to justify, even trivialise, the extreme violence in terms of defending the Catholic religion. When some perpetrators had doubts about the legitimacy or the meaning of the heinous acts they were committing, advice was sought from members of the Catholic Church. The response was forceful and unanimous: they were 'soldiers of Christ', fighting for the kingdom of God, and anything was permissible and would be forgiven if they were to beat the subversion.[80]

Studying this guidance allows some answers to be put forward to the question of how a human being becomes a perpetrator of mass murder. In the case studied here, it has been of interest to determine the nature of the ideology that allowed the Argentine perpetrators to have the moral backing and impunity to empower them to cross the threshold of socially acceptable violence, and to proceed to exercising an extreme form of violence against a negative otherness that was defined as such by that same ideological framework. Facing a largely civilian and unarmed enemy – defenceless or in retreat – and to subject them to an extreme form of violence, and to continue abusing their remains after their death, it is necessary to be convinced that committing such a crime against humanity is a positive act; and, since the perpetrators were, for the most part, state officials they would have to be convinced it was a crime whose perpetration would benefit the nation.

But this ideological framework did not just enable the slaughter. It also allowed the suffering inflicted on the enemy to be extended beyond his or her murder and to the bereaved. Murders were followed by the destruction or concealment of the remains. This allowed the fiction to be created that no crime had taken place. There were also attempts to attain documentation to accompany the crimes as part of their attempt to hide them, with the expectation that this practice would go unpunished.

In the sources consulted, no pattern can be detected that explains, in even any minimally rational way, the actions taken by the perpetrators; nor do the sources show the existence of an ordering principle – as the racist ideology in Nazism, or tribal hatred in the case of Rwanda may be considered to be – to explain the treatment of the bodies in the Argentine case. This issue was also highlighted by the EAAF, which offers a 'hypothesis'.[81]

As Hélène Piralian[82] has argued with regard to the case of genocide in Armenia, destroying the bodies, or hiding them so that relatives could not bury them according to their beliefs and wishes, ultimately meant the destruction of the death of the disappeared detainees. Attempts were made to prevent those killed in the CDCs being integrated into the community of the dead, or their families being able to mourn, remember, and venerate them. In the Argentine case, we view the destruction and concealment of corpses as an extension of the suffering inflicted on the disappeared detainees beyond biological death and an additional form of punishment that was inflicted by the perpetrators.

The perpetrators in Argentina do not seem to have sought to make their victims understand why they received their punishment. The cause of the suffering inflicted was enunciated during torture and repeated tirelessly during their captivity – their stigmatization as 'subversives', together with all sorts of insults – but there does not seem to have been an intention to bring redemption to the disappeared detainees through their punishment. This could explain why children were also tortured, something that distinguishes the Argentine case from the Rwandan genocide, during which torturers ignored children because they were deemed unable to understand why such suffering was being inflicted on them.[83]

The work carried out using judicial and forensic sources does not show, with regard to the cases studied here, the existence of an industrial logic in the management of corpses. We have been able to establish a series of recurrences in the fate of the corpses that allow an initial typology of their treatment by the perpetrators. The management of the corpses shows the need for the participation of a wider network of state officials (court officials, medical examiners, administrative staff of the armed and security forces) in the concealment and/or delivery of bodies to the relatives; these officials became a de facto part of the clandestine apparatus created by the perpetrators when the phase of mass violence began. Rather than being a true piece of technical and social engineering, there was a lot of trial and error, and irrational omnipotence, which was given strength by making use of resources that predated the slaughter, such as the judiciary.

The question is raised of why the perpetrators, in their management of the bodies, used certain procedures that were a priori destined to fail. For example, it seems unlikely that a member of the Argentine navy would not have realized that bodies thrown into the sea could be returned to shore by the tide, as indeed happened. And nor is it possible to accept that a medical examiner, in signing a death certificate that recorded the cause of death as only a 'cardiorespiratory arrest' when the body displayed multiple signs of having been tortured and mutilated, would not expect the fraud to come to light, as did happen, even before the end of the military dictatorship.

Not only did they seek to wipe out everyone whom the perpetrators considered 'challengers', but they also sought to wipe out the death, and with this erase the crime. First, nature showed them that this was not possible. By transferring bodies that had been abnormally treated to morgues, there was no way to fulfil the goal of erasing the traces of the crime. Then there were the human-rights organizations, the EAAF, and relatives of the victims who, through their struggles and work, confirmed a phenomenon that was sometimes corroborated by sectors of civil society and the perpetrators themselves.

Argentine society still owes considerable debts to its recent traumatic past. There are still many unsolved cases, many stories that are yet to be constructed, and more grieving to be done. The Argentine justice system has got back to work, and some of those debts are most likely now being paid. We believe that it is not about turning one of history's black pages, but rather of furthering our knowledge of this 'past that does not pass'.[84]

Notes

1 Local terminology has been preserved.
2 The text of this chapter was translated from the author's Spanish by Cadenza Academic Translations.
3 Due to the heterogeneity of the people targeted for destruction, they cannot be grouped into a single category, and certainly should not be considered as a part of a guerrilla movement. Guerrilla forces did, though, represent, at the time of the coup, a policing problem. In February 1975, the armed forces began to be involved in suppressing guerrilla forces using both legal and illegal methods. Towards the end of that year, one of the main guerrilla organizations (the Marxist People's Revolutionary Army) had been completely defeated, while another group (the Peronist Montoneros) was in disorderly retreat, which left it significantly weakened and facilitated the work of repressing it. Moreover, its leadership left the country for security reasons to settle first in Rome and then in Mexico.

4 For the sense in which the concept of 'challengers' is used, see Sidney G. Tarrow, *Power in Movement: Social Movements and Contentious Politics* (Cambridge: Cambridge University Press, 2011).
5 D. Feierstein, *Seis estudios sobre genocidio. Análisis de las relaciones sociales: otredad, exclusión y exterminio* (Buenos Aires: Eudeba, 2000).
6 J. Sémelin, *Purifier et détruire: les usages politiques des massacres et génocides* (Paris: Seuil, 2005).
7 CONADEP, Archivo Nacional de la Memoria (National Memorial Archive), File no. 7316.
8 Federal Capital Criminal and Correctional Court of Appeal, judgement for case no. 49.614, 'Yavico Alfredo s/ denuncia de incumplimiento de los deberes de funcionario público', 2010, p. 768.
9 CONADEP, *Nunca más* (Buenos Aires: Eudeba, 1991), p. 239; EAAF, 'The coast cases: General Lavalle, General Madariaga, and Villa Gesell cemeteries', in *EAAF 2007 Annual Report* (Buenos Aires: EAAF, 2007), pp. 32–5; P. Bernardi & L. Fondebrider, 'Forensic archaeology and the scientific documentation of human rights violations: an Argentinian example from the early 1980s', in R. Ferllini (ed.), *Forensic Archaeology and Human Right Violations* (Illinois: Charles C. Thomas, 2007), pp. 205–32.
10 Oral Federal Criminal Court No. 5, judgement in case no. 1.223, 18 July 2008, pp. 17–18 (see www.masacredefatima.com.ar, accessed January 2014), and judgement in case no. 16.441/02, 'Masacre de Fátima. Resolución procesamiento con prisión preventiva y embargo sobre Lapuyole, Marcote, y Gallone', 22 June 2004, p. 15.
11 The 'Menéndez' case was of great importance because it was the sum of sixteen other legal processes (involving crimes against humanity and other crimes) against former general Luciano Benjamin Menéndez. See Córdoba Federal Criminal Court No. 1, judgement for the case 'Menéndez, Luciano Benjamín y otros p.ss.aa: Privación ilegítima de la libertad agravada, Imposición de tormentos agravados' (Expte. M-13/09), 22 December 2010. This officer was a key figure in the junta, as a hardliner who ordered mass arrests, executions, and the torture of prisoners (to gain military intelligence). Menéndez was head of the Third Army Corps, with jurisdiction over ten Argentine provinces (Jujuy, Salta, Catamarca, La Rioja, San Juan, Mendoza, San Luis, Córdoba, Santiago del Estero, and Tucumán). He was personally involved with two clandestine detention centres, 'La Perla' and 'La Ribera'. See www.desaparecidos.org/arg/tort/ejercito/menendez (accessed February 2012).
12 CONADEP, *Nunca más*.
13 M. J. O. Sarrabayrouse, *Poder judicial y dictadura: el caso de la morgue judicial* (Buenos Aires: Defensoría del Pueblo de la Ciudad de Buenos Aires/Facultad de Filosofía Letras, Universidad de Buenos Aires, 2003).
14 G. Águila, *Dictadura, represión y sociedad en Rosario, 1976/1983: un estudio sobre la represión y los comportamientos y actitudes sociales en dictadura* (Buenos Aires: Prometeo libros, 2008).

15 The army was (and is) the most powerful of the armed forces and carried the greatest political weight; furthermore, from 1955 the police force was subordinated to the army until the end of the military dictatorship, in 1983. Although this study is limited to the Argentine army, we believe that it would not be problematic to extend the analysis presented here to the rest of the security and armed forces.
16 Prudencio García, *El drama de la autonomía militar: Argentina bajo las Juntas Militares* (Madrid: Alianza, 1995), p. 35.
17 It has been possible to identify different methods of indoctrination with regard to the Argentine army: informal meetings after the regular courses that took place in training centres; the classes of the standard courses of these centres, mainly in areas such as religion, ethics, and the history of international relations and of Argentina; spiritual retreats organized in barracks; courses and conferences organized outside barracks; and mass, which ceremony was almost mandatory for Argentine soldiers. See M. Ranalletti, *Du Mékong au Río de la Plata: la doctrine de la guerre révolutionnaire, 'La Cité catholique' et leurs influences en Argentine, 1954–1976*, doctoral thesis, Institut d'études politiques de Paris (2006); M. Ranalletti, 'Aux origines du terrorisme d'État en Argentine (1955–1976)', *Vingtième Siècle: Revue d'Histoire*, 105 (January–March 2010), 45–56.
18 A. L. Hinton, 'Why did you kill? The Cambodian genocide and the dark side of face and honor', *Journal of Asian Studies*, 57:1 (February 1998), 93–122.
19 L. Zanatta, *Del Estado liberal a la nación católica: Iglesia y Estado en los orígenes del peronismo, 1930–1943* (Bernal: Editorial de la Universidad Nacional de Quilmes, 1996).
20 M. Badaró, *Militares o ciudadanos: la formación de los oficiales del Ejército Argentino* (Buenos Aires: Prometeo Libros, 2009); P. Marchak, *God's Assassins: State Terrorism in Argentina in the 1970s* (Montreal: McGill-Queen's University Press, 1999); L. E. Tibiletti, 'La sociabilización básica de los oficiales del Ejército en el período 1955–1976', in O. Moreno (ed.), *La construcción de la Nación argentina: el rol de las fuerzas armadas. Debates históricos en el marco del Bicentenario (1810–2010)* (Buenos Aires: Ministerio de Defensa, 2010), pp. 265–6.
21 M. J. Moyano, *Argentina's Lost Patrol: Armed Struggle, 1969–1979* (New Haven: Yale University Press, 1995), ch. 4.
22 M. Ranalletti, 'Contrainsurgencia, catolicismo intransigente y extremismo de derecha en la formación militar argentina: Influencias francesas en los orígenes del terrorismo de Estado (1955–1976)', in D. Feierstein (ed.), *Terrorismo de Estado y genocidio en América Latina* (Buenos Aires: Prometeo Libros, 2009), pp. 253–84.
23 M. Ranalletti & E. Pontoriero, 'La normativa en materia de defensa y seguridad y la criminalización de las disidencias (1955–1976)', paper presented at the Fifth Workshop on Recent History (V Jornadas de trabajo sobre historia reciente), Universidad Nacional de General Sarmiento, 24 June 2010.
24 M. Ranalletti, 'La legitimación de la tortura como herramienta en

tareas de inteligencia: estudio de caso a partir de los reglamentos del Ejército argentino (1968–1976)', paper presented at the Second International Meeting 'Análisis de las Prácticas Sociales Genocidas' ('Analysis of Social Practices in Genocide'), Universidad Nacional de Tres de Febrero, Buenos Aires, 20–22 November 2007.

25 On 25 May 1973, after more than seventeen years of its proscription, the Peronist movement returned to government following the 11 March 1973 elections. This was seen as a defeat for the military and its civilian allies. See R. Fraga, *Ejército: del escarnio al poder, 1973–1976* (Buenos Aires: Editorial Planeta, 1988).

26 C. Sacheri, 'El universitario frente a la ideología marxista', speech given at a study day on Marxism, Universidad Católica Argentina, Buenos Aires, 9 June 1973.

27 Defence Council Directive No. 1/75, 'Régimen funcional de acción sicológica a la Directiva del Consejo de Defensa', PEN (Poder Ejecutivo Nacional), Ministry of Defence, October 1975, pp. 1–2.

28 See the work of the Research Group on Genocide in Tucumán (Grupo de Investigación sobre el Genocidio en Tucumán), at http://gigettucuman.blogspot.com.ar (accessed 13 June 2013).

29 The question of who would succeed General Perón as Peronist leader was settled through armed violence. One faction created paramilitary groups to attack its internal opponents, to which Peronist guerrilla forces responded with arms. Some of the members of these paramilitary groups joined the task forces which carried out the slaughter that took place under the military dictatorship. This move by paramilitaries into task forces was investigated by the Argentine justice system and journalists. See Judiciary's Office, Federal Court of Mar del Plata (Poder Judicial de la Nación, Tribunal Oral Federal de Mar del Plata), judgement for case no. 890/12, 'Colegio de Abogados de Mar del Plata y otros s/denuncia s/desaparición forzada de personas s/inc', 9 April 2008 (Universidad Nacional de Mar del Plata, 'Actividades de inteligencia de la represión ilegal'); J. C. Torre & L. de Riz, 'Argentina since 1946', in Leslie Bethell (ed.), *Argentina Since Independence* (Cambridge: Cambridge University Press, 1993), pp. 299–310.

30 There had been five previous military coups, in 1930, 1943, 1955, 1962, and 1966.

31 F. Mittelbach & J. Mittelbach, *Sobre áreas y tumbas: informe sobre desaparecedores* (Buenos Aires: Ediciones de la Urraca, 1984), pp. 11–13; Darío Olmo & Maco Somigliana, 'La huella del genocidio: los desaparecidos', *Encrucijadas*, 2:15 (2002), 29–30.

32 Cases of civilian abductions carried out with air support and also abductions of blind people through the use of military forces have been recorded.

33 CONADEP, *Nunca más*, ch. 1.

34 M. Ranalletti, 'Denial of the reality of state terrorism in Argentina as narrative of the recent past: a new case of "negationism?"', *Genocide Studies and Prevention: An International Journal*, 5:2 (August 2010), 160–73.

35 This information comes from the personal experience of one of the authors of this chapter.
36 An analysis of the documentation gathered by the judge and the judgement passed in the trial of the most important intelligence unit of the Argentine army, Intelligence Battalion 601, shows the subversion of the unit's internal hierarchy during its repressive clandestine operations. Testimonies given by perpetrators, the unit's administrative staff, and Silvia Tolchinsky (a disappeared detainee who was in various CDCs) show that this aspect of the CDCs' operations has been studied very little; see National Federal Criminal Court No. 4, judgement for case no. 16307/06, 'Guerrieri Pascual Oscar y otros s/ Privación ilegal de la libertad personal' (registro secretaría no. 8), 2010.
37 On 17 December 1976, the Chief of General Staff, General Roberto Eduardo Viola, ordered the enactment of a new regulation for the oversight of troops during combat against irregular forces, which replaced both the previous regulations (RC-8-2 and RC-8-3) and also the project which had been developed in 1975 that seems to have been used on a temporary basis during the first phase of mass violence. With regard to centralization and decentralization, see 'Operaciones contra elementos subversivos' ('Operations against subversives'), Army regulation RC-9-1, pp. 77–8.
38 Ibid., p. 82.
39 This was the title by the military dictatorship designated itself.
40 Federal Criminal Court No. 1, judgement for case no. 1.627, 'Guillamondegui, Néstor Horacio y otros s/privación ilegal de la libertad agravada, imposición de tormentos y homicidio calificado', 31 May 2011, p. 831.
41 Ibid., p. 834.
42 Córdoba Federal Criminal Court No. 1, judgement for the case 'Videla Jorge Rafael y otros, p.ss.aa Imposición de tormentos agravados, Homicidio calificado, Imposición de tormentos seguidos de muerte, Encubrimiento' (Expte. no. 172/09), 22 December 2010; and Córdoba Federal Criminal Court No. 1, judgement for the case 'Menéndez, Luciano Benjamín y otros p.ss.aa', p. 270.
43 F. Graziano, *Divine Violence: Spectacle, Psychosexuality and Radical Christianity in the Argentine 'Dirty War'* (Boulder: Westview Press, 1992), pp. 16–17.
44 Ibid., p. 13.
45 Córdoba Federal Criminal Court No. 1, judgement for the case 'Menéndez, Luciano Benjamín y otros p.ss.aa', pp. 185–8.
46 A. Becker, 'Exterminations: le corps et les camps', in G. Vigarello (ed.), *Histoire du corps: 3. Les mutations du regard. Le XXe siècle* (Paris: Editions du Seuil, 2006), pp. 321–39; C. E. Forth, 'The body', in J.-M. Dreyfus & D. Langton (eds), *Writing the Holocaust* (London: Bloomsbury Academic, 2011), pp. 166–78.
47 É. Gessat-Anstett, 'Résister à l'outrage', *Gradhiva*, 5 (2007), pp. 96–101.
48 Case no. 14.216/03, 'Suárez Mason Carlos y otros sobre privación ilegal de la libertad…', 23 May 2006, auto de procesamiento, p. 250.

49 CONADEP, Delegación Bahía Blanca, *Informe final de la actuación de la CONADEP delegación Bahía Blanca y zonas aledañas* (*Final Report of the CONADEP Delegation for and Bahía Blanca Surrounding Areas*), 4 September 1984, available at www.desaparecidos.org/arg/conadep/bahia/info.html (accessed January 2014).
50 Oliveira Sarrabayrouse worked on an administrative inquiry initiated by the National Supreme Court of Justice following a complaint about the irregular operation of the morgue and a criminal inquiry that followed the forced disappearance of Dr Norberto Gomez; see Sarrabayrouse, *Poder judicial y dictadura*.
51 Ibid., pp. 3–4.
52 According to Sarrabayrouse's reconstruction, based on a study of case no. 35.769, 'Gómez, Salvador denuncia privación ilegítima de la libertad', examination by Dr Carlos Oliveri. Ibid.
53 Ibid., pp. 21–2.
54 This was the Menéndez case. The case papers now include the following two files: '*VIDELA* Jorge Rafael y otros, p.ss.aa Imposición de tormentos agravados, Homicidio calificado, Imposición de tormentos seguidos de muerte, Encubrimiento' (Expte. N° 172/09) and '*MENÉNDEZ*, Luciano Benjamín y otros p.ss.aa. Privación ilegítima de la libertad agravada, Imposición de tormentos agravados' (Expte. M-13/09).
55 CONADEP, 'Anexo: Morgue judicial', in *Informe CONADEP Córdoba* (1999), available at www.desaparecidos.org/nuncamas/web/investig/articulo/cordoba/07.htm (accessed January 2014).
56 Córdoba Federal Criminal Court No. 1, judgement in the case 'Menéndez, Luciano Benjamín y otros p.ss.aa', pp. 185–8.
57 Ibid., pp. 191–2.
58 Judgement for case no. 836/09, 'S/ Homicidio, tormentos, privación ilegítima de la libertad, etc. E.p. de Cecilio José Kamenetzky. Imputados Musa Azar y otros', 9 November 2010, pp. 6, 48.
59 Sarrabayrouse, *Poder judicial y dictadura*, p. 22.
60 CONADEP, *Nunca más*, pp. 231, 245–8.
61 CONADEP, *Informe CONADEP Córdoba* (Córdoba: CONADEP, 1999).
62 This special court recorded several murders as fabricated clashes.
63 For example, a charred body with gunshot wounds was found abandoned on a road in the locality of Villa Esmeralda (Córdoba province); see Federal Court of Appeal, Córdoba, Court A, judgement for case no. 12.627, 'Menéndez IV', 'Barreiro, Ernesto Guillermo y otros p.ss.aa. privación ilegítima de la libertad agravada, imposición de tormentos agravados y homicidio agravado' (Expte. 756/2010), 6 August 2012, pp. 147–9.
64 CONADEP gathered testimonies and documentation relating to the discovery of corpses in waterways and seaways such as the banks of the Paraná River in the city of San Pedro (Buenos Aires province), the coast of the River Plate (Buenos Aires city), the coastline of the city of Colonia (Uruguay), and the seaside resort of Santa Teresita (Buenos Aires province). In the last instance, a judicial case was opened during the dictatorship following the appearance of thirty-seven bodies that

The treatment of corpses in Argentina 173

had been buried as 'unidentified' in General Lavalle cemetery; see CONADEP, *Nunca más*, pp. 238–44.
65 Ibid., pp. 238–9.
66 According to the statements of former naval captain Adolfo Scilingo. See Horacio Verbitsky, *El vuelo* (Barcelona: Seix Barral, 1995).
67 The sea returned several bodies to the resorts region in the south of Buenos Aires province; these remains were buried as 'unidentified'. The EAAF has established that 'Eleven were buried at General Lavalle cemetery, three at General Madariaga cemetery, and one at Villa Gesell cemetery'; see EAAF, 'The coast cases', pp. 32–5; Bernardi & Fondebrider, 'Forensic archaeology'.
68 CONADEP, *Nunca más*, p. 239.
69 Ibid., p. 240.
70 Ibid., pp. 240–1.
71 Tucumán Federal Court No. 1, Indictment for case no. 563/05, 'Arsenal Miguel de Azcuénaga CCD s/Secuestros y Desapariciones' (Expte. 400443/84), 27 December 2010. Sixty-one cases were consolidated in this case so they could be considered in the same trial.
72 San Martín City Federal Criminal Court No. 1, judgements for case nos 2005 and 2044, 'Arsinoe s/ privación ilegal de la libertad', 9 August 2009, p. 128. This source refers to CONADEP file no. 7170.
73 San Martín City Federal Criminal Court No. 1, judgement for case no. 2046, 'Campo de Mayo III', 5 May 2011.
74 Thirty people were murdered between 19 and 20 August 1976, in retaliation for an attack by a unit of Montoneros against a federal police station. See Federal Criminal Court No. 5, judgement for case no. 1.223, 18 July 2008, pp. 17–18. The remains of five of the victims were buried as 'unidentified' in the cemetery in Derqui (Buenos Aires province); see www.masacredefatima.com.ar (accessed January 2014); Federal Criminal Court No. 5, judgement for case no. 16.441/02, 'Masacre de Fátima, Resolución procesamiento con prisión preventiva y embargo sobre Lapuyole, Marcote, y Gallone', 22 June 2004, p. 15.
75 Snow and Bihurriet, taking the figure of 9,000 missing persons as a basis, estimated that 10 per cent of them were buried as 'unidentified' in cemeteries in Buenos Aires province; see C. C. Snow & M. J. Bihurriet, 'An epidemiology of homicide: *Ningún nombre* burials in the Province of Buenos Aires from 1970 to 1984', in T. B. Jabine & R. P. Claude (eds), *Human Rights and Statistics: Getting the Record Straight* (Philadelphia: University of Pennsylvania Press, 1992), pp. 328–63.
76 EAAF, '2006 case investigations and identifications: province of Buenos Aires', in *EAAF 2007 Annual Report* (Buenos Aires: EAAF, 2007), pp. 22–3. The same results were obtained by forensic anthropologists in their work relating to other cemeteries in the region (Lomas de Zamora, Berazategui, and Ezpeleta).
77 Federal Criminal Court No. 1, judgement for case no. 1.627, 'Guillamondegui, Néstor Horacio y otros', pp. 253–5. The EAAF is currently working on the identification of eight bodies (including that of a woman in an advanced stage of pregnancy) found on 16 October

1976 in drums that had been filled with cement and dumped in the San Fernando canal (Buenos Aires province). Three have now been identified, and these remains have been handed over to relatives.
78 CONADEP discovered this procedure at the 'La Perla' CDC (Córdoba province), and the Federal Court of Tucumán has discovered, thanks to the EAAF's expertise, a similar burial at the former Miguel de Azcuénaga Arsenal Battalion, also in Córdoba province. See CONADEP, *Nunca más*, pp. 226–9.
79 J. Waller, 'The ordinariness of extraordinary evil: the making of perpetrators of genocide and mass killing', in O. Jensen & C.-C. W. Szejnmann (eds), *Ordinary People as Mass Murderers: Perpetrators in Comparative Perspective* (Basingstoke: Palgrave Macmillan, 2008), pp. 145–57.
80 This is how it was put by one of the perpetrators, former naval captain Adolfo Scilingo, a member of a task force that operated out of the CDC at the School of Naval Mechanics; see Verbitsky, *El vuelo*. Years later, Lieutenant Colonel Guillermo Enrique Bruno Laborda, accused of using torture on political detainees, said that his chaplain had said to him during confession that having tortured and 'taken out' the enemies of God was commendable, and that he would be rewarded for it in the hereafter; see Horacio Verbitsky, 'Confesiones de un teniente coronel: Mancha venenosa', *Página/12* (9 June 2004). The journalist and writer Carlos del Frade made a complaint made to CONADEP against the priest Eugenio Zitelli, the former chaplain of the Rosario police (1976–83) and archbishop of the diocese (from 1988). According to del Frade, Zitelli confessed to another priest – Angel-Presello – that he approved of the practice of torture, because without torture it was not possible to get information from detainees; see C. del Frade, *El Rosario de Galtieri y Feced*, ch. 7, at www.nuncamas.org (accessed January 2014); also email interview with Carlos del Frade, 21 April 2004. CONADEP's case no. 683 includes the testimony of an officer of the Buenos Aires provincial police, Julio Alberto Emmed, which states that the then chaplain of this force, Father Christian von Wernich, was present at torture sessions of detainees, and carried out intelligence work in different CDCs in Buenos Aires province. According to Emmed, after he had beaten three detainees to death, von Wernich told him that what he had done had been necessary and 'a patriotic act', adding that 'God knew that it was for the good of the country'. Von Wernich is mentioned by several disappeared detainees as being present at torture sessions; see CONADEP case files 6949, 2852, 2818, 2820, 2821, 2822, and 6982; CONADEP, *Nunca más*, pp. 189–90; Hernán Brienza, *El caso von Wernich: Maldito tú eres: Iglesia y represión ilegal* (Buenos Aires: Editorial Marea, 2003).
81 Olmo & Somigliana, 'La huella del genocidio', p. 29.
82 H. Piralian, *Génocide et transmission: sauver la mort, sortir du meurtre* (Paris: Editions L'Harmattan, 1994), pp. 33–4, cited in C. Fournet, *The Crime of Destruction and the Law of Genocide: Their Impact on Collective Memory* (Ashford: Ashgate Publishing, 2007), p. 16.

83 J. Hatzfeld, *Une saison de machette* (Paris: Le Seuil, 2004), p. 159, cited in Frédéric Baillette, 'Stratégies de la cruauté: figures de la mort qui rôde', *Quasimodo*, 2:9 (2006), 12.

84 E. Conan & H. Rousso, *Vichy, un passé qui ne passe pas* (Paris: Fayard, 1994).

Bibliography

Judicial sources

Case no. 14.216/03, 'Suárez Mason Carlos y otros sobre privación ilegal de la libertad...', auto de procesamiento, 23 May 2006

Córdoba Federal Criminal Court No. 1 (Tribunal Oral en lo Criminal Federal No. 1 de Córdoba), judgement for the case 'Menéndez, Luciano Benjamín y otros p.ss.aa: Privación ilegítima de la libertad agravada, Imposición de tormentos agravados' (Expte. M-13/09), 22 December 2010

Córdoba Federal Criminal Court No. 1, judgement for the case 'Videla Jorge Rafael y otros, p.ss.aa Imposición de tormentos agravados, Homicidio calificado, Imposición de tormentos seguidos de muerte, Encubrimiento' (Expte. no. 172/09), 22 December 2010

Federal Capital Criminal and Correctional Court of Appeal (Cámara Nacional de Apelaciones en lo Criminal y Correccional de la Capital Federal), judgement for case no. 49.614, 'Yavico Alfredo s/ denuncia de incumplimiento de los deberes de funcionario público', 2010

Federal Court of Appeal, Córdoba, Court A (Cámara Federal de Apelaciones de Córdoba, Sala A), judgement for case no. 12.627, 'Menéndez IV', 'Barreiro, Ernesto Guillermo y otros p.ss.aa. privación ilegítima de la libertad agravada, imposición de tormentos agravados y homicidio agravado' (Expte. 756/2010), 6 August 2012

Federal Criminal Court No. 1 (Tribunal Oral en lo Criminal Federal No. 1), judgement for case no. 1.627, 'Guillamondegui, Néstor Horacio y otros s/privación ilegal de la libertad agravada, imposición de tormentos y homicidio calificado', 31 May 2011

Federal Criminal Court No. 5, judgement for case no. 1.223, 'Lapuyole, Juan Carlos; Gallone, Carlos Enrique; Timarchi, Miguel Angel s/ inf. arts. 55, 80 inc. 2 y 144 bis inc 1º-Ley 14.616-CP', 18 July 2008

Federal Criminal Court No. 5, judgement for case no. 16.441/02, 'Masacre de Fátima, Resolución procesamiento con prisión preventiva y embargo sobre Lapuyole, Marcote, y Gallone', 2 June 2004

Federal Oral Court of Santiago del Estero (Tribunal Oral en lo Federal de Santiago del Estero), judgement for case no. 836/09, 'S/ Homicidio, tormentos, privación ilegítima de la libertad, etc. E.p. de Cecilio José Kamenetzky. Imputados Musa Azar y otros', 9 November 2010

Judiciary's Office, Federal Court of Mar del Plata (Poder Judicial de la Nación, Tribunal Oral Federal de Mar del Plata), judgement for case no. 890/12, 'Colegio de Abogados de Mar del Plata y otros s/denuncia s/ desaparición forzada de personas s/inc', 9 April 2008

National Federal Criminal Court No. 4 (Juzgado Nacional en lo Criminal y Correccional Federal No. 4), judgement for case no. 16307/06, 'Guerrieri Pascual Oscar y otros s/ Privación ilegal de la libertad personal' (registro secretaría no. 8), 2010

Oral Federal Criminal Court No. 5 (Tribunal Oral en lo Criminal Federal No. 5), judgement in case no. 1.223, 18 July 2008 (see www.masacredefatima.com.ar, accessed January 2014), and judgement in case no. 16.441/02, 'Masacre de Fátima', Resolución procesamiento con prisión preventiva y embargo sobre Lapuyole, Marcote, y Gallone', 22 June 2004

San Martín City Federal Criminal Court No. 1 (Juzgado Federal nº 1 de la Ciudad de San Martín), judgements for case nos 2005 and 2044, 'Arsinoe s/ privación ilegal de la libertad', 9 August 2009

San Martín City Federal Criminal Court No. 1, judgement for case no. 2046, 'Campo de Mayo III', 5 May 2011

Tucumán Federal Court No. 1 (Tribunal Oral Federal No. 1 de Tucumán), Indictment for case no. 563/05, 'Arsenal Miguel de Azcuénaga CCD s/Secuestros y Desapariciones' (Expte. 400443/84), 27 December 2010

Books, chapters, and articles

Águila, G., *Dictadura, represión y sociedad en Rosario, 1976/1983: un estudio sobre la represión y los comportamientos y actitudes sociales en dictadura* (Buenos Aires: Prometeo libros, 2008)

Badaró, M., *Militares o ciudadanos: la formación de los oficiales del Ejército Argentino* (Buenos Aires: Prometeo Libros, 2009)

Baillette, F., 'Stratégies de la cruauté: figures de la mort qui rôde', *Quasimodo*, 2:9 (2006), 7–50

Becker, A., 'Exterminations: le corps et les camps', in G. Vigarello (ed.), *Histoire du corps: 3. Les mutations du regard. Le XXe siècle* (Paris: Editions du Seuil, 2006), pp. 321–39

Bernardi, P. & L. Fondebrider, 'Forensic archaeology and the scientific documentation of human rights violations: an Argentinian example from the early 1980s', in R. Ferllini (ed.), *Forensic Archaeology and Human Right Violations* (Chicago: Charles C. Thomas, 2007), pp. 205–32

Brienza, H., *El caso von Wernich: Maldito tú eres: Iglesia y represión ilegal* (Buenos Aires: Editorial Marea, 2003)

CONADEP (Comisión Nacional sobre la Desaparición de Personas), 'Anexo: Morgue judicial', in *Informe CONADEP Córdoba* (1999), available at www.desaparecidos.org/nuncamas/web/investig/articulo/cordoba/07.htm (accessed January 2014)

CONADEP, *Informe CONADEP Córdoba* (Córdoba: CONADEP, 1999)

CONADEP, *Nunca más* (Buenos Aires: Eudeba, 1991)

CONADEP, Delegación Bahía Blanca, *Informe final de la actuación de la*

CONADEP delegación Bahía Blanca y zonas aledañas (*Final Report of the CONADEP Delegation for and Bahía Blanca Surrounding Areas*), 4 September 1984, available at www.desaparecidos.org/arg/conadep/bahia/info.html (accessed January 2014)

Conan, E. & H. Rousso, *Vichy, un passé qui ne passe pas* (Paris: Fayard, 1994)

Defence Council Directive No. 1/75, 'Régimen funcional de acción sicológica a la Directiva del Consejo de Defensa', PEN (Poder Ejecutivo Nacional), Ministry of Defence, October 1975

Del Frade, C., *El Rosario de Galtieri y Feced*, ch. 7, at www.nuncamas.org (accessed January 2014)

EAAF (Equipo Argentino de Antropología Forense), *EAAF 2007 Annual Report* (Buenos Aires: EAAF, 2007)

EAAF, 'The coast cases: General Lavalle, General Madariaga, and Villa Gesell cemeteries', in *EAAF 2007 Annual Report* (Buenos Aires: EAAF, 2007), pp. 32–5

EAAF, '2006 case investigations and identifications: province of Buenos Aires', in *EAAF 2007 Annual Report* (Buenos Aires: EAAF, 2007), pp. 22–3

Eagle, G., *Dictatorship, Repression and Society in Rosario, 1976/1983: un estudio sobre la represión y los comportamientos y actitudes sociales en dictadura* (Buenos Aires: Prometeo libros, 2008)

Feierstein, D., *Seis estudios sobre genocidio. Análisis de las relaciones sociales: otredad, exclusión y exterminio* (Buenos Aires: Eudeba, 2000)

Forth, C. E., 'The body', in J.-M. Dreyfus & D. Langton (eds), *Writing the Holocaust* (London: Bloomsbury Academic, 2011), pp. 166–78

Fournet, C., *The Crime of Destruction and the Law of Genocide: Their Impact on Collective Memory* (Ashford: Ashgate Publishing, 2007)

Fraga, R., *Ejército: del escarnio al poder, 1973–1976* (Buenos Aires: Editorial Planeta, 1988)

García, P., *El drama de la autonomía militar: Argentina bajo las Juntas Militares* (Madrid: Alianza, 1995)

Gessat-Anstett, É., 'Résister à l'outrage', *Gradhiva*, 5 (2007), 96–101

Graziano, F., *Divine Violence: Spectacle, Psychosexuality and Radical Christianity in the Argentine 'Dirty War'* (Boulder: Westview Press, 1992)

Hatzfeld, J., *Une saison de machette* (Paris: Le Seuil, 2004)

Hinton, A. L., 'Why did you kill? The Cambodian genocide and the dark side of face and honor', *Journal of Asian Studies*, 57:1 (February 1998), 93–122

Marchak, P., *God's Assassins: State Terrorism in Argentina in the 1970s* (Montreal: McGill-Queen's University Press, 1999)

Mittelbach, F. & J. Mittelbach, *Sobre áreas y tumbas: informe sobre desaparecedores* (Buenos Aires: Ediciones de la Urraca, 1984)

Moyano, M. J., *Argentina's Lost Patrol: Armed Struggle, 1969–1979* (New Haven: Yale University Press, 1995)

Olmo, D. & Somigliana, M., 'La huella del genocidio: los desaparecidos', *Encrucijadas*, 2:15 (2002), 29–30

Piralian, H., *Génocide et transmission: sauver la mort, sortir du meurtre* (Paris: Editions L'Harmattan, 1994)

Ranalletti, M., 'Aux origines du terrorisme d'État en Argentine (1955–1976)', *Vingtième Siècle: Revue d'Histoire*, 105 (January–March 2010), 45–56

Ranalletti, M., 'Contrainsurgencia, catolicismo intransigente y extremismo de derecha en la formación militar argentina: Influencias francesas en los orígenes del terrorismo de Estado (1955-1976)', in D. Feierstein (ed.), *Terrorismo de Estado y genocidio en América Latina* (Buenos Aires: Prometeo Libros, 2009), pp. 253–84.

Ranalletti, M., 'Denial of the reality of state terrorism in Argentina as narrative of the recent past: a new case of "negationism?"', *Genocide Studies and Prevention: An International Journal*, 5:2 (August 2010), 160–73

Ranalletti, M., *Du Mékong au Río de la Plata: la doctrine de la guerre révolutionnaire, 'La Cité catholique' et leurs influences en Argentine, 1954-1976*, doctoral thesis, Institut d'études politiques de Paris (2006)

Ranalletti, M., 'La legitimación de la tortura como herramienta en tareas de inteligencia: estudio de caso a partir de los reglamentos del Ejército argentino (1968–1976)', paper presented at the Second International Meeting 'Análisis de las Prácticas Sociales Genocidas' ('Analysis of Social Practices in Genocide'), Universidad Nacional de Tres de Febrero, Buenos Aires, 20–22 November 2007

Ranalletti, M. & E. Pontoriero, 'La normativa en materia de defensa y seguridad y la criminalización de las disidencias (1955–1976)', paper presented at the Fifth Workshop on Recent History (V Jornadas de trabajo sobre historia reciente), Universidad Nacional de General Sarmiento, 24 June 2010

Sarrabayrouse, M. J. O., *Poder judicial y dictadura: el caso de la morgue judicial* (Buenos Aires: Defensoría del Pueblo de la Ciudad de Buenos Aires/Facultad de Filosofía Letras, Universidad de Buenos Aires, 2003)

Sémelin, J., *Purifier et détruire: les usages politiques des massacres et génocides* (Paris: Seuil, 2005)

Snow, C. C. & M. J. Bihurriet, 'An epidemiology of homicide: *Ningún nombre* burials in the Province of Buenos Aires from 1970 to 1984', in T. B. Jabine & R. P. Claude (eds), *Human Rights and Statistics: Getting the Record Straight* (Philadelphia: University of Pennsylvania Press, 1992), pp. 328–63

Tarrow, S. G., *Power in Movement: Social Movements and Contentious Politics* (Cambridge: Cambridge University Press, 2011)

Tibiletti, L. E., 'La sociabilización básica de los oficiales del Ejército en el período 1955-1976', in O. Moreno (ed.), *La construcción de la Nación argentina: el rol de las fuerzas armadas. Debates históricos en el marco del Bicentenario (1810-2010)* (Buenos Aires: Ministerio de Defensa, 2010), pp. 265–6

Torre, J. C. & L. de Riz, 'Argentina since 1946', in L. Bethell (ed.), *Argentina Since Independence* (Cambridge: Cambridge University Press, 1993), pp. 299–310

Verbitsky, H., 'Confesiones de un teniente coronel: Mancha venenosa', *Página/12* (9 June 2004)
Verbitsky, H., *El vuelo* (Barcelona: Seix Barral, 1995)
Waller, J., 'The ordinariness of extraordinary evil: the making of perpetrators of genocide and mass killing', in O. Jensen & C.-C. W. Szejnmann (eds), *Ordinary People as Mass Murderers: Perpetrators in Comparative Perspective* (Basingstoke: Palgrave Macmillan, 2008), pp. 145–57
Zanatta, L., *Del Estado liberal a la nación católica: Iglesia y Estado en los orígenes del peronismo, 1930–1943* (Bernal: Editorial de la Universidad Nacional de Quilmes, 1996)

Part III: Logics

7

State violence and death politics in post-revolutionary Iran[1]

Chowra Makaremi[2]

From 9 January to 19 July 2012, the Iranian daily *Gooya News*, one of the Iranian diaspora's main information sites, published a series of forty-one articles, entitled 'Interviews with a torture and rape witness'. The tortures and rapes in question were from the period of violent state repression that gripped the Islamic Republic throughout the 1980s. The interviews give voice to the anonymous testimony of an official involved in the penitentiary and judicial sphere of that period. In this respect, they constitute a rare document, though secrecy still surrounds the administrative practices and chains of command that organized state violence in Iran, which remain in place and in effect in some cases. Interview number 19 is entitled 'The cadavers from the mass graves from the 1981 massacre in the riverbed'.[3] The interviewee, an official at the Ministry of Justice in the city of Shiraz, recounts being summoned to appear before the revolutionary tribunal during the summer of 1981. Majid Torabpour, the director of Shiraz city prison, is waiting for him there, joined by about fifteen members of the prison's administrative staff, and asks him to approach the Islamic judge (*hakeme sha'r*[4]) about managing the 'thirty-six cadavers remaining' on their hands. The story continues like this:

> I went into the office of the Islamic judge Qorbani ... he was talking out loud to himself: 'It's no longer clear who to turn to: you write to the office of the Imam [Khomeini], no answer; Mr Montazeri's office doesn't reply either, the same goes for Ardebili.'[5] Then he took three

sheets of paper on his desk and handed them to me, and only then did I understand the scope of the disaster. Due to heavy rains, the river, which flowed from the Derāk mountains[6] and passed behind the villages of Hassan Abad and Ahmad Abad, had overflowed and stirred up several communal pits where bodies had been buried in bulk just under the surface. The flood had strewn the bodies all along the river's course. When people saw the bodies, they immediately informed the Sepāh [militias that are part of the Guardians of the Islamic Revolution]. Local members of the Sepāh and of the Basij [volunteer militia corps] were mobilized to collect the bodies. Thirty-six had been gathered up to the present moment; they had put them in two trucks and had brought them to the prison. The Islamic judge continued explaining to me how he was completely in the dark about this matter, and did not know whose cadavers they were, how they had been killed, or how they had been buried. He had seen the bodies, and the murders [sic] were just one or two weeks old.

Astonished, I asked: 'Do you mean that there has been no legal judgement?' 'That's impossible', the judge told me: 'I told you that I am completely in the dark about this, and whenever I try to get explanations, I'm told what I have the habit of telling people [who ask for news about their family and friends]. Try to see *Haj-agha*[7] on your own.' Given the situation, I suggested that he begin by authorizing burial of the bodies, since the bodies would be a cause for concern if they stayed the way they were: then I suggested that the investigation of the case continue after they were put in the ground. At first, he was not won over and replied: 'Sir, I have a responsibility; what answer will I give the officials? What answer will I give God? They [the penitentiary administration] don't want to listen to reason and keep claiming that these people died during combat between opposition groups.' In reply, I told the judge that it was useless to be naïve about this; it was well known who and what institutions were behind this work, and I convinced him to authorize burying the bodies on the condition that they be identified beforehand and provided that, for my part, I would be conducting the investigation.

They were all gathered in Hamid Baneshi's[8] office, calmly smoking with sangfroid, and talking among themselves.... We set off for the courtyard at the rear of the prison ... where there was room for manoeuvring and transport: a blue, tarp-covered Nissan and a small red lorry were parked there. There they had piled the bodies which the rainwater had washed up. I asked that they be unloaded. Hamid whistled and they all gathered together; they lined up the bodies on the ground. Most of the faces were in the process of decomposing; there were visible whip marks and wounds on several people's faces and bodies. I asked for a cigarette. Jahfar Ebrahimi was beside me; he was an *akhound* [mullah] in civilian clothing who was responsible for collecting the bodies. I said: 'I believe there are more here than indicated.' Jahfar replied: 'Shahrokh knows more about it than I do. That said, water carried off the majority; we were only able to gather up the ones over there. And don't bother with the *Haj-agha* identification. Shahrokh knows who they all are; he has lists.' We went to see Shahrokh, who ended up talking: 'Those bodies there, we got them in the collective houses or in the street, and some went away under *ta'zir*.[9] I'm the one who had the responsibility of burying them and I have their names; we know the number of common graves, 25–26 of them, and their location, too.' I was in disbelief. I counted the cadavers; there were 48. They separated the men and women and left to bury them.

I worked two weeks on this question. The number of pits that the flood had moved was 28, and the total number of bodies was at least 485.

When this affair came to light, there were changes in posts among the officials: Seyyed Reza Mir'emad was named prosecutor in Tehran, and Mohamad Reza Ramezani became his replacement. As for the Islamic judge Qorbani, he became a representative in the National Assembly (I no longer remember if this is in Samnan or in Dagheman)![10]

In this testimony, the handling of cadavers raises various issues involving state violence and the organization of death in the case of Iran.[11] The violence described in this story is a complex violence, in tension between the juridical and administrative order, which possesses an internal coherence anchored in a theological ideology, and the unleashing of a destructive undertaking. Thus, the dialogue between the Islamic judge and the narrator, an official from the Ministry of Justice, hinges on the fact that the cadavers were allegedly produced without a legal judgement, without a preliminary death sentence, which is judged unthinkable. A majority of the documented cases of the suppression of Iranian citizens in the 1980s are indeed the product of the judicial and penitentiary systems, as we will see below. What is at issue, moreover, in this dialogue is the production of the judge's written authorization to rebury the cadavers unearthed by the flooding river. The handling of these unwieldy bodies unleashes a crisis that allows us to glimpse a second type of organization that is grafted on and connected to the administrative order: orders circulate orally and mark an economy of silence, which not only passes between repressive organs and society but also inside the apparatus of repression. The crisis of the cadavers illustrates how this economy of secrecy is also interconnected with moral universes. The Islamic judge complains, 'whenever I try to get explanations, I'm told what I have the habit of telling people'. He initially refuses to give the written order for reburial, invoking his deontological responsibility before his hierarchical superiors, and his moral one before God. On the one hand, the Islamic judge, who is in charge of prison sentences and execution in the revolutionary tribunal, sketches the ideological and moral horizon that organizes the administration of death. On the other, this 'moral economy'[12] is limited to the interior of the repressive apparatus: the judge complains about the arbitrariness and secrecy that he reproduces on a daily basis on the outside, since he has the habit of not giving a response 'to the people' who have come to ask for news about their deceased relations. Indeed, revolutionary tribunal hearings – and often their very location – are secret, without a barrister or other protagonists aside from the judge, the prosecutor, and the accused.

An initial picture suggested by the crisis is one of a violent mechanism characterized by a rupture between inside and outside: it functions around an internal organizational and discursive-logical coherence, but operates behind closed doors, showing a discreet face to the social enemy located outside. But the confusion to which the judge is exposed suggests a second tableau superimposed over the first. The internal organization is itself binary and traversed by an economy of secrecy that brings two value systems into opposition with one another. Indeed, the bodies that are spit out along the river make visible a violence that parallels the violence of the repressive apparatus organized around the revolutionary tribunal, detention centres, and execution squads. The story of this crisis is constructed around an opposition between those in office – between men possessing a certain sensibility (the narrator asks for a cigarette, the judge talks out loud to himself all alone) and morality – and those unpolished people out in the field. Juxtaposed with the ordered violence that the one group oversees – cadavers stretched out in the courtyard of the prison – is the disorder of hasty, shallow graves dug by the others. The condemnation and the confusion of officials stem from the work being poorly executed: it imperils the economy of silence essential for the functioning of the repressive mechanism, and causes a resurgence of the nightmarish texture of violence – potentially troubling for some of the repression's actors – by way of a pile of women and men's bodies mixed together, washed by the rain, in the process of decomposing.

The bodies are those of men and women killed 'in collective houses or in the street', or while being tortured, entailing forms of violence that indicate a situation of civil war[13] or of politicide.[14] These actions are conducted and supervised (lists are drawn up, accounts are made) by members of the militia, who form a command structure with informal boundaries: a religious man in civilian clothing in charge of 'gathering the bodies', who next introduces the narrator to the operations official: 'Shahrokh knows who they all are, he has the lists'. These two faces of state violence – a non-explicit duality, albeit one of which actors are aware ('useless to be naïve about this; it was well known who and what institutions were behind this work') – are re-articulated with each other as a result of the handling of the cadavers crisis. This crisis introduces us to the different strata of the state's discretion and violence at the same time that it illustrates the manner in which the administrative and juridical order of the new republican Islamic state absorbed, codified, and legalized the violent practices of Islamist militias.

This narrative poses several challenges that delineate the analysis that we offer here: What became of the victims' bodies? What does this handling of bodies teach us about the simultaneously concrete and ideological organization of death that marked the establishment of the Islamic Republic? What are the effects of these violent practices on the social body, and in what way are the living governed via management of the dead (of *their* dead) in post-revolutionary society?

The organization of death

State violence targeted those with more or less clearly established links with political organizations opposing the Islamic Republic.[15] On 29 June 1981, waves of collective executions began of prisoners who were arrested during demonstrations. It is probable that other, lesser-known, collective executions took place in 1984. Finally, in the summer of 1988, shortly after the peace treaty with Iraq was signed, members of the opposition still in prison were liquidated in a massacre that claimed thousands of victims. As in the majority of the episodes of state violence, the number of victims is difficult to assess, and access to figures and evidence is difficult because the administrations and actors who led those crackdowns are still in place. The historian Ervand Abrahamian concluded in 1999 that more than 7,900 dissidents had been eliminated between 1981 and 1985. In 2012, the Iran Human Rights Documentation Center (IHRDC), based at Yale, estimated 20,000 to be the number of documented executions and political deaths in the period through to 1988. The initiative International People's Tribunal on the Abuse and Mass Killings of Political Prisoners in Iran (1981–88) has published a list of 15,116 people executed between 1981 and 1988, including 4,677 between July and October 1988.[16]

The suppression of dissidents was administered through a juridical and ideological apparatus organized around revolutionary tribunals. Though officially recognized when they were instituted in 1979, these courts did not enjoy legal status until the beginning of 1983, but remained even then in contradiction with certain constitutional articles concerning the public character of judicial hearings, the right to a defence, and the right to appeal.[17] These hearings, at the margin of the judicial system, took place in prisons and typically lasted only five to twenty minutes. These were held in secret, albeit they did have legal status. Likewise, the 'religious ordinance' (the *fatwa*) giving the order for the 1988 massacre was kept secret, but it was legally authorized. The 'special commission' responsible for carrying out this command had no official existence or legal basis, but was composed of officials from the Ministry of Justice. Thus the organization of death arose at different scales of a juridical and administrative system with two faces, one public and the other secret. The passing of a sentence was not, however, the only cause of death: different militias that were part of the Sepāh (the Revolutionary Guard), of Hezbollah, of VEVAK (the Ministry of Intelligence and Security) conducted extra-judicial executions, especially between 1979 and 1984.[18] Death could also come under torture, or as a disciplinary sanction in prison.[19]

To come now to this chapter's main question: what was done with the executed prisoners' bodies? What relations can we establish, to the extent permitted by our knowledge of the facts, between this treatment and the logics of overseeing death? Beyond the physical suppression of dissidents, what functions did this treatment of bodies play in the relationship between state and society?

The management of the dead has been an essential process in making state violence invisible and normal, by virtue of rendering any overall assessment of this violence impossible, and by creating silence and amnesia in the social body. With different testimonials juxtaposed together, this management of bodies can be understood according to two challenges: firstly, the respect of rules about separating Muslims and non-Muslims (*najes*) during burial; and secondly, the visibility of state violence to family and friends, and more widely in society. The treatment of bodies of executed prisoners thus indicates an organization of social space and an organization of symbolic space. This analysis brings out the connections between burial practices and the methods used to suppress dissidents, which are of two orders: ideological and socio-political.

Najes

As Khosrokhavar has indicated, the management of the dead in this period of Iran's history must, before anything else, be resituated in the religious and cultural context of the Shi'ism that was redefined by the Islamic Republic.[20] This observation makes it possible to grasp how, in practice, the respect for Islamic rules concerning purity and impurity (*najes*) is at the core of an ideological mechanism that categorizes victims as 'others', killable with impunity.

Shi'ite funerary rites require that bodies, which are washed according to a specific procedure, be wrapped in a white shroud and placed directly in the ground, with the head pointing towards Mecca. Incineration is not practised. The separation of the pure and the impure is a fundamental principle in daily practice, and it occurs in mortuary rites as well. Contact with what is considered impure (*najes*) thus contaminates practising Muslims, who must guard against this or purify themselves through ablutions. The list of what is taken to be impure is precise and explicit (it includes, for example, pork and alcohol). In the Shi'ite tradition, there are two supplementary elements that are important in our analysis: non-believers and dead bodies. So, in theory, and to a certain extent in practice, those who are in charge of the administration of the dead must not transgress the rules of *najes* or contaminate themselves. It is in the name of this prohibition that daily life is organized inside prisons in such a way that contact with prisoners defined as *kāfer*, that is to say non-Muslim (a category including Marxists, Baha'i minorities, etc.), does not soil the penitentiary personnel. The prison stories emphasize, however, the fact that this prohibition, which plays an important role in daily interactions and in the organization of prison space, falls away in the torture room.[21] Other rules are more directly concerned with the administration of death. It is thus forbidden to kill a pregnant woman or a virgin woman; these prohibitions were not systematically respected as we will see, however. Several testimonials report the practice of raping unmarried female prisoners before their execution.[22] Burying Muslims and non-Muslims in the same space is forbidden as well. This rule seems to have been particularly important in the management of human remains, all the more so because cemeteries, major political sites since the 1978 insurrections, had been constituted as a public space overinvested by state propaganda during the war, due to the cult of martyrdom that developed.[23] Therefore, those executed prisoners who were categorized as non-Muslims ('at war against God', a crime punishable by death) were supposed to be buried separately, in non-Muslim sections of cemeteries. In certain cases, the leadership saw to it that families respected this rule; in other cases, it buried the executed prisoners itself in distinct spaces and would later inform their relatives.

These different rules organized the administration of death, but they did not constitute a fixed and rigorous system. To give an idea of the manner in which this complex mechanism functioned in practice, one can refer to a testimonial, which to my knowledge is the only one produced by an eye witness of the 1988 massacre, in the province of Khuzestan in the south-west of the country. It is the story of Mohammad-Reza Ashooq, a prisoner who succeeded in escaping the bus that would take a group of mojahedin in August 1988 to the site of the shooting, where trenches had been dug.

> '[Once we arrived] at the [military] base [in Kharileh], they forced us into the communal showers. The walls and the doors were covered with photos of [martyred] Basijis who had been there before us. They gave us a shroud and some camphor. They ordered us to remove our clothes and to put on the shroud [the narrator refuses and is beaten, finally led away fully clothed with his fists tied together]. They made us get in the minibus. They led me off to the vehicle and made me sit down in a seat in the back. All the others who got in the minibus were dressed in white, wearing blindfolds, with their hands tied together. I believe that the bindings on my fists were loosened when I was beaten; I was able to free my hands. It was around 3:30 in the morning then, and everyone was tired, including the revolutionary guards [the Sepāh militiamen], who seemed frightened themselves. Everyone was yelling. The prisoners were shouting insults at Khomeini.' The narrator manages to escape by jumping through the minibus's window. He goes on: 'I must have run about a kilometre towards the river when I heard gunfire. At first, there were machine guns, then individual gunshots. The shots came from a corner far away, close to the shacks, where there was light.'[24]

According to this testimony, the funeral rites (the washing of bodies anointed with camphor and placed in a white shroud) are, so to speak, subcontracted out to the prisoners themselves. The prisoners are taken to and shot at the burial site itself. Several survivors of Tehran's prisons, where the massacres began at the end of July 1988, report that the method used in the first weeks was hanging. It must be said that, beginning in 1983, hanging seems to have been given systematic preference over shooting in Iranian prisons. This is the same period when national newspapers stopped publishing lists of the names of executed prisoners. It is possible that the authorities began to practise more discretion at that time, and that execution methods were adapted to this imperative. Still, the testimonials agree that in 1988 recourse to hanging was abandoned after several weeks in Tehran, and firing squads were brought back into use[25] by an administration that had less time at its disposal to complete the massacres. It seems to me that, in light of a comparative reading of the various sources of available information, between the first wave of hangings at the beginning of August 1988, in Evin Prison in Tehran, and the scene reported by Mohammad-Reza Ashooq in Khuzestan, a sort of method had been clarified (judging from what is currently known, it is not clear whether this happened locally or more widely), finding a balance between the requirements of discretion, efficiency, and respect for the ideological frameworks that justified administering death.

As shown by the categorizations that preside over the massacre and the management of bodies during and after it, state violence and terror – and the passage from one to the other – conform to an economy and organization. The latter two simultaneously make possible and frame instinctual, violent release, putting it in the service of a precise government objective, which is the domination of the social body by the state apparatus. On the one hand, they produce conditions favouring violence, firstly through mental operations producing dangerous 'others', now well known in the contexts of extreme violence,[26] and which one finds in the work of revolutionary tribunals and special commissions, and secondly through an administrative and judicial apparatus which rewards brutality by offering social advancement to those who know how to demonstrate it and by excluding moderates and those who are reluctant, as illustrated by the fate of the Ayatollah Montazeri, eliminated from succession to the role of Supreme Guide and placed under house arrest after protesting against the 1988 massacres. On the other hand, they ideologically frame this violence by grasping it in a series of symbolic, religious, and political representations that justify it and render its exercise acceptable in the systematic, reasoned context of a chain of command. The management of cadavers shows the implementation and the function, in this ideological framework, of justifying and regularizing the situation with regard to the religious laws.

La'nat ābād (the quarter of the damned)

And the effect of this treatment of bodies was not limited to the universe of the actors of violence. I wish to show, rather, that it assumed broader social functions.[27] This can seem paradoxical with regard to the secrecy that surrounds the practices of repression and elimination, as has just been seen. It appears, however, as has been shown elsewhere by studies devoted to the *desaparecidos* in Argentina, that the process of rendering violence invisible is not solely a negative operation of stifling discretionary practices, but itself produces effects that are useful for the objective of social control. If one re-examines the prohibitions that regulate burial practices, it appears, through interviews with close family and friends and the testimonials gathered, that the burial of the executed did not exclusively target their spatial separation from the community of Muslims with which the state wished to make the social body coincide. Indeed, the question was not only where the authorities buried these bodies – but how. Several testimonials and some photographs indicate that the victims were buried without a shroud, in their clothes, and even in their shoes, which seems even more blasphemous in relation to rules concerning burial. They were laid to rest as a group in shallow, mass graves, while tradition requires a tomb more than a metre and a half deep. Thus these practices run counter to traditional burials, and to the usual rites and traditions that hold the community together; more than just separation and exclusion, they represent instances of blasphemy and profanation.

To understand the specific significance of blasphemy and the political use made of it by the authorities, it is useful to revisit the social functions of sepulchral rites as they were analysed by the anthropologist Robert Hertz at the beginning of the twentieth century. He identified across different types of societies a constant that one could call the second life of dead bodies, that is to say, the treatment reserved for them: the material transformations, the spatial movements that they undergo, and the temporality and specific steps of this processing, which can go on for several months. In the following way, he emphasizes the function, simultaneously social and psychological, that is assumed by the treatment of bodies after death:

> Because it has faith in itself, a healthy society cannot admit that an individual who is part of its own substance, on which it has imprinted its mark, could be gone forever; life must have the last word: in various ways, the deceased will emerge from the throes of death to return to the peace of human communion.... [It is] the promise that every religious Society implicitly makes to its members ... exclusion gives way to a new integration.[28]

It is this reintegration that is attacked by profane burial, by putting religious taboos in motion that render it impossible. Beyond the physical elimination of those who are identified as outside of post-revolutionary society, the apparatus of repression aimed for their symbolic and enduring removal from the social world. Islamic ideology, fabricated ad hoc by the protagonists of violence, and the manner in which this ideology took control of religious rules, thus offer a privileged view of the symbolic orders through which social cohesion and inclusion were defined. The treatment reserved for the bodies of the dead – their being rendered invisible, their profanation, their exclusion – did not merely follow, reinterpret, or subvert the rules that symbolically and socially ordered public space: it mobilized them in favour of a drive to maintain the order of the Islamic society dreamt of by the state. Or, rather, to produce and maintain a disorder whose simultaneously social and psychological effects, echoed in the private and public spheres, served a government objective: controlling the population.

An economy of silence

As Robert Hertz underscores in his analysis of funerary rites,[29] the management of the dead thus connects back to two essential dimensions, which are the position of the deceased in a family and community network, and the maintenance of the symbolic order through the respect of funerary rites. These involve, as we have mentioned, a treatment of the body and a temporality through which the work of mourning for close friends and family develops, along with a resorption of the disorder caused by the intrusion of death into the symbolic order and the social body. The 'double and painful work of disaggregation and mental syntheses'[30] that is carried out through this mourning, that is to say the work of separating members of the community and family from a deceased person, 'who is too big a part of themselves' ('fait trop partie d'(eux-)mêmes') (disaggregation), and reintegrating the deceased member in a symbolic order and a continuity (synthesis), are a condition of the order and continuity of society itself. It is at this sensitive pivot – where affects, symbolic representations, and the social order develop – that the practices of sepulchre-confiscation attack: through them, as Antonius Robben has analysed in the case of Argentina,[31] the violence deployed on executed prisoners reverberates in concentric circles or produces new effects of constraint and control over the surviving close family and friends, as well as wider (activist, neighbourhood) social networks. This is what is shown by the testimony of Aziz Zarei, father of a female Mujahed prisoner[32] executed in October 1982:

> With my body empty, back bent, knees shaking, and mouth dry, I went into the sentencing office and introduced myself. The official handed me an envelope that was already ready and said to me: 'Go to the morgue to retrieve the body, you can move it where you wish.' At that moment, I felt so weak, so powerless, that I couldn't say a word, not even: 'But that poor woman was pregnant!'
>
> ... My wife and I went to the forensic doctor's office, ... I told him: 'We've come to ask you to keep our daughter, entrusting her to you while we telephone Shiraz so that one or two people can come help us move the body since the two of us, an old man and an old woman, don't have the means or the strength to do it.'
>
> [He replied] 'Before coming here, I contacted the Sepāh so that they would come and remove the body, which is the only one we have here, since the morgue's generator is broken.'
>
> It was such an oppressive situation for me that I didn't know what to do: I didn't have the strength to move and did not know anyone who could help me. I couldn't even speak. Everything turned dark in front of me: my body shook. My wife sat in a corner like a madwoman, indifferent and shedding tears. I had no other choice but to bury her there in Bandar-Abbas.
>
> ... Out of compassion, that man decided to help me. He requested an ambulance, and, with help from the driver, we removed my child's bloodied corpse from the morgue drawer, a sight that left me speechless.... With help from the driver, we loaded the body in the ambulance and set off ... we arrived at the cemetery. The official in charge of preparing bodies asked us to go sit down somewhere: 'We are going to wrap her in a shroud and put her in the ground.' Despite her mother's and her mother-in-law's insistence that they be permitted in the preparation room so they could see their child for the last time, they refused, adding that if the women were insistent, they would not even touch the remains to administer the final preparations since the preparers had not been ordered to do so. As time was short, we gave up our request. Her mother's goal was to find out if her daughter had been killed while she was still pregnant, or if, in one way or another, they had made her abort beforehand. Alas, she could not see her child this final time.[33]

Two distinct, albeit interconnected, challenges arose around the treatment of the remains of the executed: keeping certain aspects of state violence secret; and imposing silence on direct witnesses who were the close friends and family of the deceased. In this perspective, the management of bodies was generally organized according to two factors which determined the location and the manner of burial: on one hand, the option of whether or not to return the remains to the families; on the other hand, the option of whether or not to make the execution visible in the form of a tomb.

Thus, the remains of executed prisoners could be returned to their families: a sum could be requested in order to get reimbursement for the bullets used for the execution.[34] The families sometimes had the right to bury their relative in a cemetery section reserved for non-Muslims, as is attested by the story cited above; in other cases, more rarely, they were forbidden to do so, and the remains were then put in the ground by family and friends, on their own, in the garden or out in nature.[35]

Not only that, the administration could also refuse to return remains to families, as was systematically the case after the 1988 massacre. In some cities, there were administrative efforts to bury the dead individually in cemeteries.[36] But in the majority of cases, the evidence of the massacres was erased by refusing to make the executions visible with tombs: the victims were buried in common graves whose location still remains unknown, except for the most significant one in Khavaran.[37] This vast, non-Muslim cemetery is separated into different sections allotted to religious minorities – Christians, Baha'i, Jews, and Buddhists – and sits on the side of the road 15 km north of the capital. After the first massacres over the course of the summer of 1981, the prisoners affiliated with the Marxist left were secretly buried in a vast wasteland bordering the Baha'i section at the far end of Khavaran cemetery. They were among the victims whose remains were not given back to their families, and whose death was not marked with the presence of a tomb either. The news concerning the existence of a mass grave in Khavaran gradually spread among the families searching for their deceased imprisoned relatives at the court building. In 1988, this would also serve as the execution site for a large number of leftist prisoners. The bodies were summarily laid to rest there in shallow pits, with their clothing and shoes on. The penitentiary authorities, when they told relatives where to find the deceased, called this place *kāferestan*, the country of non-Muslims, or *la'nat ābād*, the quarter of the damned. As the daughter of a dead woman probably interred there remembered:

> We went to Khavaran, but that was not a cemetery there. Everyone knows what a cemetery looks like: there it was clods of soil turned over, mothers in tears sitting on the ground who poured earth over their faces.... We came from Kermanshah, and each time we reached

Khavaran, we saw a woman seated on my mother's tomb. She was from Tehran proper, and was permanently sitting in the same spot. It was customary for families to visit various tombs out of solidarity; later it was gathered that she thought it was her own daughter who was buried at this very spot. One time when we were in Khavaran, this woman showed a piece of navy blue clothing to my grandmother and asked her if her daughter Sousan (my mother) had a garment that colour. It turned out that she had dug in the ground, she had excavated the tomb because she was looking for her daughter's cadaver, and she had found a body that had been decomposing for a year and which was unrecognizable, wearing clothing with this fabric. And no one would ever figure that out.[38]

Thus, the four cases that we have been able to distinguish (whether the remains are returned or not, whether marking a tomb is permitted or refused) are articulated around an essential issue, the issue of the visibility of state violence. The tomb is tangible and enduring proof of violence. But beyond this trace, whose erasure is at stake, violence's invisibility is secured by also forbidding a network of practices. These prohibitions and confiscations participate in what one could call an economy of silence. In this way, the treatment of bodies demarcates circles of silence around the closed world of detention centres. A part of what goes on there must not filter out, to the families: this is why the bodies of prisoners executed while undergoing torture are not returned to the families.[39] Likewise, what families know must not filter out to broader social networks: commemorative ceremonies at home are suppressed and their participants arrested;[40] those close to the deceased also continue to be kept under surveillance by *komitehs*, to which they are regularly summoned for routine interrogation. These different practices, which coexisted through the 1980s, are connected to the question of the governance of the living by way of the dead. From this perspective, the economy of silence does not rest uniquely on the intimidation of families by force and their psychological weakening through the production of open mourning. It also creates the conditions for a marginalization that results from both the exclusion and the withdrawal of families facing a reality that differs from the social reality shared by the majority: a reality organized around denial, in which the massacres did not take place and the eliminated individuals did not exist.

And so, in the current context, it is of this violent story's very nature to be partly written by rumours and oral testimony. Several of these sources agree that a flood took place at the Khavaran site in 2001. A flood, caused by heavy rains, unearthed several bodies that had been interred close to the surface. The bodies were reportedly carried by the current all the way to the Buddhist section of the cemetery, whose guardians supposedly claimed that those were gifts from nature there and allegedly took the opportunity to give them decent burials in individual tombs. Neither the Khavaran flood nor the one near Shiraz in 1981, reported in the introduction to this chapter, can be verified today. But these stories tell a truth that matters to us: it is perhaps a matter of hope – promise, dressed in that messianic dimension that makes up the texture of history for Walter Benjamin.[41] It may quite simply consist of a shared fable that sutures the symbolic order upset by confiscation and desecration, and thus recreates the possibility of the continuity of the social: the story of an unleashing of elements, nature's rage, under whose impact the earth itself ends up spitting up the state's secrets, which are – in every sense of the word – poorly buried.

Notes

1 The text of this chapter was translated from the author's French by Cadenza Academic Translations.
2 My field research was funded by the Wenner-Gren Foundation for Anthropological Research, which I thank for its support.
3 M. Noqrekar, 'The cadavers from the communal graves from the 1981 massacre in the riverbed', *Gooya News*, 18 April 2012, available at http://news.gooya.com/columnists/archives/139248.php (accessed 20 January 2013). *Gooya News* is a Persian-language paper, and all translations here are the author's own.
4 A Sharia judge, the title given to judges of the revolutionary tribunals.
5 High-ranking ayatollahs: Mousavi Ardebili headed the Supreme Court, and Montazeri was Khomeini's presumed successor for the office of Supreme Guide.
6 Situated north-west of the city of Shiraz.
7 A respectful way to address a person who possesses a certain influence.
8 Actors in the carceral world would generally use pseudonyms.
9 The victims were killed when they were arrested or while being tortured. *Ta'zir* is an Arabic term present in the Koranic source of the law, which means administering strong corporal punishment: the word is used to designate torture in the prison system.
10 Noqrekar, 'The cadavers from the communal graves'. Extract reproduced with the permission of Massoud Noqrekar at *Gooya News*.
11 It is not possible to attest to the veracity of this story, although it has gained a certain notoriety in the public sphere. See for instance I. Mestaghi, 'A look at the erroneous interpretations of a Ministry of Justice agent in the Islamic regime', *Gooya News*, 10 July 2012, available at http://news.gooya.com/politics/archives/2012/07/143359.php

(accessed 20 January 2013). This is the only detailed testimony gathered from an actor of state violence: the precise view that he offers of the organization of the mechanism of repression and the conditions of collecting testimony leaves little doubt on the position of the witness, a former member of the judicial and security apparatus. With regard to our topic, the question is not the veracity of the testimony, nor that of the figures that it gives, but its verisimilitude, and the mental representations, the cultural institution, and the range of concrete practices that it sets in motion. The latter practices consistently correspond to what the testimonials and scientific works published on this period say. Indeed, these representations and these practices offer us (this is why I have chosen to begin with this story) useful and heuristic angles for approaching the material in the remainder of this chapter, which relies on a field investigation and an archival search that has been underway since 2009. Thus, this testimony is not the basis that I use to draw the analysis that I derive from it; rather, I use it to introduce in a synthetic fashion, around the questions connected to this chapter, a series of observations that have taken shape over the course of the research process.

12 See D. Fassin, 'Les économies morales revisitées', *Annales: Histoire, Sciences Sociales*, 6 (2009), 1237–66.

13 M.-D. Demelas-Bohy, 'La notion de guerre civile en question', *CLIO: Histoire, Femmes et Sociétés* (online) 5 (1997), at http://clio.revues.org/412 (accessed 2 January 2013); N. Sambanis, 'Resort to arms: international and civil war, 1816–1980. Conceptual and empirical complexities of an operational definition', *Journal of Conflict Resolution* 48 (2004), 814–56; M. Small & J. D. Singer, *What Is Civil War?* (Beverly Hills: Sage, 1982). There are several factors constantly found in the definitions of civil war discussed in these works: the framework of the nation state, the number of deaths, and the existence of an effective resistance.

14 This notion, forged in reference to forms of mass violence in which numerous people are eliminated due to their ideology or political opinion, was discussed in W. H. Moore, 'Repression and dissent: substitution, context, and timing', *American Journal of Political Science*, 42:3 (1998), 851–73; G. Sjoberg, E. Gill, N. Williams & K. E. Kuhn, 'Ethics, human rights and sociological inquiry: genocide, politicide and other issues of organizational power', *American Sociologist*, 26:1 (spring 1995), 8–19.

15 This theme has been treated in several analytical works: E. Abrahamian, *Tortured Confessions: Prisons and Public Recantations in Modern Iran* (Berkeley: University of California Press, 1999); S. A. Arjomand, *The Turban for the Crown: The Islamic Revolution in Iran* (New York: Oxford University Press, 1988); M. Behrooz, 'Reflections on Iran's prison system during the Montazeri years (1985–1988)', *Iran Analysis Quarterly*, 2:3 (2005), 11–24; H. Dabashi, *Theology of Discontent: The Ideological Foundation of the Islamic Revolution in Iran* (New Brunswick: Transaction Publishers, 2005); K. Katzman, *The Warriors of Islam:*

Iran's Revolutionary Guard (Boulder: Westview Press, 1993); A. Matin-Asgari, 'Twentieth century Iran's political prisoners', *Middle Eastern Studies*, 42:5 (2006), 689–707; D. M. Rejali, *Torture and Modernity: Self, Society, and State in Modern Iran* (Boulder: Westview Press, 1994); K. Shahrooz, 'With revolutionary rage and rancor: a preliminary report on the 1988 massacre of Iran's political prisoners', *Harvard Human Rights Journal*, 20 (2007), 227–61; H. Sorg (C. Makaremi), 'Le massacre des prisonniers politiques de 1988 en Iran: une mobilisation forclose?', *Raisons Politiques*, 30:2 (2008), 59–87. It is also the subject of a series of testimonials: A. Agah, S. Mehr & S. Parsi, *We Lived to Tell: Political Prison Memoirs of Iranian Women* (Toronto: McGilligan Books, 2007); Iran Human Rights Documentation Center (henceforth IHRDC), *Deadly Fatwa: Iran's 1988 Massacre* (New Haven: IHRDC, 2009); IHRDC, *Speaking for the Dead: Survivor Accounts of Iran's 1988 Massacre* (New Haven: IHRDC, 2010); International People's Tribunal on the Abuse and Mass Killings of Political Prisoners in Iran (1981–88), *Findings of the Truths Commission held 18th–22nd June, 2012* (Farsta, Sweden: Iran Tribunal Press, 2012); C. Makaremi, *Le Cahier d'Aziz* (Paris: Gallimard, 2011); I. Mesdaghi, *Neither Life nor Death, Volume 3: Restless Raspberries*, 2nd edition (Kista, Sweden: Alfabet Maxima Publishing, 2006); N. Mohajer (ed.), *The Book of Prison: An Ontology of Prison Life in the Islamic Republic of Iran* (Berkeley: Noghteh Books, 1998); H.-A. Montazeri, *Khaterat-e Hossein-Ali Montazeri (Memoirs of Hossein-Ali Montazeri)* (Los Angeles: Ketab Corp., 2001); G. Robertson, *The Massacre of Political Prisoners in Iran, 1988: Report of an Inquiry* (Washington, DC: Abdorrahman Boroumand Foundation, 2010); S. Talebi, *Ghosts of Revolution: Rekindled Memories of Imprisonment in Iran* (Stanford: Stanford University Press, 2011).
16 Abrahamian, *Tortured Confessions*, p. 135; IHRDC, *Deadly Fatwa*; International People's Tribunal on the Abuse and Mass Killings of Political Prisoners in Iran (1981–88), 'List of political mass executions in 1980s', at www.irantribunal.com/index.php/en/resourses/documents/27-list-of-political-mass-executions-in-1980s (accessed 20 January 2013).
17 See articles 32, 34, and 35 of the Constitution of the Islamic Republic of Iran adopted in 1979 (amended in 1989).
18 The database of the Boroumand Foundation (ABF) documents 138 extra-judicial executions between February 1979 and January 1989.
19 See Agah *et al.*, *We Lived to Tell*.
20 F. Khosrokhavar, *L'Islamisme et la mort: le martyre révolutionnaire en Iran* (Paris: Harmattan, 1995), p. 212.
21 Mesdaghi, *Neither Life nor Death*; Agah *et al.*, *We Lived to Tell*.
22 IHRDC, *Surviving Rape in Iran's Prisons* (New Haven: IHRDC, 2011); Justice for Iran (JFI), *Crimes and Impunity: A Pioneering Report on Sexual Torture in Iranian Prisons* (London: JFI, 2012).
23 The ideological and political construction of the Islamic Republic around a reinvestment of the figure of the martyr, inherited from Shi'ism, took place during the insurrectionary period of 1978–79 as

much as it did during the post-revolutionary period and the war with Iraq (1980–88), as shown by: M. J. Fischer, 'Islam and the revolt of the petit bourgeoisie', *Daedalus*, 111:1 (winter 1982), 101–25; P. Chelkowski, 'Iran: mourning becomes revolution', *Asia*, 3 (1980), 30–45; J. D. Swenson, 'Martyrdom, mytho-cathexis and the mobilization of the masses in the Iranian revolution', *Ethos*, 3 (summer 1985), 121–49; Khosrokhavar, *L'Islamisme et la mort*; P. Khosronejad (ed.), *Unburied Memories: The Politics of Bodies, and the Material Culture of Sacred Defense Martyrs in Iran*, special issue of the *Journal of Visual Anthropology*, 25:1 (2012), 1–20.

24 Testimony from Mohammad-Reza Ashooq, in IHRDC, *Deadly Fatwa*, p. 41, and Robertson, *The Massacre of Political Prisoners*, p. 51. This instance of escape and the name of the fugitive were also mentioned in the memoirs of Ayatollah Montazeri, *Khaterat-e Hossein-Ali Montazeri*.

25 IHRDC, *Deadly Fatwa*, pp. 37, 38, 44; Robertson, *The Massacre of Political Prisoners*, p. 59.

26 H. Arendt, *Eichmann in Jerusalem: A Report on the Banality of Evil* (New York: Viking Press, 1963); H. G. Kelman, 'Violence without moral restraint: reflections on the dehumanization of victims and victimizers', *Journal of Social Issues*, 29:4 (1973), 25–61.

27 D. Bigo, 'Disparitions, coercition et violence symbolique', *Cultures & Conflits*, 13–14 (1994), 3–16; D. Hermant, 'L'espace ambigu des disparitions politiques', *Cultures & Conflits*, 14 (1994), 118–89; A. C. G. M. Robben, *Political Violence and Trauma in Argentina* (Philadelphia: University of Pennsylvania Press, 2005), pp. 339–51; A. C. G. M. Robben & M. M. Suárez-Orozco (eds), *Cultures Under Siege: Collective Violence and Trauma* (Cambridge: Cambridge University Press, 2000), pp. 48–101.

28 R. Hertz, *Sociologie religieuse et folklore* (1928) (Paris: Les Presses Universitaires de France, 1970), p. 71.

29 Ibid.

30 Ibid., p. 79.

31 A. C. G. M. Robben, 'State terror in the netherworld', in A. C. G. M. Robben (ed.), *Death, Mourning and Burial: A Cross-Cultural Reader* (Oxford: Blackwell, 2004), p. 135.

32 The organization Mujahedin-e Khalq was the Islamic Republic's principal opposition party. It began an armed struggle in June 1981.

33 Makaremi, *Le Cahier d'Aziz*, pp. 46–9.

34 Testimony from Roya Sadeghi, at the International People's Tribunal on the Abuse and Mass Killings of Political Prisoners in Iran (1981–88), *Findings of the Truths Commission*, p. 219.

35 Testimony from Esmat Vatanparast, ibid., p. 250. *Le Colonel*, a novel by M. Dowlatabadi (London: Haus Publishing, 2009) (the original version is in Persian, but it did not secure the right to be published), recounts the burial of a young female dissident by her father in the family garden. The story, which unfolds on the night of the burial, excavates this situation as a symbolic representation of the experience of post-revolutionary violence.

36 Makaremi, *Le Cahier d'Aziz*, pp. 98–106.
37 These facts are drawn from six ethnographic interviews with those close to deceased people buried in Khavaran, twenty testimonials written and entered in the database of the Boroumand Foundation, and forty-three hearings of witnesses before the investigation commissions of the International People's Tribunal on the Abuse and Mass Killings of Political Prisoners in Iran (1981–88), *Findings of the Truths Commission* at Amnesty International, London (18–22 June 2012) and the Court of International Justice, the Hague (25–27 October 2012).
38 Testimony of Sahar Mohammadi at the International People's Tribunal on the Abuse and Mass Killings of Political Prisoners in Iran (1981–88), *Findings of the Truths Commission*, p. 295.
39 Makaremi, *Le Cahier d'Aziz*, pp. 78–9; testimony from Roya Rezai Jahromi, at the International People's Tribunal on the Abuse and Mass Killings of Political Prisoners in Iran (1981–88), *Findings of the Truths Commission*, p. 136.
40 The daughter of a female militant executed in 1984 gives this report: 'The first year we organized a memorial ceremony for my mother, they showed up wearing masks and took all the young people gathered there away for an interrogation. For fear of putting young people in danger, there were no more ceremonies organized.' Testimony of Sahar Mohammadi at the International People's Tribunal on the Abuse and Mass Killings of Political Prisoners in Iran (1981–88), *Findings of the Truths Commission*, p. 295.
41 W. Benjamin, 'Sur le concept d'histoire', in *Œuvres III* (Paris: Gallimard, 2000), pp. 427–43.

Bibliography

Abrahamian, E., *Tortured Confessions: Prisons and Public Recantations in Modern Iran* (Berkeley: University of California Press, 1999)

Agah, A., S. Mehr & S. Parsi, *We Lived to Tell: Political Prison Memoirs of Iranian Women* (Toronto: McGilligan Books, 2007)

Amnesty International, *Iran: Le site de Khavaran doit être préservé en vue d'une enquête sur les massacres* (Index AI: MDE 13/006/2009, Public Document), 20 January 2009

Arendt, H., *Eichmann in Jerusalem: A Report on the Banality of Evil* (New York: Viking Press, 1963)

Arjomand, S. A., *The Turban for the Crown: The Islamic Revolution in Iran* (New York: Oxford University Press, 1988)

Behrooz, M., 'Reflections on Iran's prison system during the Montazeri years (1985–1988)', *Iran Analysis Quarterly*, 2:3 (2005), 11–24

Benjamin, W., 'Sur le concept d'histoire', in *Œuvres III* (Paris: Gallimard), 2000, pp. 427–43

Bigo, D., 'Disparitions, coercition et violence symbolique', *Cultures & Conflits*, 13–14 (1994), 3–16

Chelkowski, P., 'Iran: mourning becomes revolution', *Asia*, 3 (1980), 30–45
Dabashi, H., *Theology of Discontent: The Ideological Foundation of the Islamic Revolution in Iran* (New Brunswick: Transaction Publishers, 2005)
Demelas-Bohy, M.-D., 'La notion de guerre civile en question', *CLIO: Histoire, Femmes et Sociétés* (online) 5 (1997), at http://clio.revues.org/412 (accessed 2 January 2013)
Dowlatabadi, M., *Le Colonel* (London: Haus Publishing, 2009)
Fassin, D., 'Les économies morales revisitées', *Annales: Histoire, Sciences Sociales*, 6 (2009), 1237–66
Fischer, M. J., 'Islam and the revolt of the petit bourgeoisie', *Daedalus*, 111:1 (winter 1982), 101–25
Foucault, M., 'Nietzsche, la généalogie, l'histoire', in *Hommage à Jean Hyppolite* (Paris: PUF, 1971), pp. 145–72
Hermant, D., 'L'espace ambigu des disparitions politiques', *Cultures & Conflits*, 14 (1994), 118–89
Hertz, R., *Sociologie religieuse et folklore* (1928) (Paris: Les Presses Universitaires de France, 1970)
IHRDC (Iran Human Rights Documentation Center), *Deadly Fatwa: Iran's 1988 Massacre* (New Haven: IHRDC, 2009)
IHRDC, *Speaking for the Dead: Survivor Accounts of Iran's 1988 Massacre* (New Haven: IHRDC, 2010)
IHRDC, *Surviving Rape in Iran's Prisons Iran* (New Haven: IHRDC, 2011)
International People's Tribunal on the Abuse and Mass Killings of Political Prisoners in Iran (1981–88), *Findings of the Truths Commission held 18th–22nd June, 2012* (Farsta, Sweden: Iran Tribunal Press, 2012)
International People's Tribunal on the Abuse and Mass Killings of Political Prisoners in Iran (1981–88), 'List of political mass executions in 1980s', at www.irantribunal.com/index.php/en/resoursces/documents/27-list-of-political-mass-executions-in-1980s (accessed 20 January 2013)
Justice for Iran, *Crimes and Impunity: A Pioneering Report on Sexual Torture in Iranian Prisons* (London: JFI, 2012)
Katzman, K., *The Warriors of Islam: Iran's Revolutionary Guard* (Boulder: Westview Press, 1993)
Kelman, H. G., 'Violence without moral restraint: reflections on the dehumanization of victims and victimizers', *Journal of Social Issues*, 29:4 (1973), 25–61
Khosrokhavar, F., *L'Islamisme et la mort: Le martyre révolutionnaire en Iran* (Paris: Harmattan, 1995)
Khosronejad, P. (ed.), *Unburied Memories: The Politics of Bodies, and the Material Culture of Sacred Defense Martyrs in Iran*, special issue of the *Journal of Visual Anthropology*, 25:1 (2012), 1–20
Makaremi, C., *Le Cahier d'Aziz* (Paris: Gallimard, 2011)
Matin-Asgari, A., 'Twentieth century Iran's political prisoners', *Middle Eastern Studies*, 42:5 (2006), 689–707
Mesdaghi, I., 'A look at the erroneous interpretations of of a Ministry of Justice agent in the Islamic regime', *Gooya News*, 10 July 2012, available at http://news.gooya.com/politics/archives/2012/07/143359.php (accessed 20 January 2013)

Mesdaghi, I., *Neither Life nor Death, Volume 3: Restless Raspberries*, 2nd edition (Kista, Sweden: Alfabet Maxima Publishing, 2006)
Mohajer, N. (ed.), *The Book of Prison: An Ontology of Prison Life in the Islamic Republic of Iran* (Berkeley: Noghteh Books, 1998)
Mohini, M. R., 'Khavaran is a name that means not forgetting', *Bidaran*, 22 September 2004, available at www.bidaran.net/spip.php?article48 (accessed 20 January 2013)
Montazeri, H. A., *Khatorat o Hossein Ali Montazeri (Memoirs of Hossein Ali Montazeri)* (Los Angeles: Ketab Corp, 2001)
Moore, W. H., 'Repression and dissent: substitution, context, and timing', *American Journal of Political Science*, 42:3 (1998), 851–73
Noqrekar, M., 'Interviews with a witness of tortures and rapes', *Gooya News*, 2012, available at http://news.gooya.com/columnists/archives/cat_noghrehkar.php (accessed 20 January 2013)
Noqrekar, M., 'The cadavers from the communal graves from the 1981 massacre in the riverbed', *Gooya News*, 18 April 2012, available at http://news.gooya.com/columnists/archives/139248.php (accessed 20 January 2013)
Nora, P., *Les Lieux de mémoire* (Paris: Editions Quarto Gallimard, 1997).
Rejali, D. M., *Torture and Modernity: Self, Society, and State in Modern Iran* (Boulder: Westview Press, 1994)
Robben, A. C. G. M., *Political Violence and Trauma in Argentina* (Philadelphia: University of Pennsylvania Press, 2005)
Robben, A. C. G. M., 'State terror in the netherworld', in A. C. G. M. Robben (ed.), *Death, Mourning and Burial: A Cross-Cultural Reader* (Oxford: Blackwell, 2004)
Robben, A. C. G. M. & M. M. Suárez-Orozco (eds), *Cultures Under Siege: Collective Violence and Trauma* (Cambridge: Cambridge University Press, 2000)
Robertson, G., *The Massacre of Political Prisoners in Iran, 1988: Report of an Inquiry* (Washington, DC: Abdorrahman Boroumand Foundation, 2010)
Sambanis, N., 'Resort to arms: international and civil war, 1816–1980. Conceptual and empirical complexities of an operational definition', *Journal of Conflict Resolution*, 48 (2004), 814–56
Shahrooz, K., 'With revolutionary rage and rancor: a preliminary report on the 1988 massacre of Iran's political prisoners', *Harvard Human Rights Journal*, 20 (2007), 227–61
Sjoberg, G., E. Gill, N. Williams & K. E. Kuhn, 'Ethics, human rights and sociological inquiry: genocide, politicide and other issues of organizational power', *American Sociologist*, 26:1 (spring 1995), 8–19
Small, M. & J. D. Singer, *What Is Civil War?* (Beverly Hills: Sage, 1982)
Sorg, H. (C. Makaremi), 'Le massacre des prisonniers politiques de 1988 en Iran: une mobilization forclose?', *Raisons Politiques*, 30:2 (2008), 59–87
Swenson, J. D., 'Martyrdom, mytho-cathexis and the mobilization of the masses in the Iranian revolution', *Ethos*, 3 (summer 1985), 121–49
Talebi, S., *Ghosts of Revolution: Rekindled Memories of Imprisonment in Iran* (Stanford: Stanford University Press, 2011)

8

Death and dismemberment: the body and counter-revolutionary warfare in apartheid South Africa[1]

Nicky Rousseau

As resistance intensified in what would turn out to be apartheid's final decade, security forces in South Africa began covertly to execute opponents extra-judicially, despite a formidable arsenal of security legislation and a state of emergency from 1985 to 1990.[2] A noteworthy aspect of these executions is that the modes of killing varied, sometimes along regional lines, or according to the particular security unit involved. Disposal of the bodies was similarly varied.

This chapter traces these different methods of killing and pays particular attention to the disposal of bodies, which signalled a new frontier of hostility, namely the 'war on the corpse'.[3] Of course, instances of extra-judicial killing are not especially noteworthy in the annals of counter-revolutionary warfare, documented across a variety of global settings. However, contrary to the state's oft-repeated intention to annihilate the enemy – an intention seemingly realized in the common depiction of the apartheid state as exercising an untrammelled sovereignty – extra-judicial killings by state security forces occurred on a relatively limited scale, running into the hundreds, rather than the thousands. Despite close ties with various South American juntas, security police were unable to translate intent into anything like the mass disappearances perpetrated by those regimes. This scale, it is argued, arises less from a sense of *restraint* than one of *constraint*, suggesting a need for more nuanced understandings of what facilitates or hinders large-scale executions.

The war comes home

Among the many omissions laid at the door of South Africa's Truth and Reconciliation Commission (TRC) is the absence of statistics indicating the number of persons killed as a result of political violence during the thirty-four-year period covered by its remit (1 March 1960 to 10 May 1994). This seems surprising for a commission specifically mandated to discover the 'nature, causes and extent of gross violations of human rights'[4] – of which killing was one such violation – and to determine the identity of both victims and perpetrators. Yet this was no lapse of memory. Firstly, determining what constituted a politically motivated killing proved a tricky enterprise, especially for the period 1990–94, which accounted for a significant majority of deaths. Secondly, determining the identity of perpetrators proved even more intractable: in numerous instances the killer's hand was either hidden, or misconstrued; in other instances, violence between opposing groups formed part of a deliberate strategy of counter-mobilization by the South African state. Instead of hard numbers, then, the TRC offered instead a categorization of killings: judicial executions, assassinations, elimination during arrest, enforced disappearances followed by elimination, ambushes, entrapment operations, killing of own forces.[5]

Apartheid legislation allowed for the killing of political suspects through judicial execution when found guilty of offences of terrorism, sabotage, or treason.[6] Additionally, generous indemnity regulations protected police officers responsible for shooting 'rioters' in civil unrest.[7] If apartheid is understood as a regime that relied on coercion with respect to its black subjects, then the legislative right to kill in certain circumstances would seem to represent its ultimate sanction. Yet increasingly during the 1980s, funerals in particular were transformed into occasions of defiance, often resulting in further shootings and deaths at the hands of the police. Townships, both in urban centres and rural towns, designed spatially as locations of control, had become instead centres of concentrated insurgency, in which the body was central to mobilization. Images of coffins draped in flags, and surrounded by young activists dressed in khaki with fists or wooden replicas of AK47s aloft, became a common sight in townships and, via the media, abroad. Thus, the enactment of apartheid's ultimate sanction – to kill – visibly demonstrated not its power but its illegitimacy.

This crisis was reflected in state security documents in the mid-1980s, as the dual strategy of keeping the line of defence well beyond South Africa's border through a policy of regional destabilization and internal reform unravelled under the impact of resistance. As returning to rule by force had the effect only of increasing resistance, the regime turned instead to acting outside of its own legal framework. Bodies that had produced illegitimacy and impotence thus produced as well a move to secret killings.[8] The TRC tracked a movement through which South Africa's internal security situation was increasingly seen and enacted through the lens of war, and security policy and practice begin to mirror those of the external regional wars in which liberation movement figures had been assassinated or attacked.[9]

The authorization of 'extraordinary measures' did not, however, mean setting aside the legalism of the apartheid state, even despite majority support by the white electorate for tough security measures.[10] Alongside calls to annihilate the enemy, therefore, security sub-committees debated at length about how to restrict internal opposition movements within the framework of a legally enacted state of emergency, and parliament passed successive amendments to existing security legislation.[11]

While the military played a key role in formulating security strategy,[12] it was primarily police structures that engaged in extra-judicial eliminations inside South Africa.[13] Sometimes, such killings were conducted by official police units; in other instances, security commanders deployed trusted operatives to conduct such operations, or units emerged which, although not officially authorized, included such senior personnel that they can be regarded as 'unofficial-official'. A large number of security police involved in these actions had prior experience of deployment in South Africa's own direct theatres of war, namely Zimbabwe and Namibia,[14] 'location[s] par excellence ... where violence of the state of exception [was] deemed to operate in the service of "civilization".'[15]

A common political and scholarly depiction of this period has been of a militarized state, where parliamentary government acted as a mere rubber stamp for a highly centralized State Security Council (SSC) led by the state President, which, through a network of structures, reached from the pinnacle of government to the smallest locality in South Africa and back again. In this view, the SSC decided, authorized, and oversaw all security operations, both lawful and unlawful.[16] This view is challenged by the work of the TRC, which suggests instead that, although extra-judicial killing represents a wider authorization and sanction, it took place in a more contingent and haphazard way.[17] Unlike the external theatre where the right to self-defence could be called upon (even if illegitimately), the move to eliminating political suspects inside South Africa was unlawful. Consequently, no standing rules of engagement or operating procedures could be specified, except for what has been termed the unwritten eleventh commandment, 'Thou shalt not be found out'.[18]

Modes of killing

Modes of killing were multiple and varied. As one tactic, security forces used the cover of lawful killings to conduct executions. Thus, for instance, a security policy document suggests that during 'riots', police should target 'ringleaders'.[19] Another was to shoot rather than arrest suspects, on the pretext of acting in self-defence against armed combatants, or to prevent a suspect from escaping.[20]

Enforced disappearances followed by killing accounted for a number of other covert murders. Security police based in the major cities of Johannesburg, Pretoria (including security police headquarters), Durban, and Port Elizabeth all later applied for amnesty for 'disappearing' combatants and/or activists in their region, including several abductions from neighbouring states such as Lesotho or Swaziland. The pattern was similar – activists would be taken into informal custody or lured into traps by agents, and then transported to rural areas. Here the rural functioned as a 'safe zone'.[21] Abductees would be interrogated (sometimes tortured) for varying periods of time and then executed unless they agreed to collaborate. Here the exact form of execution varied – Pretoria security police strangled several captives, three were slowly electrocuted using an electric generator, others were sedated before being blown up; Durban police seemed to prefer death by a single shot to the back of the head; Port Elizabeth security police shot or stabbed several activists as well as killing four of their own (black) colleagues in a car bomb.[22]

Aside from ambushes, which sometimes targeted groups of six to seven, most of the above were directed at individuals or very small groups of mainly guerrilla suspects. In several entrapment operations, security police targeted young political activists who were 'recruited' by undercover agents purporting to be guerrilla commanders and then killed. For example, in 1985, in an operation code-named Zero Zero approved by the minister of police, young men from the townships of Duduza and Tsakane near Johannesburg were 'recruited' and trained before being supplied with hand-grenades for the purpose of a simultaneous attack on identified collaborators in their communities. Seven youths were killed and a further eight seriously injured when the zero-timed devices exploded in their hands. In another, jointly run with military special forces, 'recruits' were driven to an ambush site, injected with sedatives, and placed back in their vehicle together with an AK47 and a limpet mine. The vehicle was then crashed into a tree and set alight, killing and burning the ten young men. Such operations were replicated in several regions.[23]

The war on the corpse

If the move to extra-judicial elimination is one in which the strategies and tactics of a wider regional war were adopted, then the variety of means and modes of killing outlined above speak to difficulties and constraints in relocating this war internally. For example, Koevoet, the police unit in which many security police officers had served in counter-insurgency operations in Namibia, shot dead guerrilla suspects and displayed their bodies openly, 'tied onto spare tyres, bumpers, mudguards and were left there until [they] got back to the base camp'.[24] Veteran photographer of the Namibian war, John Liebenberg, describes one such incident:

> Under the baobab close to the shop of Johannes Andjamba, Guy Tillim and I stopped for a coke [i.e. Coca-Cola] and a little shade. Excited voices pointed to a Koevoet patrol returning to the base. 'Look,' murmured Guy. On the side of the vehicle lay slumped the body of man. The Casspirs stopped outside a *cuca* shop and the occupants disappeared inside. I cannot recall how we got to the vehicles. All I remember was the deathly silence. We both took some frames....[25]

Kill ratios were carefully recorded by individual units, as their members received bounties accordingly. Reputedly, the taking of trophies or fetishes, body parts such as ears, was not uncommon.[26] In contrast to this, inside South Africa killing was forced to happen under cover of secrecy, or to masquerade in other forms, or to be conducted in ways that seemed little different from criminal murder. The resulting 'difficult' corpses could not be left on the side of the road like road kill nor displayed publicly strapped to the front or rear bumper of military or police vehicles, nor captured in photographs that mimicked the big-game safari shot, which also circulated semi-surreptitiously in regional war zones.[27]

Again, there were no standing rules regarding the disposal of corpses, and so each team was had to develop its own modus operandi. As with killing, a range of methods emerged, and although certain patterns or preferences can be discerned, sometimes crossing regions, they retain a sense of improvisation and of being driven by opportunity. A number of bodies were concealed. For example, police in the Natal region threw a body over a densely wooded cliff, one was buried in a sugar-cane field, some were dumped in the territory of opposing political groups, while several more were buried, covered with limestone to hasten decomposition, in secret graves.[28] Such bodies remained available for possible discovery at a later stage, presenting perhaps some degree of risk. Other security police units attempted to ensure the complete obliteration of the corpse by different methods. In one case, the body of an activist killed in custody was allegedly thrown into a crocodile-infested river, while in at least three known separate cases the bodies of abductees were repeatedly blown up.[29]

Other security police burnt their dead bodies. These cases narrated at public TRC amnesty hearings have achieved iconic notoriety. A commander of one unit provided a cavalier description in which he detailed the burning process, as well as describing how the unit barbecued (in South African parlance, *braaied*) meat on an adjacent fire.[30] Another unit attempted a more clinical register, seemingly at pains to dispel the image that had been conjured up of beer-swilling men eating barbecued meat while their victims burnt alongside them. Nonetheless, they recounted taking bodies to a farm, dousing them with diesel, and placing them on a fire which had to be fed all night. Even then, not all the remains were incinerated, demonstrating the difficulty of burning adult human bodies on an open pyre. According to the testimony, the remaining pieces of burnt flesh and bone were gathered into plastic bags and thrown into a river.[31] However, some twenty-five years later, exhumations on the farm discovered 6 kg of diesel-coated burnt human bone fragments in two septic tanks, just metres from where the bodies had been burnt.[32]

By contrast, Pretoria security police chose not to conceal the bodies of those whom they had abducted and killed. Taking the 'war on the corpse' to new levels, bodies were displayed openly but their very publicity acted to obfuscate. In one case involving a victim who had been strangled to death, a tyre was placed around the victim's neck and then set alight to suggest a death by 'necklacing'; in several other cases, bodies were transported from the city to outlying rural areas, and placed on a landmine or several limpet mines which were then detonated.[33] As this coincided with a period in which the armed wing of the African National Congress (ANC) was engaged in a landmine campaign, these incidents passed off as cases where 'terrorists' had accidentally blown themselves up. In a few instances, the victim was still alive at the time of detonation, having allegedly been sedated; thus the explosion served both to kill and to dispose of the corpse. A similar modus operandi was used in at least two other regions, although here bodies were placed on railway lines (a frequent target of guerrilla attacks, aimed at disrupting transport systems).[34]

Ironically in these cases, the mode of disposal converted the bodies of 'black operations' to those able to enter the normal bureaucracy of death, as it did for other bodies resulting from executions which masqueraded as legitimate killings, such as those of people in 'combat' or 'escaping' from custody. Here, bodies would be processed in the usual manner for unnatural deaths: after the crime scene had been marked out, photographed, and sketched, and, where possible, fingerprints taken, the body would be removed to the nearest police mortuary.

Mortuary records tell their own story of unnatural and violent death of Africans under apartheid. In one region's records, listings for the bodies resulting from counter-revolutionary warfare operations interrupt the columns of numerous stillborn and infant deaths, homicides, winter deaths of the elderly, suicides, and untimely deaths in motor vehicle or mining accidents. In almost all cases, the bodies resulting from counter-revolutionary warfare were recorded among the extraordinarily high number of 'Unknown black males' recorded in death registers across South Africa, reflecting the historical legacies of migrant labour, which resulted in high numbers of unidentified and unclaimed bodies; sometimes they were distinguished from the rest by the appellation *terroris*.[35]

Criminal investigations in South Africa do not require forensic pathologists to examine the crime scene. With no state pathologists outside of the main urban areas, post-mortems were conducted by the closest district surgeon – 'state employed doctors whose work combined medico-legal duties with caring for indigent patients pro bono' – as well as certain categories of civil servants.[36] District surgeons had the most rudimentary of forensic training from medical school, were rarely willing to risk a confrontation with security police, and squeezed in post-mortem duties between their routine medical duties. Post-mortems could take place days, in some cases even weeks, after the death, and many noted little more than race, cause of death, and a rudimentary marking up of injuries on a diagrammatic representation of the body. Thereafter, the corpse (or remains thereof) would be released to the undertaker responsible for indigent burials, placed in a coffin, and buried in an unmarked pauper's grave in the local cemetery.

Much has been written of the human impulse to rescue dead and decaying matter from its material and animal origins through various rituals. Posel and Gupta suggest that 'exceptional and demeaning' defilement of human remains, or burial as unknown and unclaimed, may reflect an opposite and 'symbolically potent' intent – to reduce the victim to mere dead meat.[37] This resonates with the accounts above, especially those accounts of burning accompanied by the cooking and consumption of animal meat, blurring the boundaries of human and animal, and conjuring the taboo of cannibalism.

In his meditation on the tensions between justice and mourning, Laqueur argues that precisely because victims of mass genocide and killing die like dogs or beasts, the work of identifying and naming is an important re-humanizing gesture.[38] But were the bodies of those claimed to be terrorists reduced to mere animal matter or dead meat? Here, perhaps ironically, by staging such incidents as the deaths of 'terrorists' who had blown themselves up, the security police attached an identity that remained essentially human, part of a political community, even if, for some, they may have been regarded as inhumane. Indeed, what has been termed here as the routine bureaucracy of death served only to reinforce the fact that these were humans. Thus, for instance, the pieces of flesh from blown-up bodies near the village of Buanja, which led a villager to investigate why 'carnivorous birds' were in the area, set in motion a process that is indisputably a human one. The remains (two feet, fragmented parts of a skull, vertebrae, ribcage segments, a left shoulder joint, as well as a portion of the lower abdomen) were not left for the vultures to pick over and consume, or incinerated, but were ultimately placed in a coffin, and buried in a cemetery as a human body.[39] At the same time, apartheid did not end with death, and the often cursory and demeaning treatment of the dead body served to 'reaffirm racial hierarchies of personal worth in death as much as in life'.[40]

These cases point to how the human may in certain circumstances unexpectedly return, even if in ways that remain ideologically circumscribed. Similarly, in the public recounting of these incidents, public revulsion functioned perhaps to reveal the perpetrators not only to be inhumane but to be inhuman, and, in this move, enabling those bodies reduced and burnt like dead meat to be re-humanized.[41]

The tactical invasion of the body[42]

Scholars warn against seeking to explain violence through examining its causes or functions and the instrumentalization thereof. To do so may reduce violence 'to a practical tool used by opposing social actors in pursuit of conflicting ends. Whether treated as a cause, function, or instrument, violence is generally assumed rather than examined in its concreteness.'[43] While mindful of this warning, the concern here is not to explain violence but to explore an aspect of necropolitics,[44] namely the corpse as 'thing' and how, even after its separation from a prior self, it remains available as a 'medium for searing assertions of power'.[45] This interest intersects with certain aspects regarding the agency of the dead body as well as the 'return to materiality' in conditions of violence.[46]

If, as has been argued, the move to extra-judicial elimination suggests not unfettered power of the apartheid state but rather its limits, nonetheless the above account demonstrates how this constraint became generative of new forms of power over the body. While bodies buried or obliterated had no further value (except perhaps as a boast), other approaches to disposal seemed to suggest that a corpse, although lifeless, had not yet escaped the binds of counter-revolutionary warfare.

At a most basic and passive level, bodies produced by ambushes or entrapment operations functioned to conceal intent, or the identity of the killers. Thus, for example, where a forensic examination of the scene of an ambush might identify a police officer as the trigger-puller, the scene and the corpses would be restaged to suggest a combat or escape scenario. On the other hand, those killed in entrapment operations or blown up by landmines spoke not to 'murder most foul' but to death 'by their own hands'. In such circumstances, the security police acted as creative director, landmines or limpet mines were the active agents, while bodies, sometimes alive, were mere matter to be acted upon. More than concealing authorship, these were acts where the very display of bodies was intended to convey a message. As the commander of the Pretoria security police put it:

> These [bodies] would be destroyed by means of explosives, so that firstly, the identity could not be established and secondly so that the South African public would be brought under the impression that they [the insurgents] were so badly trained that they would blow themselves up.[47]

In several instances, a parallel scene rolled: the sole purpose of the collection of statements, and of the filling and filing of forms and documents (post-mortem reports, photographs, and maps of the crime scene, fingerprints) was to make visible and fix a particular version of the incident, namely one that sought to whiten the blackest of operations.

The bodies and possessions of those killed in ambushes produced information. Through the 'tactile invasion' of the body or, more aptly here, dismemberment, a visual archive of fingerprint cards, crime scene photographs, and post-mortem body shots worked 'to "arrest" and "capture" the criminal-[terrorist]'.[48] Bodies yielded fingerprints used to identify individuals and connect them to biographies of resistance; photographs of suspects, matched to earlier mug shots, or even of the dead body, were routinely used in interrogations of other terror suspects. Indeed, in some documented cases, detainees were literally taken to the scene or the mortuary or shown photographs of the deceased both to inculcate fear as well as to collect information.[49] Weaponry, clothing, and possessions, possibly notes or documents, could provide further information. This kind of information, forwarded to security headquarters and entered into a database, would become available, sometimes for years afterwards, in further investigations, and in possible future court cases, as well as operationally.

Bodies could also function as faulty intelligence, able to disrupt the fabric of trust that is always critical to resistance in repressive regimes. Several of the disappeared were rumoured to have 'sold out' or 'crossed sides'. In one instance, a young activist was necklaced at the funeral of the young militants killed in Operation Zero Zero, after suspicion fell on her because she had been a passenger in the car of the security police agent who had posed as the guerrilla commander and supplied the young men with the zero-timed devices. In such instances, one could say that the body served to function in a more active and pernicious way – to disrupt its own forces.⁵⁰ The same can be said where those killed by security police officers were staged as victims of inter- or intra-party conflict between rival resistance movements, or as 'accidental deaths' of an incompetent guerrilla army whose poorly trained combatants had 'blown themselves up'.

While the resort to killing may be understood as a register of the failure to turn the resister into a compliant subject – in other words, marking a certain kind of limit – then these instrumental displays by the security police functioned to turn back this failure onto the enemy itself. Here, where the tactics (or imagined tactics) of the enemy are returned to that enemy, we have the classic move of what J. J. McCuen refers to as 'the art of counter-revolutionary warfare', a move made more potent by turning the body itself into a weapon.⁵¹ This 'weaponization' of the dead body as an active agent of the war against its own comrades marked a new frontier of the 'war on the corpse'.

At the same time, the capacity thus to conscript and to deploy the corpse in the service of counter-insurgency remained risky, and the efficacy of such carefully staged performances could not be guaranteed. Multiple explosions, for example, could unnerve the white electorate; for supporters of the liberation movements, those killed could retain the status of heroic resister, the good comrade who had sacrificed all; organizations and their members could reject attempts to ascribe killings to rival groups or bungled operations.

In this regard, nowhere was the power of corpse to call forth multitudes more evident than the killing of four men in the Eastern Cape. The Cradock Four,⁵² as they are colloquially referred to, were abducted in June 1985, just weeks after one of the incidents described above involving the burning of three bodies. In this instance, however, the victims were variously stabbed or shot, their bodies mutilated and set alight in bushes alongside a road. Despite attempts by security police to lay the blame at the door of a rival political movement, by leaving a pamphlet of that organization next to the victims' burnt-out car, their killings produced one of the largest political funerals in the history of apartheid South Africa.⁵³

Perhaps here one should note both the power of the body to generate resistance, and the use of the body as a weapon of counter-revolutionary warfare. Does this require some rethinking of the notion of the agency of the dead body (and, as things/objects, of the return to the material itself)? While this debate is far wider than mere questions of human intent or instrumentalization, it nonetheless calls attention to more limited concerns posed by the notion of 'bodies of evidence' or the 'unsettled body' that calls for justice or recovery.[54] Where bodies have acted as weapons of counter-revolutionary warfare, they have done so not with their own but another's agency, challenging the claim that the dead body can be a 'witness beyond the grave', capable of providing an 'alternative form of testimony'.[55] Without confessions from the killers, these bodies would most likely have remained as the bodies of guerrillas who had accidentally fallen victim to their own explosives. In these cases, as Domanska suggests, the bodies served 'the living, becoming the space of conflict between different interests of power ... [and] knowledge'.[56] In a similar vein, Crossland warns that the 'mediating interpretants' of 'the body of evidence' – including those who research and study dead bodies – may act to endow 'the dead with an agency that is carefully channelled and constrained'.[57] Thus, while the confessional text may not provide the truth, the material body may mislead.

Indeed, the bodies themselves seem to obfuscate. Thus the body fragments scattered across the landscape following the detonation of a landmine call in multiple ways – as prey to vultures, as possibly human to local villagers, and as terrorist to police – suggesting a movement of the body from unhuman to human, or human-but-inhumane, yet nonetheless one that cannot be left as prey and must be returned to the category of racialized human subject through burial as an unknown pauper or terrorist. In turn, the post-apartheid era has enabled a further movement to named beloved through exhumation, or named hero, via the state's memorial practices.[58] If agency is understood as the capacity of the body (thing) to affect or 'perform a socializing function',[59] then it demonstrates here the power to do so. In a different context, Gaston Gordillo suggests that 'What makes corpses affectively unpredictable is that their power to affect is liberated from the capacity to be affected. This gives corpses ... a potent political afterlife'.[60] The body that enables a misreading and misleading produces as well a site of contestation.

Hundreds rather than thousands

And yet. These killings, as noted at the outset, number not in the thousands, but amount to a few hundred. They are on the same scale, possibly even less, than the sum of the victims of South Africa's most notorious serial killers – even if we were to add an extra few hundred on the grounds that any existing statistic represents only those whose fate is known, and for whom apartheid security forces are the indisputable killers. One could hypothesize that more combat deaths were in fact killings. And the security forces must have been responsible for the deaths of some of the close to 500 persons the TRC noted as 'still missing'; in the latter group, just over 100 were classified as probable enforced disappearances, 64 of whom were last seen in the company of members of the security forces, and a further 117 as having disappeared during periods of unrest.[61] This would certainly increase, possibly even double, the total, but would not substantially alter the overall picture. Occasional rumours of mass graves, and proliferating bodies, that surface from time to time are regarded as improbable by investigators responsible for post-TRC investigations.[62] These rather small numbers seem at odds with the general depiction of apartheid, not only as cruel and evil, but as a highly militarized police state. They are contrary to apartheid's self-representation of itself at the time when it vowed to annihilate the enemy, as well as to how it is remembered and depicted in memorialization initiatives, which appear to share much of that self-representation.

There are different ways of answering this puzzle. One is to point to the fact that the vast majority of those killed by the apartheid state were not murdered by its security forces, but rather by forms of deliberately engineered and enforced structural violence, such as the restrictions on movement that garrisoned the majority of black South Africans away from the cities in so-called 'homelands', where mortuary registers would be filled with records of premature deaths. Thus South Africa's mass graves would be in the cemeteries of resettlement camps such as Dimbaza, or the hundreds of migrant workers buried anonymously as paupers in city cemeteries.[63] In other words, following a well worn critique, a focus on bodies of mass killing is in danger of obscuring colonial or apartheid pasts in its failure to recognize that, in certain parts of the world, mass killing is invisible and a consequence of the slow attrition of structural violence.

A further argument may be that other security strategies were found to be more effective and indeed account for considerably more deaths. Thus, the policy of keeping the line of defence as far as possible beyond South Africa's borders was directly responsible for thousands upon thousands of deaths of non-South Africans mainly in South Africa's own theatre of war, Namibia and southern Angola, and at least partially accountable for many thousands more in a proxy war in Mozambique, as well as lower numbers of deaths in Zimbabwe, Zambia, Botswana, Lesotho, and Swaziland.[64] Then, too, within South Africa, civilian protest played a far more significant role than the armed struggle, and deaths arising from civilian protest are certainly higher than these security police killings. However, by far the highest number of deaths arising from direct political violence inside South Africa is of those killed in inter-civilian conflict between liberation movements and Inkatha, an ethnically mobilized movement primarily based in the KwaZulu-Natal region of South Africa and the migrant hostels of Johannesburg.[65] Certainly political violence in these areas most closely approximates the description Mbembe provides of 'zones in which war and disorder, internal and external figures of the political, stand side by side or alternate with each other … the location par excellence where the controls and guarantees of judicial order can be suspended'.[66]

But here we are returned to the conundrum faced by the TRC. As with the proxy wars in Angola and Mozambique, apportioning responsibility for such deaths is no easy matter. Certainly, counter-mobilization, including the deliberate fomenting of violence, was a key component of the apartheid government's counter-revolutionary warfare strategy, and the TRC tracked overall support from the apartheid government for Inkatha, including political support, the training and arming of a covert hit squad, as well as the supply of arms during the early 1990s.[67] As a former member of a covert military unit put it:

> The emphasis was more placed on disruption by … indirect means of getting the enemy to kill itself, to detain itself and to disrupt itself. And physically killing them was placed more or less … [a]s a last resort, sort of method. But emphasis … was placed on sowing confusion and distrust between these different organisations.[68]

Yet this conflict is not reducible to a simple state project, but has a more muddled authorship, and it is impossible, for example, to disaggregate deaths arising from a hit squad trained by the security forces from the wider cycle of killing and revenge killing that the actions of the hit squad may have encouraged. Counter-mobilization's success relied on the capacity to mobilize along pre-existing fault-lines; despite efforts to replicate their success in KwaZulu-Natal and Johannesburg, the security forces were unable to do so elsewhere in any significant way, despite the considerable resources of the military, which largely drove this strategy.[69]

What, then, is the significance of the killings outlined earlier? Likening the violence that accompanied the partition of India and Pakistan to that in Rwanda, Ashis Nandy notes that killing did 'not come easy', as those engaged in the violence were 'ordinary people' rather than the 'centralized killing machine' of the state.[70] While Nandy clearly refers here to the will or psychological capacity of 'ordinary people' to kill, for state agents, trained less to protect than to kill (or to protect by killing), who may have the will to kill and are in fact authorized to do so, killing may still not 'come easy'.

If, following Mbembe, sovereignty is 'the power and capacity to dictate who may live and who must die',[71] how does one account for the seeming difficulty the late apartheid state had in exercising this sovereign right, even while at the same time his outline of sovereign power mirrors that of the apartheid state? A key argument here has been that this difficulty points to a form of constraint, a limit. While 'the sovereign right to kill' may not have been 'subject to legal and institutional rule', the sovereign's capacity to 'kill at any time or in any manner'[72] was nonetheless considerably constrained. Whites were (and are) vastly outnumbered in South Africa, and were never able to effect mass killing or genocide (notwithstanding certain fantasies and research by some sectors of the military and civilian society).[73] Beyond this, a series of factors – international condemnation of apartheid, a political system that represented itself as a political democracy hitched to the West's 'war against communism', the huge financial cost attached to external and internal wars in the context of a serious economic crisis – disabled its capacity to embark on the open slaughter of political opponents or the kind of mass disappearance programmes of the Latin American dictatorships such as those in Argentina and Chile with which it had close relationships.

Provided only with the political and institutional endorsement to kill political opponents, each security police unit had to devise its own modus operandi and rules of engagement, while seeking to remain undetected. Killing one by one in covert conditions was logistically difficult, and required not just time and planning resources, but the devising of a means and method each time. In this regard, killing operations were in fact not dissimilar from serial killing – each operation had to be imagined, planned, and executed.[74] Thus, although the security police acted with seeming impunity with regard to individual cases and operations, they did not have the capacity to engage in mass disappearances or mass killings. Indeed, it is possible that 'the engorged gaze over the politically prone body'[75] was the effect of failure and impotence on the part of a once powerful security police system, rather than that of untrammelled power. Exercising the power to kill may have aimed more to shore up a (fading) sense of power and control rather than demonstrating a capacity to contain, let alone end, insurgency.

Notes

1 This chapter is based on research conducted as part of the South African Truth and Reconciliation Commission (TRC) and an uncountable number of discussions with my former TRC colleague, Madeleine Fullard. It also draws on some of the arguments developed in an earlier paper – Nicky Rousseau, 'The farm, the river and the picnic spot: topographies of terror', *African Studies*, 68:3 (2009), 351–69. Thanks to Patricia Hayes and Riedwaan Moosage for their valuable comments.
2 For details see www.sahistory.org.za/topic/state-emergency-south-africa-1960-and-1980s (accessed 1 December 2012).
3 Deborah Posel & Pamila Gupta, 'The life of the corpse: framing questions and reflections', *African Studies*, 68:3 (2009), 299–309, at p. 305.
4 Promotion of National Unity and Reconciliation Act 34 of 1995, available at www.justice.gov.za/legislation/acts/acts_full.html (accessed 1 December 2012).
5 Although the TRC database coded killings according to method as well, much of the 'perpetrator volume' of the seven-volume final report of the TRC is organized according to these listed categories. TRC, *Truth and Reconciliation Commission of South Africa Report*, Vol. 2 (Cape Town: Jutas, 1998–2003), vol. 2.
6 Definitions of terrorism, sabotage, and treason were extremely wide, enabling prosecution for acts of political opposition regarded as lawful in most democracies. A. S. Matthews, *Law, Order and Liberty in South Africa* (Berkeley: University of California Press, 1972), pp. 175–7.
7 TRC, *Report*, vol. 2, p. 181.
8 The intention is not to suggest that resistance was responsible for the move to extra-judicial killing; rather, what is indexed here is Foucault's notion of power as productive. Michel Foucault, 'The subject and power', in H. L. Dreyfus & P. Rabinow (eds), *Michel Foucault: Beyond Structuralism and Hermeneutics*, 2nd edition (Chicago: University of Chicago Press, 1983), pp. 208–26.
9 TRC, *Report*, vol. 2, pp. 14–40.
10 This refers to the way in which apartheid was carefully codified into a myriad of laws, and the manner in which the then government 'placed a premium on law and order; on rule based formal legalism'. Dikgang Moseneke, 'A journey from the heart of apartheid darkness towards a just society', Philip Hart Memorial Lecture, Georgetown University, 4 April 2012, available at http://scholarship.law.georgetown.edu/

cgi/viewcontent.cgi?article=1000&context=hartlecture (accessed 20 January 2013).
11. For a discussion of the contestation around the meaning of words such as 'annihilate' and 'eliminate', see TRC, *Report*, vol. 5, pp. 214–18.
12. Annette Seegers, *The Military in the Making of Modern South Africa* (London: Tauris Academic Studies, 1996).
13. 'Analysis of security force perpetrators', document extracted from TRC database and amnesty hearings in the author's possession.
14. 'Analysis of security force perpetrators'; Rousseau, 'The farm, the river', p. 363.
15. Achille Mbembe, 'Necropolitics', *Public Culture*, 15:1 (2003), 11–40, at p. 24.
16. Phillip Frankel, Noam Pines & Mark Swilling (eds), *State, Resistance and Change in South Africa* (Johannesburg: Southern Book Publishers, 1988); Jacklyn Cock & Laurie Nathan (eds), *War and Society: The Militarisation of South Africa* (Cape Town: David Philip, 1989).
17. Madeleine Fullard & Nicky Rousseau, 'Who gave the orders?', unpublished paper, pp. 8–9.
18. TRC, *Report*, vol. 1, p. 43.
19. Ibid., vol. 2, p. 176.
20. Ibid., pp. 250–7.
21. In devising a modus operandi, security police drew on what was familiar and often personal. The rural was a key aspect of certain operatives' 'imaginary of violence'. Rousseau, 'The farm, the river'.
22. 'Analysis of security force perpetrators'.
23. TRC, *Report*, vol. 2, pp. 257–67, vol. 6, pp. 198–203.
24. Sean Callaghan, TRC Health Sector Hearing, available at www.justice.gov.za/trc/special/health/health01.htm (accessed 1 December 2012).
25. John Liebenberg & Patricia Hayes, *Bush of Ghosts: Life and War in Namibia, 1986–1990* (Fernwood: Umuzi/Random House, 2010), p. 247.
26. Etienne van Heerden, 'My Cuban', in *Mad Dog and Other Stories* (Cape Town: New Africa Books, 1992), p. 74.
27. Jacque Pauw, *Into the Heart of Darkness: Confessions of Apartheid's Assassins* (Johannesburg: Jonathan Ball, 1997), p. 82; SWAPO, 'SWATF/Koevoets not war veterans', available at www.swapoparty.org/swatf_koevoets_not_war_veterans.html (accessed 7 December 2012).
28. TRC, *Report*, vol 2, pp. 240–2, 269, 545, 547, 549.
29. Ibid., vol. 3, p. 623, vol. 2, p. 240; TRC Amnesty Committee, 'AC 2001/241', available at www.justice.gov.za/trc/decisions/2001/ac21241.htm (accessed 1 December 2012).
30. TRC Amnesty Hearing, available at www.justice.gov.za/trc/amntrans/durban/coetzee1.htm (accessed 1 December 2012); D. Coetzee, 'Hitsquads. Testimony of a South African security policeman: the full story', unpublished manuscript, section 5.4.8.3.
31. TRC Amnesty Hearing, 15–19 September 1997, 22–26 September 1997, 3–13 November 1997, available at www.justice.gov.za/trc/amntrans/am1997.htm (accessed 1 December 2012).

32 Missing Persons Task Team, *Report: The Search for Missing Activists at Post Chalmers near Cradock, Eastern Cape* (August 2009). The author was part of the team responsible for exhuming the remains.
33 'Necklacing' describes a method used to kill so-called collaborators whereby a petrol-soaked tyre is placed around the victim's neck and set alight. For the disposal of bodies, see TRC, *Report*, vol. 6, pp. 236–40; Rousseau, 'The farm, the river', pp. 357–9.
34 TRC, *Report*, vol. 2, pp. 242–3.
35 An Afrikaans word meaning terrorist.
36 Paul Gready, 'Medical complicity in human rights abuses: a case study of district surgeons in apartheid South Africa', *Journal of Human Rights*, 6:1 (2007), 415–32, at p. 416.
37 Posel & Gupta, 'The life of the corpse', p. 301.
38 Thomas Laqueur, 'The dead body and human rights', in S. Sweeney & I. Hodder (eds), *The Body* (Cambridge: Cambridge University Press, 2002), pp. 75–93; see also B. Honig, 'The other is dead: mourning, justice and the politics of burial', in Alexander Keller Hirsch (ed.), *Theorizing Post-conflict Reconciliation: Agonism, Restitution and Repair* (Oxford: Routledge, 2012), pp. 149–50.
39 Rousseau, 'The farm, the river', p. 353.
40 Posel & Gupta, 'The life of the corpse', p. 304.
41 This effect may also account for a phenomenon noticed by some TRC staff members, that the more brutal an account provided by perpetrators was, the more believable it seemed to be for victims' families and a wider public. Perhaps this was valued not for its evidentiary value but because it reasserted what was properly regarded as human and inhuman.
42 This plays on Allen Feldman's formulation of the 'tactile invasion' of the body, in 'Violence and vision: the aesthetics and prosthetics of terror', *Public Culture*, 10:1 (1997), 24–60, at p. 27.
43 Fernando Coronil & Julie Skurski, 'Dismembering and remembering the nation: the semantics of political violence in Venezuela', *Comparative Studies in History and Society*, 33:2 (1991), 288–337, at p. 289.
44 Mbembe, 'Necropolitics'.
45 Coronel & Skurski, 'Dismembering and remembering', p. 289.
46 Joost Fontein, 'Between tortured bodies and resurfacing bones: the politics of the dead in Zimbabwe', *Journal of Material Culture*, 15:4 (2010), 423–48; Cara Krmpotich, Joost Fontein & John Harries, 'The substance of bones: the materiality and affective presence of human remains', *Journal of Material Culture*, 15:4 (2010), 371–84; Zoë Crossland, 'Of clues and signs: the dead body and its evidential traces', *American Anthropologist*, 111:1 (2009), 69–80; Ewa Domanska, 'The material presence of the past', *History and Theory*, 45:3 (2006), 337–48; Bruno Latour, 'How to talk about the body: the normative dimensions of science study', *Body and Society*, 10:2–3 (2004), 205–29; Ciraj Rassool, 'Bone memory and the disciplines of the dead: human remains, transitional justice and heritage transformation', available at www.worddocx.com (accessed 1 December 2012).

47 'Jack' Cronje, TRC Amnesty Hearing, Pretoria, 21 October 1999, testimony available at www.justice.gov.za/trc/amntrans/1999/99101228_pre_991021.htm (accessed 1 December 2012).
48 Allan Sekula, cited in Crossland, 'Of clues and signs', p. 72.
49 Telephone interview with FMR, 3 November 1999; and LWM statement, both in the exhumation notes of Nicky Rousseau & Madeleine Fullard.
50 TRC, *Report*, vol. 3, pp. 628–31, 667–8.
51 J. J. McCuen, *The Art of Counter-Revolutionary Warfare* (London: Faber & Faber, 1966).
52 So-named after the small town from which they came, and which had become an important centre of rural resistance.
53 TRC, *Report*, vol. 2, pp. 227–8.
54 Domanska, 'The material presence of the past'; Crossland, 'Of clues and signs'; Fontein, 'Between tortured bodies and the resurfacing of bones'.
55 Domanska, 'The material presence of the past', p. 344.
56 Ibid.
57 Crossland, 'Of clues and signs', p. 75.
58 Rousseau, 'The farm, the river'.
59 Damanska, 'The material presence of the past', p. 340.
60 Gaston Gordillo, 'The afterlife of a sovereign corpse: Gaddafi', *Critical Legal Thinking*, 28 October 2011, available at http://criticallegalthinking.com/2011/10/28/the-afterlife-of-a-sovereign-corpse-gaddafi(accessed 1 December 2012).
61 TRC, *Report*, vol. 6, pp. 512–49. These figures are contested by the victim organization Khulumani, which – using a far wider definition of 'political' than prescribed in the TRC mandate requiring the act to be politically motivated and carried out by members or supporters of a bona fide political structure – has 6,800 people on its database of missing persons from the apartheid era. See www.khulumani.net/truth-a-memory/item/718-a-story-of-a-disappearance-resolved-mr-buti-mqakelana.htm (accessed January 2014).
62 Personal communication with Madeleine Fullard, head of the Missing Persons Task Team, a governmental, post-TRC unit responsible for investigations into unsolved TRC cases.
63 Such a point is part of a wider critique of initiatives, such as the TRC, that focused on a narrowly conceived understanding of political violence, ignoring the more systemic violence of apartheid.
64 TRC, *Report*, vol. 2, pp. 93–7, 144–54. South Africa's military forces were engaged in both a direct and a proxy war in Angola.
65 CASE, *The Role of Political Violence in South Africa's Democratisation* (Johannesburg: Community Agency for Social Enquiry, 2003); TRC, *Report*, vol. 3, ch. 2; Anthony Minnaar, *Conflict and Violence in Natal/Kwazulu: Historical Perspectives* (Pretoria: Human Sciences Research Council, 1990).
66 Mbembe, 'Necropolitics', p. 24.
67 TRC, *Report*, vol. 2, pp. 463–9, 605–10.
68 Ibid., p. 222.

69 Louise Flannagan, 'Covert operations in the Eastern Cape', in C. Schutte, I. Liebenberg & A. Minnaar (eds), *The Hidden Hand: Covert Operations in South Africa* (Pretoria: HSRC, 1998), pp. 213-22.
70 Ashis Nandy, 'Coming home: religion, mass violence and the exiled and secret selves of a citizen-killer', *Public Culture*, 22:1 (2010), 127-47, at pp. 144-5.
71 Mbembe, 'Necropolitics', p. 11.
72 Ibid., p. 25.
73 Included in documents associated with South Africa's chemical and biological warfare (CBW) programme were records of experiments into restricting the fertility of black people, as well as of contact with a British scientist regarding the development of a toxin that would target black people only. Also see Marlene Burger & Chandre Gould, *Secrets and Lies* (Cape Town: Zebra Press, 2002).
74 See Rousseau, 'The farm, the river', pp. 359-63, for elaboration of this point.
75 Feldman, 'Violence and vision', p. 27.

Bibliography

'Analysis of security force perpetrators', document extracted from TRC database and amnesty hearings in the author's possession

Burger, M. & C. Gould, *Secrets and Lies* (Cape Town: Zebra Press, 2002)

CASE, *The Role of Political Violence in South Africa's Democratisation* (Johannesburg: Community Agency for Social Enquiry, 2003)

Cock, J. & L. Nathan (eds), *War and Society: The Militarisation of South Africa* (Cape Town: David Philip, 1989)

Coetzee, D., 'Hitsquads. Testimony of a South African security policeman: the full story', unpublished manuscript

Coronil, F. & J. Skurski, 'Dismembering and remembering the nation: the semantics of political violence in Venezuela', *Comparative Studies in History and Society*, 33:2 (1991), 288-337

Cronje, J., TRC Amnesty Hearing, Pretoria, 21 October 1999, testimony available at www.justice.gov.za/trc/amntrans/1999/99101228_pre_991 021.htm (accessed 1 December 2012)

Crossland, Z., 'Of clues and signs: the dead body and its evidential traces', *American Anthropologist*, 111 (2009), 69-80

Domanska, E., 'The material presence of the past', *History and Theory*, 45:3 (2006), 337-48

Feldman, A., 'Violence and vision: the aesthetics and prosthetics of terror', *Public Culture*, 10:1 (1997), 24-60

Flannagan, L., 'Covert operations in the Eastern Cape', in C. Schutte, I. Liebenberg & A. Minnaar (eds), *The Hidden Hand: Covert Operations in South Africa* (Pretoria: HSRC Press, 1998), pp. 213-22

Fontein, J., 'Between tortured bodies and resurfacing bones: the politics of the dead in Zimbabwe', *Journal of Material Culture*, 15:4 (2010), 423-48

Foucault, M., 'The subject and power', in H. L. Dreyfus & P. Rabinow (eds), *Michel Foucault: Beyond Structuralism and Hermeneutics*, 2nd edition (Chicago: University of Chicago Press, 1983), pp. 208–26

Frankel, P., N. Pines & M. Swilling (eds), *State, Resistance and Change in South Africa* (Johannesburg: Southern Book Publishers, 1988)

Fullard, M. & N. Rousseau, 'Who gave the orders?', unpublished paper

Gordillo, G., 'The afterlife of a sovereign corpse: Gaddafi', *Critical Legal Thinking*, 28 October 2011, http://criticallegalthinking.com/2011/10/28/the-afterlife-of-a-sovereign-corpse-gaddafi (accessed 1 December 2012)

Gready, P., 'Medical complicity in human rights abuses: a case study of district surgeons in apartheid South Africa', *Journal of Human Rights*, 6:1 (2007), 415–32

Hansen, T. B. & F. Stepputat, 'Sovereignty revisited', *Annual Review of Anthropology*, 35 (2006), 295–315

Honig, B., 'The other is dead: mourning, justice and the politics of burial', in A. K. Hirsch (ed.), *Theorizing Post-conflict Reconciliation: Agonism, Restitution and Repair* (Oxford: Routledge, 2012), pp. 149–65

Krmpotich, C., J. Fontein & J. Harries, 'The substance of bones: the materiality and affective presence of human remains', *Journal of Material Culture*, 15:4 (2010), 371–84

Laqueur, T., 'The dead body and human rights', in S. Sweeney & I. Hodder (eds), *The Body* (Cambridge: Cambridge University Press, 2002), pp. 75–93

Latour, B., 'How to talk about the body: the normative dimensions of science study', *Body and Society*, 10:2–3 (2004), 205–29

Liebenberg, J. & P. Hayes, *Bush of Ghosts: Life and War in Namibia, 1986–1990* (Fernwood: Umuzi/Random House, 2010)

Matthews, A. S., *Law, Order and Liberty in South Africa* (Berkeley: University of California Press, 1972)

Mbembe, A., 'Necropolitics', *Public Culture*, 15:1 (2003), 11–40

McCuen, J. J., *The Art of Counter-Revolutionary Warfare* (London: Faber & Faber, 1966)

Minnaar, A., *Conflict and Violence in Natal/Kwazulu: Historical Perspectives* (Pretoria: Human Sciences Research Council, 1990)

Missing Persons Task Team, *Report: The Search for Missing Activists at Post Chalmers near Cradock, Eastern Cape* (August 2009)

Moseneke, D., 'A journey from the heart of apartheid darkness towards a just society', Philip Hart Memorial Lecture, Georgetown University, 4 April 2012, available at http://scholarship.law.georgetown.edu/cgi/viewcontent.cgi?article=1000&context=hartlecture (accessed 20 January 2013)

Nandy, A., 'Coming home: religion, mass violence and the exiled and secret selves of a citizen-killer', *Public Culture*, 22:1 (2010), 127–47

Pauw, J., *Into the Heart of Darkness: Confessions of Apartheid's Assassins* (Johannesburg: Jonathan Ball, 1997)

Posel, D. & P. Gupta, 'The life of the corpse: framing questions and reflections', *African Studies*, 68:3 (2009), 299–309

Rassool, C., 'Bone memory and the disciplines of the dead: human remains, transitional justice and heritage transformation', available at www.worddocx.com (accessed 1 December 2012)

Rousseau, N., 'The farm, the river and the picnic spot: topographies of terror', *African Studies*, 68:3 (2009), 351–69

Seegers, A., *The Military in the Making of Modern South Africa* (London: Tauris Academic Studies, 1996)

SWAPO, 'SWATF/Koevoets not war veterans', available at www.swapoparty.org/swatf_koevoets_not_war_veterans.html (accessed 7 December 2012)

TRC (Truth and Reconciliation Commission of South Africa), *Report* (Cape Town: Jutas, 1998–2003), vols 1–7

TRC Amnesty Committee, 'AC 2001/241', available at www.justice.gov.za/trc/decisions/2001/ac21241.htm (accessed 1 December 2012).

TRC Amnesty Hearing, 5–7 November 1996, available at www.justice.gov.za/trc/amntrans/durban/coetzee1.htm (accessed 1 December 2012)

TRC Amnesty Hearing, 15–19 September 1997, 22–26 September 1997, 3–13 November 1997, available at www.justice.gov.za/trc/amntrans/am1997.htm (accessed 1 December 2012)

van Heerden, E., 'My Cuban', in *Mad Dog and Other Stories* (Cape Town: New Africa Books, 1992), pp. 74–83

9

The Tutsi body in the 1994 genocide: ideology, physical destruction, and memory

Rémi Korman

Since 1994, bodies have been at the centre of the memorialization of the Tutsi genocide. For, in addition to constituting evidence in the context of forensic investigations, they are publicly exhibited in memorials to the genocide. The display of bodies aims principally to remind visitors of the historical facts of the genocide: not only the sites of massacres, but also the form these took.

Far from being an incidental detail, the methods employed by the killers are an important source of information on the ideology of genocide which developed at the beginning of the 1990s. Spurred on by 'hate media', this ideology targeted the country's Tutsi minority, more than 80 per cent of whom were exterminated between 7 April and 4 July 1994. This process of extermination was accompanied by practices of cruelty involving the infliction of specific forms of violence upon Tutsi bodies, in particular using edged weapons.

In order to understand these practices, it is crucial to examine the history of bodily representations since the colonial era, and in particular the Hamitic myth which was elaborated in this period.[1] While the terms 'Hutu', 'Tutsi', and 'Twa' used today did exist before colonization, they were reinforced by the arrival in the area of the first European colonizers, who exercised social control through the implementation of an ideology of racial inequality. According to Hamitic ideology, the Hutus were the country's true indigenous inhabitants, of 'Bantu' stock, while the Tutsis were foreign invaders, of 'Nilotic' or 'Hamitic' origin. The former were generally described as simple 'peasants', and the latter as a more calculating, 'feudal' class.[2] This system of classification was based on stereotypical racial representations, Tutsis being described as tall with thin noses and a lofty bearing, as opposed to Hutus, who were short, stocky, and flat-nosed. The Tutsis were sometimes even described as 'false negroes', as Europeans with black skin. This system of classification was the official policy of the Belgian colonialists, and was even extended to identity cards, which stated the holder's ethnic origin from 1931 onwards.

While these representations of the Tutsi body formulated in the colonial era remained throughout the twentieth century, the meanings they carried changed over time. An idealized 'Tutsi beauty' became a mark of stigma following the fall of the Tutsi monarchy and the establishment of the first exclusively Hutu Rwandan republic at the beginning of the 1960s. However, it was at the beginning of the 1990s that these representations underwent a radical shift. With the emergence of economic tensions at the end of the 1980s, the introduction of multi-party politics, and, above all, the start of the civil war on 1 October 1990, the Tutsis were increasingly made scapegoats for the country's problems. The new free press, of which extremist media sources formed a major part, would seek to redefine how the Tutsi body was imagined, and then incorporate these representations within the planning for future massacres. The Tutsi body was thus at the heart of the practices of cruelty organized by the genocidaires in 1994.

The Tutsi body in genocide ideology

The incessant repetition of the Hamitic myth under the country's first two republics helps to explain the stereotypes circulating in Rwanda at the beginning of the 1990s. What, then, were the specific bodily and physiological features which were supposed to characterize the Tutsis in 1994, according to the extremist media, and how were these representations used during the massacres?[3]

It must be borne in mind that, during the genocide, the body served as a pendant to the identity card. The body could be read, seen, scrutinized by the killers, who sought to isolate the differences which would allow them to locate the 'enemy'. Militias would probe every part of the body in which features specific to a certain notion of 'Tutsiship' were supposedly to be found. Extremist media sources such as Kangura or Radio Télévision Libre des Milles-collines

(RTLM) encouraged listeners to recognize Tutsis by sight alone, for the cunning Tutsis were supposedly trying to dupe the rest of the population by passing themselves off as Hutus. Esther Mujawayo, co-founder of an association for widows of the genocide, Avega, recalls having heard an RTLM journalist broadcasting the following address on the radio in the very first days of the genocide:[4]

> How can you distinguish the cockroach from the Hutu?
> You have several methods to choose from.
> The cockroach has a gap between his front teeth.
> The cockroach has narrow heels.
> The cockroach has eight pairs of ribs.
> The cockroach has stretch marks on his thighs near the buttocks.
> The cockroach has a thin nose.
> The cockroach's hair is not so curly.
> The cockroach's skull is long at the back, and his forehead is sloped.
> The cockroach is tall and there is haughtiness in his eyes.
> The cockroach has a pronounced Adam's apple.

As ludicrous as they may seem, these ideas were pressed into service at the barriers, the mobile checkpoints where militias thought they could establish the ethnicity of individuals on the basis of these descriptions. In practice, it was very difficult for the armed gangs to know for sure which ethnic group the people arrested at the barriers belonged to. They were particularly reliant on two sources of information: the knowledge of the local population, as neighbours would know the ethnicities of those arrested; and identity cards. In the absence of an identity card, physical appearance would dictate survival or death. As one woman survivor recounts:

> They started shouting as soon as they saw me. One of them knew me well and wanted to save me. He claimed that I was not a Tutsi. He said 'Look at her carefully. She does not have the features of a Tutsi.' They began to examine me, so as to judge my Tutsiship.[5]

The examinations carried out by the militias sought to identify the supposedly characteristic indicators of a Tutsi body. Height was the determining element, although other features were also taken into account, such as the form of the nose and teeth. According to Karen Krüger,[6] the nose was, quite literally, at the centre of these representations. Impossible to hide, the nose thus became a tool with which to measure ethnicity. A joke printed in a newspaper supporting the Rwandan Patriotic Front (RPF) in 1992 stated that, in order to be a member of the Coalition pour la Défense de la République (CDR), an extremist party belonging to the Hutu power tendency, one had to be able to insert two fingers into each nostril.[7] The implication was that this party was reserved for Hutus. This joke was then picked up on by the extremists and integrated within numerous texts, finally becoming, in the minds of the genocidaires in 1994, an actual method of checking the ethnicity of people arrested at the barriers. Victims were, for example, made to insert two fingers into their nostrils in order to measure the width of their nose. One militiaman, when interrogated on this subject, gave the following account:

> I was told that the Tutsi is the enemy of the Hutu because he has a slender nose. One can easily slip a finger into a Hutu's nostrils as his nose is wide. In order to find out whether a Hutu or a Tutsi was in front of us, we always tried putting a finger in his nose … if the finger did not fit we knew it was a Tutsi.[8]

Within this geography of the body, then, the nose had a predominant role, being the principal marker, highly visible and easily measured. For this reason it became a particular target of propaganda, with Kantano Habimana, the famous RTLM journalist, declaring in one of his programmes that 'We are talking about a single ethnic group. Take a person and look at their height and physical appearance; *just* take a look at their pretty little nose and then break it'.[9]

Teeth were another feature scrutinized by the killers, who saw the Tutsis as being marked out by their dentition. According to their imagined representations, the Tutsis, seen as a pastoral people, consumed excessive quantities of milk, to the extent that they would 'strip dairies bare'.[10] For the ideologues of the genocide, the Tutsis had particularly prominent teeth. It is possible that, specifically, the teeth of King Musinga, visible in numerous photographs from the colonial era, played a role in these stereotyped representations. The killers also went to great lengths to find teeth with gaps between them (*inyinya*). The journalist Kantano Habimana, who very probably delivered the address heard by Esther Mujawayo, talked at length in a programme broadcast on the RTLM in January 1994 about the gap between Major Rose Kabuye's incisors, which, in his view, was an indicator of her Tutsiship. Lastly, the genocidaires also paid close attention to skin colour. A darker complexion (*igikara*) was supposedly Hutu, while lighter skin (*inzobe*) was seen as Tutsi.

It is important to bear in mind that many Hutus, referred to as moderates, were also victims of the ideology of the genocide. These political opponents of the extremist parties were generally given nicknames implying that their bodies were marked by Tutsi characteristics. Laurent Kanamugire has noted the use of such negative expressions as *ingondeka*, denoting a tall and stooping stature, *muzuru*, an excessively long nose, *mbavu*, a large number of ribs, *gasongo*, a lanky physique, and *mujosi*, a long neck.[11]

The ideology of the genocide thus served to define the Tutsi as different, foreign bodies. It also served to legitimize the cruelty to the victims.

Practices of cruelty during the massacres

One of the defining features of the genocide committed against the Tutsi in 1994 was the range of practices of cruelty committed by the killers, violence without useful purpose, aiming as much to inflict suffering upon as to eliminate its victims. How, though, can we define this cruelty? What were the specific elements that defined it in 1994?[12] Véronique Nahoum-Grappe defines cruelty as a specific form of violence, identifiable by its intensity.[13] Whereas violence can cause varying degrees of pain, cruelty has the explicit objective of inflicting suffering and humiliation. It forms part of a framework of asymmetric power, and this was very clearly the case during the genocide.[14]

In Rwanda, a first aspect of this cruelty was the carrying out of killings in broad daylight. During the genocide of the Tutsi in 1994, the killers openly committed their crimes, in full view of the population. This public nature of their crimes was made possible by an ideology which meant that these acts carried no consequences. This social impunity, which facilitated the murders, was accompanied by the humiliation of the victims. The latter were stripped, once again in front of the population, who laughed, joined in the beatings, and picked up abandoned possessions. The act of stripping victims naked also had the aim of revealing the supposed somatic difference of the Tutsis, thus preventing them from hiding their 'abnormality'. As well as being perpetrated in broad daylight, the massacres were also committed by neighbours of the victims. Most of the killings were carried out in the hills of Rwanda, giving a very close-knit character to the murders. Teachers killed their students, neighbours killed their neighbours, and the crime of genocide even reached down to the level of relations within families.

It is to be noted that, of the 'ten commandments of the Muhutu', proclaimed in December 1990 by the extremist magazine *Kangura*, the first denounces mixed marriages:[15] 'Every Muhutu must know that Umututsikazi [a Tutsi woman], wherever she may be, is in the pay of the Tutsi people. Consequently, any Muhutu who marries an Umututsikazi, who takes an Umututsikazi as his concubine, who makes an Umututsikazi his secretary or his protégée, is a traitor.' Many so-called mixed families were caught up in the genocide. There were two possible situations: mixed couples where the husband was a Tutsi, and those where the husband was a Hutu. It is important to note that in Rwandan culture ethnic affiliation is patrilineal (ethnicity is 'transmitted' by the father). In the case of families where the father was a Tutsi, only the Hutu mother could hope to survive. Some women in this situation killed their own children, the latter now considered as 'children of the enemy'. Conversely, many Hutu husbands were forced to kill their Tutsi wives by the militias in order to save their children. Nicknamed 'Hutsi', the latter have subsequently been torn by their dual status as the children of killers and the children of victims of the genocide.[16] In some cases, Hutsi children were even killed by their Hutu father, demonstrating the extreme racialization of social and family relationships at the time of the genocide.

Another characteristic feature of the genocide was the choice of weapons used to inflict suffering upon the victims. It is a striking fact that the tools used for killing were in general not weapons, but everyday objects. This situation led to the creation of euphemisms for the violence carried out. Claudine Vidal has pointed out the use of the expression 'to cut' (*gutema*) in place of 'to kill' (*kwica*). The tools employed thus 'contaminated' the vocabulary denoting the act of killing.[17] However, some weapons were given explicit names, such as the club called *Nta mpongano y'umwanzi* (no pity for the enemy). The use of this type of weapon inevitably involved coming face to face with the victim, as well as 'transgressing the anatomical barrier',[18] and thus coming into contact with blood, for the killers as much as for the victims.

Nevertheless, one should be wary of some interpretations that have made the use of edged weapons a condition of the cruelty of the massacres. Some have seen the rudimentary character of the agricultural implements employed as, in itself, explaining the degree of suffering inflicted. Yet this image of a poor person's genocide, or an agricultural genocide, needs to be challenged.[19] Traditionally, the machete has never been considered a weapon in Rwanda, unlike the spear, sword, or bow. While there certainly were practices of cruelty involving edged weapons, these were not a mere consequence of the implements being used, but rather a literal enactment of the ideology of the genocide. Several studies have shown the role of firearms during the massacres.[20] Whenever attacks were carried out in large groups, they almost always followed an identical format. Militias with guns and grenades would attack first, breaking any resistance and preventing escape; then other people would finish off the survivors with machetes, clubs, hoes, and so on. Bladed (or blunt) weapons were used in order to cause suffering to victims' bodies, and to destroy them according to a predetermined process. This is not to say that a degree of inventiveness was absent from these practices of cruelty.[21] Alongside the ideology of the genocide went a certain amount of autonomy on the part of the killers, even if the meaning of their acts referred back to shared representations. For, as Mary Douglas argues, 'what one sculpts from human flesh is an image of society'.[22]

The killers, then, sought to cut, to shorten the Tutsi, who were considered taller in stature. The expression 'to shorten tall trees' has been used by some.[23] Some victims had their feet and legs cut off; others were decapitated. The killers would often begin by severing victims' Achilles' tendons in order to prevent them from escaping. Now unable to stand, they were also seen as no longer being able to boast of their stature. Cutting their bodies into pieces also functioned as a signifier of the uprooting of the Tutsi 'growth'. The official memorial song for the seventeenth commemoration of the genocide, entitled 'We refuse to allow our history to be falsified' ('Twanze gutoberwa Amateka'), echoes this plant metaphor. In the middle of the chorus, the composer and genocide survivor Kizito Mihigo sings the words 'Twanze kuba insina ngufi', meaning 'we refuse to be little banana trees'. This is a reference to a Rwandan proverb that states that little banana trees are easier to uproot. These are powerful words for survivors, affirming their refusal to be uprooted, to be cut down and prevented from growing.

During the genocide, bodily extremities and all such 'outgrowths' were a target of the killers; they sought to destroy what, according to collective representations, were recognizable traits, and this 'hystericalization of small differences'[24] led them to cut off those extremities that were supposedly characteristic of a Tutsi body. Noses and little fingers were thus cut off, from the dead as well as the living. This ideology drove some killers to attack objects and even animals. The most striking examples of this involved religious objects, and in particular statues which, in the minds of the killers, bore 'the marks of a Tutsi body'. Militias thus broke the nose off

The Tutsi body in the 1994 genocide 233

a statue of the Virgin Mary in Kibeho, an important site for the Catholic Church in Rwanda, while others decapitated a statue of Christ on the cross inside a church in Nyarubuye.

How can these practices of cruelty ever be made intelligible? What possible meaning can be assigned to such acts? Several anthropological hypotheses seeking to understand such forms of violence have been put forward since 1994.[25] They focus on the idea of a culture of violence and obedience in Rwanda, as well as on the mythical and cosmogonical beliefs and representations found among the country's population. While these approaches may at first glance seem stimulating, some of them do tend to rely on a highly culturalist model which is somewhat problematic. For the cultural aspect of the violence must not be allowed to overshadow the genocide's political dimension.

According to the anthropologist Danielle de Lame, the economic and political situation at the beginning of the 1990s cannot account entirely for the violence of the genocide.[26] She puts forward several hypotheses relating to traditions of cruelty and violence as a 'structure within Rwandan history', as well as to the role of fear, and also a 'mythico-religious' vision of history centred on the figure of the king. She explains how, in the past, whenever the king became weak, the resulting chaos produced a violent reaction from the people. These ideas, in conjunction with the context of political crisis at the beginning of the 1990s, have been used to legitimize the violence committed during the genocide. It is to be noted that this culturalist hypothesis is regularly invoked by defence teams at the International Criminal Tribunal for Rwanda in order to explain the events of the genocide.[27]

Far more useful are those anthropological analyses which focus on the representation of the body. Danielle de Lame also points out that the circulation of forces within boundaries, and within the body in particular, is an essential paradigm within Rwandan culture, thus providing an explanation for the fury with which the limbs of Tutsi victims were hacked off. This hypothesis has been taken up by Christopher Taylor,[28] who 'relates the various forms of killing and practices of cruelty ... to systems of traditional symbolic logic'.[29] According to Taylor, the Tutsi were likened to obstacles that had to be removed from circulation. This theory would account for the traditional practices of execution employed, as well as various beliefs relating to the violence committed during the genocide, although it clearly has to be seen alongside other attempts to understand this violence.

Investigations of the methods used in the genocide

Right from the outset, in 1994, the series of inquiries produced by Rwandan institutions all made specific reference to the cruelty of the acts committed during the genocide. The horrors suffered by the victims are not simply evoked in vague terms; instead, the cruelty is analysed in detail, being considered by the investigators as a crucial element of the act of genocide. The inventiveness evident in the various ways of inflicting suffering and in the form taken by the massacres is a central concern of these reports into the atrocities.

In its investigative report into the massacres produced after the genocide, the Human Rights Commission of the Rwandan Patriotic Front, at that time led by Tito Rutaremara,[30] devoted considerable space to this question, listing more than twenty ways of killing used during the massacres. Concurrently, CLADHO, a Rwandan human rights group, in partnership with the survivors' organization Ibuka and the non-governmental organization Huridocs, developed a database that allowed the sites of the genocide to be catalogued, along with the names of the victims, the names of the killers, as well as the specific instruments used in the massacres. While the idea of a collaborative effort between these groups quickly foundered, the database, christened Genosys,[31] would form the basis of the work done by Ibuka in its investigation of the genocide in the Kibuye prefecture, in western Rwanda. When one reads Ibuka's report, the importance for survivors of the question of exactly how the genocide was carried out is immediately apparent. A significant amount of it is devoted to describing the implements used by the killers during the genocide. On the official publication in December 1999 of the resulting *Dictionnaire nominatif des victims du génocide en préfecture de Kibuye*,[32] Ikuba's president, Frédéric Mutagwera, spoke at some length on the 'twenty-nine ways' in which victims were murdered during the genocide, the list of which runs as follows:

> 1. Sexual abuse (raped to death), 2. Tearing out the eyes, 3. Tearing out the heart, 4. Burning alive, 5. Castration, 6. Devouring by dogs, 7. Knives, 8. Crushing (of babies) against a wall or floor, 9. Burying alive (Nyange church), 10. Sword, 11. Starvation, 12. Beating to death, 13. Suffocation, 14. Shooting, 15. Club with nails, 16. Club, 17. Hand grenade, 18. Axe, 19. Hoe, 20. Spear, 21. Stoning, 22. Cess pit, 23. Machete, 24. Hammer, 25. Drowning, 26. Hanging, 27. Staking, 28. Poison, 29. Torture.

Subsequently, other Rwandan reports would look into this question, such as the *Dénombrement des victimes du génocide et des*

The Tutsi body in the 1994 genocide   235

massacres, published by the Ministry of Local Administration and Social Affairs in 2001. The latter study analyses the distribution of methods of killing during the genocide according to geographical location. The authors conclude that some weapons, such as the machete and club, were predominant throughout the country. However, the patterns of their use differed from one area to another. Firearms appear to have been used particularly extensively in Gikongo and Butare prefectures, indicating the presence of armed units, most probably from the army. Several local studies of the genocide have also examined the mistreatment of victims' bodies, in particular the monograph on the genocide in Nyarubuye written by Privat Rutazibwa and Paul Rutayisire,[33] and another on the genocide in the town of Mugina edited by Faustin Rutembesa and Ernest Mutwarasibo. In the latter study, Rutembesa examines practices of cruelty, termed *ibikorwa bya kinyamaswa*,[34] and sexual violence in particular.

This interest in the specific methods employed serves to remind us that the memory of the genocide committed against the Tutsi is not founded solely upon the bodies of the victims.[35] The weapons of the killers also hold significant memorial value. These objects, abhorrent as they are, are the 'prolongation of the body' of the killer, and even of that of the victim. For this reason, a great number of genocide memorials exhibit these implements of torture next to the remains of victims. At the memorial site in Nyamata, the guides show visitors the various ways in which bodies were abused, pointing out cut marks on bones, arrows stuck in skulls, and a wall against which children were crushed. At the memorial site in Nyarubuye, a log used for the preparation of *urwawa* (banana beer) is exhibited; during the genocide it was used for beheading Tutsis.[36]

This conscious museological decision seeks to highlight the meaning placed by the killers on the destruction of these bodies. By targeting specific parts of the body, they symbolically attacked the 'Tutsiship' of their victims. By dismembering the corpses, by destroying them, they attacked their very humanity, seeking in this way to render any funeral rites impossible. These acts explain the appearance following the genocide of a new expression: 'burial with dignity' (*Gushyingura mu cyubahiro*).[37] These bodies must be buried with dignity, buried properly, because these victims were killed wrongly, suffering a 'bad death' (*Bapfuye nabi*) – bad in the sense not only of the torture suffered by the victims, but also of the way in which their corpses were treated. This notion of bad death is an important element of traditional Rwandan culture, and is one of the reasons why Christian religious discourse, based as it is on the notion of salvation after death, has encountered such difficulty in adapting to a Rwandan context.[38]

A bad burial also amounts to a bad death. Victims suffered this fate, being buried in unmarked mass graves by the killers, whereas collective burial is quite alien to Rwandan notions and practices; the dead are generally buried on the land surrounding the family home. However, it is also a fact that, beneath the veneer of rationalist discourse often heard in Rwanda, the fear of the spirits of the dead still persists, particularly in the countryside. Monseigneur Aloys Bigirumwami, the first Rwandan bishop, wrote in 1969 in his celebrated writings on the customs of Rwanda:

> The spirit of the deceased, the *muzimu*, will be either good or bad according to the subsequent good or bad fortune enjoyed by those who outlive him. Earthly successes are attributed to him, but so too are any instances of illness, sterility, or death afflicting members of his family, their livestock and other possessions. It is his way of gaining respect or exacting revenge. This is why Rwandans take many careful precautions before, during and after the burial in order to ensure that the spirit of the deceased leaves on good terms with the family.[39]

There are also specific beliefs associated with each type of spirit. The spirit of a person who has died far from their family, without a burial, is called *umuzimu w'umugwagasi*. The testimony of many survivors shows that the spirit of the deceased who has not had a proper burial, the *umugwagasi*, is particularly dreaded.

Conclusion

It is clear that the practices of cruelty in 1994 were rooted in a complex ideological humus. They were linked both to the collective representations developed over the course of the twentieth century which transformed the Tutsi and Hutu body into a site of political antagonism, and also to the genocide ideology which became widespread at the beginning of the 1990s. The specific nature of the violence inflicted upon bodies at a local level remains largely unknown. Detailed local studies of the genocide are still rare, and analysis of the archives of the Gacaca courts is only now beginning. Above all, there has been no real comparative study of the massacres carried out in 1994 and those committed in 1963 and 1973.

More generally, a history of the modalities of violence in Rwanda and the African Great Lakes region in the twentieth century has yet to be written. While the genocide committed against the Tutsi had a certain number of specific features, the massacres in Burundi in both 1972 and 1993, along with those carried out in Uganda under the rule of Idi Amin, also require further analysis. A comparative study of this violence and of the different abuses inflicted on bodies during these events will allow the potential role to be assessed of migrations and movements of refugees in the diffusion of new practices of violence.

The intensity of the sexual violence currently being committed in the Democratic Republic of Congo is the most striking example of this process. Rape, used on a massive scale in Rwanda in 1994 and recognized as a genocidal crime by the International Criminal Tribunal for Rwanda (ICTR),[40] has become one of the main instruments of the violence committed by armed militias in the Democratic Republic of Congo. As well as rape, however, a whole range of violent practices originating in specific mass crimes seem to have been exported throughout the Great Lakes region. Gaining an understanding of this process of migration of knowledge and techniques of violence is thus a priority for researchers working on the status of bodies in situations of mass violence.

Notes

1 See J.-P. Chrétien, *Le Défi de l'ethnisme: Rwanda et Burundi, 1990–1996* (Paris: Karthala Editions, 1997); F. Baillette, 'Figures du corps, ethnicité et génocide au Rwanda', *Quasimodo*, 6 (2000), 7–37.
2 See J.-P. Chrétien, 'Le Génocide du Rwanda un négationnisme structurel', *Hommes & Libertés*, 151 (2010), 29–31.
3 I would like to thank Hélène Dumas for her advice relating to this section.
4 F. Baillette, 'Figures du corps', p. 9.
5 K. Krüger, 'The destruction of faces in Rwanda 1994', *L'Europe en Formation*, 357 (2010), 91–105, at p. 103.
6 Ibid., p. 94.
7 See *Kangura*, 35, p. 4: 'Iyo umuntu yatse ikarita ya CDR bashyira intoki ebyiri muri buri zuru rye zakwirwamo akabona kwemererwa kuba umuyoboke w'iryo shya' ('When someone asked for a CDR membership card, they would stick two fingers into each of his nostrils and, if they went in, he would be accepted as a member of the party'). It should be noted that a certain degree of humour surrounds these questions, of a type similar to kinship jokes. Kinship jokes, a classic object of anthropological study, are social practices which allow members of a family, or of different clans or peoples, to mock one another without causing offence. Few studies have been devoted to this question in

Rwanda. See J. Freedman, 'Joking, affinity and the exchange of ritual services among the Kiga of northern Rwanda: an essay on joking relationship theory', *Man*, 12:1 (1977), 154–65, at p. 154.

8 Krüger, 'The destruction of faces', p. 103 (testimony of Alphonse N., Gikondo prison, 6 September 2003).

9 'Il s'agit d'une seule ethnie. Regardez donc une personne et voyez sa taille et son apparence physique; regardez *seulement* son joli petit nez et cassez-le'. Baillette, 'Figures du corps', p. 8.

10 Kantano Habimana declared in a programme broadcast on 5 or 6 January 1994 on RTLM that: 'It's surprising to see someone drinking two or three litres of milk from Nyabisindu or Rubilizi etc...., there was supposed to have been a shortage of milk in the dairies. Someone wrote to me saying "Help! They've emptied the dairy!" I've seen it with my own eyes. They have a very large stock of milk.' ('C'est surprenant de voir quelqu'un boire deux ou trois litres du lait provenant de Nyabisindu ou de Rubilizi etc...., il y aurait dû y avoir pénurie de lait dans les laiteries. Quelqu'un m'a écrit ceci: "Au secours! Ils ont vidé la laiterie !" J'ai vu cela de mes propres yeux. Ils possèdent un très grand stock de lait.') See the judgement and sentence passed by the judge for case ICTR-99-52-T, International Criminal Tribunal for Rwanda, 3 December 2003.

11 L. Kanamugire, *Le Rôle de l'État dans le génocide des Tutsi d'avril– juillet 1994: Cas de l'ex-commune urbaine de Ngoma* (Butare: Université nationale du Rwanda, 2003).

12 See C. Vidal, 'Le Génocide des rwandais tutsi: cruauté délibérée et logiques de haine', in F. Héritier (ed.), *De la violence* (Paris: Odile Jacob, 1996), pp. 325–66. This ground-breaking chapter, published in 1996, offers essential insights into the question of the violence committed during the genocide.

13 V. Nahoum-Grappe, 'L'Usage politique de la cruauté: l'épuration ethnique (ex-Yugoslavia, 1991–1995)', in F. Héritier (ed.), *De la violence* (Paris: Odile Jacob, 1996), pp. 273–323.

14 E. Mailänder, 'Work, violence and cruelty', *L'Europe en Formation*, 357 (2010), 29–51, at p. 29.

15 See *Kangura*, 6 December 1990, p. 6–8.

16 J. Ruremesha, 'Rwanda: les enfants 'hutsi' écartelés et rejetés', *Syfia Grands Lacs*, 20 January 2004.

17 See the contribution by Stéphane Audoin-Rouzeau in L. de Vulpian, *Rwanda, un génocide oublié? Un procès pour mémoire* (Paris: Editions Complexe, 2004), p. 55.

18 Ibid.

19 C. Vidal, 'Un "génocide à la machette"', in M. Le Pape, J. Siméant & C. Vidal (eds), *Crises extrêmes: face aux massacres, aux guerres civiles et aux génocides* (Paris: La Découverte, 2006), pp. 21–35.

20 P. Verwimp, 'Machetes and firearms: the organization of massacres in Rwanda', *Journal of Peace Research*, 43 (2006), 5–22.

21 J. Kagabo, 'Après le génocide. Notes de voyage', *Les Temps Modernes*, 583 (1995), 102–25.

22 '[C]e que l'on sculpte de la chair humaine, c'est une image de la société.' M. Douglas, *De la souillure: essai sur les notions de pollution et de tabou* (Paris: Maspero, 1971), p. 35, quoted in J. Dufour, *Présence des corps: mémoriaux et politique mémorielle du génocide des Tutsi au Rwanda: 1994–2011* (Paris: École des Hautes Études en Sciences Sociales, 2011), p. 49.

23 This expression was much used around the time of the 2004 film *Hotel Rwanda*. It is possible that it was invented in this context.

24 A. Brossat, *Le Corps de l'ennemi: hyperviolence et démocratie* (Paris: La Fabrique, 1998), quoted in J. Dufour, *Présence des corps*, p. 55.

25 Studies of the Tutsi genocide have mainly been carried out by political scientists. Analysis by historians or anthropologists remains rare.

26 D. de Lame, 'Le génocide rwandais et le vaste monde, les liens du sang', in F. Reyntjens & S. Marysse (eds), *L'Afrique des Grands-Lacs, annuaire 1996–1997* (Paris: L'Harmattan, 1997), pp. 157–77.

27 See for example the report by Lucien Hounkpatin, 'Analyse ethno-psychiatrique de la tragédie rwandaise d'avril 1994', Trial of the Cyangugu group at the International Criminal Tribunal for Rwanda, 8 July 2002 (case no. ICTR-99-46-T).

28 C. Taylor, *Terreur et sacrifice: une approche anthropologique du génocide rwandais* (Toulouse: Octarès Editions, 2000).

29 C. Vidal, 'Rwanda 1994: l'imaginaire traditionnel perverti par le génocide', *L'Homme*, 163 (2002), 205–16, at p. 211.

30 J.-P. Schreiber, 'Rwanda, janvier 1995: voyage au cœur de l'abomination', in R. Boulal & P. Kalisa (eds), *N'épargnez pas les enfants! Mémoire d'un génocide de proximité* (Brussels: Aden Editions, 2009), pp. 41–63.

31 B. Verstappen, *Micro-thesauri: A Tool for Documenting, English* (Huridocs, 2001).

32 Ibuka, *Dictionnaire nominatif des victimes du génocide en Préfecture de Kibuye* (Kigali: Ibuka, 1999).

33 P. Rutazibwa & P. Rutayisire, *Génocide à Nyarubuye: monographie sur l'un des principaux sites du génocide des Tutsi de 1994 au Rwanda* (Kigali: Editions Rwandaises, 2007).

34 F. Rutembesa & E. Mutwarasibo, *Amateka ya Jenoside yakorewe Abatutsi muri Mugina* (Kigali: CNLG, 2009). *Kinyamaswa* refers to the concept of ferocity or savagery.

35 H. Dumas & R. Korman, 'Espaces de la mémoire du génocide des Tutsis au Rwanda', *Afrique contemporaine*, 238 (2011), 11–27.

36 N. Rera, *Nyarubuye: quelque part, entre les vivants et les morts* (Paris: Génocides et politiques mémorielles, 2011), available at http://chs.univ-paris1.fr/genocides_et_politiques_memorielles (accessed 9 October 2013).

37 R. Korman, *Le Rwanda face à ses morts ou les cimetières du génocide comme lieux de mémoire* (Paris: Génocides et politiques mémorielles, 2012), available at http://chs.univ-paris1.fr/genocides_et_politiques_memorielles/?Le-Rwanda-face-a-ses-morts-ou-les (accessed 9 October 2013).

38 On funerary rites in Rwanda and the role of Christianity in the evolution

of representations of death, see G. van't Spijker, *Les Usages funéraires et la mission de l'Eglise: une étude anthropologique et théologique des rites funéraires au Rwanda* (Kampen: Uitgeversmaatschappij J. H. Kok, 1990).

39 '[L]'esprit du défunt, le muzimu, sera bon ou mauvais suivant le sort heureux ou malheureux des survivants. On lui attribue les réussites terrestres, mais aussi les maladies, la stérilité, la mort qui peuvent frapper les membres de sa famille, le bétail et tous ses biens. C'est son moyen de se faire respecter ou de se venger. C'est pour cela que le Rwandais a recours à de multiples précautions très minutieuses avant, pendant et après l'enterrement pour que l'esprit du défunt s'en aille en bons termes avec la famille.' See A. Bigirumwami, 'Les rites rwandais autour de la mort', in *Colloque: ethique chrétienne et valeurs africaines* (Kinshasa, 1969), pp. 40–58.

40 On this point see the trial of Jean-Paul Akayesu, at the International Criminal Tribunal for Rwanda (case no. TPIR-96-4-T).

Bibliography

Baillette, F., 'Figures du corps, ethnicité et génocide au Rwanda', *Quasimodo*, 6 (2000), 7–37

Bigirumwami, A., 'Les rites rwandais autour de la mort', in *Colloque: ethique chrétienne et valeurs africaines* (Kinshasa, 1969), pp. 40–58

Brossat, A., *Le Corps de l'ennemi: hyperviolence et démocratie* (Paris: La Fabrique, 1998)

Chrétien, J.-P., *Le défi de l'ethnisme: Rwanda et Burundi, 1990–1996* (Paris: Karthala Editions, 1997)

Chrétien, J.-P., 'Le génocide du Rwanda un négationnisme structurel', *Hommes & Libertés*, 151 (2010), 29–31

de Lame, D., 'Le génocide rwandais et le vaste monde, les liens du sang', in F. Reyntjens & S. Marysse (eds), *L'Afrique des Grands-Lacs, annuaire 1996–1997* (Paris: L'Harmattan, 1997), pp. 157–77

de Vulpian, L., *Rwanda, un génocide oublié? Un procès pour mémoire* (Paris: Editions Complexe, 2004)

Douglas, M., *De la souillure: essai sur les notions de pollution et de tabou* (Paris: Maspero, 1971)

Dufour, J., *Présence des corps. Mémoriaux et politique mémorielle du génocide des Tutsi au Rwanda: 1994–2011* (Paris: École des Hautes Études en Sciences Sociales, 2011)

Dumas, H. & R. Korman, 'Espaces de la mémoire du génocide des Tutsis au Rwanda', *Afrique contemporaine*, 238 (2011), 11–27

Freedman, J., 'Joking, affinity and the exchange of ritual services among the Kiga of northern Rwanda: an essay on joking relationship theory', *Man*, 12:1 (1977), 154–65

Hounkpatin, L., 'Analyse ethnopsychiatrique de la tragédie rwandaise d'avril 1994', Trial of the Cyangugu group at the International Criminal Tribunal for Rwanda, 8 July 2002 (case no. ICTR-99-46-T)

Ibuka, *Dictionnaire nominatif des victimes du génocide en Préfecture de Kibuye* (Kigali: Ibuka, 1999)

Kagabo, J., 'Après le génocide. Notes de voyage', *Les Temps Modernes* (1995), 102–25

Kanamugire, L., *Le Rôle de l'État dans le génocide des Tutsi d'avril-juillet 1994: Cas de l'ex-commune urbaine de Ngoma* (Butare: Université nationale du Rwanda, 2003)

Korman, R., *Le Rwanda face à ses morts ou les cimetières du génocide comme lieux de mémoire* (Paris: Génocides et politiques mémorielles, 2012), available at http://chs.univ-paris1.fr/genocides_et_politiques_memorielles/?Le-Rwanda-face-a-ses-morts-ou-les (accessed 9 October 2013)

Krüger, K., 'The destruction of faces in Rwanda 1994', *L'Europe en Formation*, 357 (2010), 91–105.

Mailänder, E., 'Work, violence and cruelty', *L'Europe en Formation*, 357 (2010), 29–51

Nahoum-Grappe, V., 'L'usage politique de la cruauté: l'épuration ethnique (ex-Yugoslavia, 1991-1995)', in F. Héritier (ed.), *De la violence* (Paris: Odile Jacob, 1996), pp. 273–323.

Rera, N., *Nyarubuye: quelque part, entre les vivants et les morts* (Paris: Génocides et politiques mémorielles, 2011), available at http://chs.univ-paris1.fr/genocides_et_politiques_memorielles (accessed 9 October 2013)

Ruremesha, J., 'Rwanda: les enfants 'hutsi' écartelés et rejetés', *Syfia Grands Lacs*, 20 January 2004

Rutazibwa, P. & P. Rutayisire, *Génocide à Nyarubuye: monographie sur l'un des principaux sites du génocide des Tutsi de 1994 au Rwanda* (Kigali: Editions Rwandaises, 2007)

Rutembesa, F. & E. Mutwarasibo, *Amateka ya Jenoside yakorewe Abatutsi muri Mugina* (Kigali: CNLG, 2009)

Schreiber, J.-P., 'Rwanda, janvier 1995: voyage au cœur de l'abomination', in R. Boulal & P. Kalisa (eds), *N'épargnez pas les enfants! Mémoire d'un génocide de proximité* (Brussels: Aden Editions, 2009), pp. 41–63

Taylor, C., *Terreur et sacrifice: une approche anthropologique du génocide rwandais* (Toulouse: Octarès Editions, 2000)

van't Spijker, G., *Les Usages funéraires et la mission de l'Eglise: une étude anthropologique et théologique des rites funéraires au Rwanda* (Kampen: Uitgeversmaatschappij J. H. Kok, 1990)

Verstappen, B., *Micro-thesauri: A Tool for Documenting, English* (Huridocs, 2001).

Verwimp, P., 'Machetes and firearms: the organization of massacres in Rwanda', *Journal of Peace Research*, 43 (2006), 5–22

Vidal, C., 'Le génocide des rwandais tutsi: cruauté délibérée et logiques de haine', in F. Héritier (ed.), *De la violence* (Paris: Odile Jacob, 1996), pp. 325–66

Vidal, C., 'Rwanda 1994. L'imaginaire traditionnel perverti par le génocide', *L'Homme*, 163 (2002), 205–16

Vidal, C., 'Un "génocide à la machete"', in M. Le Pape, J. Siméant & C. Vidal (eds), *Crises extrêmes: face aux massacres, aux guerres civiles et aux génocides* (Paris: La Découverte, 2006), pp. 21–35

Index

abductions 207, 214
Abdülhalik, Mustafa 97
Abrahamian, Ervand 187
Abuharar camps 104
Adenauer, Konrad 125–6
African National Congress 210
Agamben, Giorgio 9
agency of the dead body 214–15
Águila, Gabriela 149
Aleppo 98, 101
Algeria 8
Ambros, Otto 127
Amin, Idi 237
Andonian, Aram 100, 107
Angola 216–17
Ankut, Krikor 103–4
anthropological studies 4, 6, 233
anti-Semitism 131
apartheid 204–6, 210–12, 216–18
Arakelian, Alphonse 93
Arendt, Hannah 1, 131
Argana Maden 92
Argentina 5–8, 146–67, 192–3, 218
Armenia 6–9, 89, 166
Arslanian, Dajad 100
Ashooq, Mohammad-Reza 190–1
Aumeier, Hans 52
Auschwitz 4, 7, 47, 49, 53, 56–7, 117–22, 127–30, 136–40

Avellaneda Cemetery 148
Azaz camp 99–100

Bab camp 100
Balakian, Krikoris 99, 101
'bandit' (use of term) 74–5
Bauman, Zygmunt 124, 129–30
beheading 21
Belzec 120–1
ben Gamliel, Shimon 119
ben Teradion, Hanina 119
Benjamin, Walter 197
Bethmann-Hollweg, Theobald von 99
Bigirumwami, Aloys 236
Bihać 29
biopower and biopolitics 7–8
Birkenau 4, 53, 117–22, 129–30
Black, Monica 80
blasphemy 192
book burnings 117, 126
Boričevac 23–4
Borrisow 69–70
Bosnia 6–7
  see also Kulen Vakuf
Botswana 217
Brissel, Charles P. 100–1
Brod, Martin 25–6
Brotnja 20

Index

Buanja 211
Bubanj 20
Buchenwald 3
Buenos Aires city judicial morgue 158–62
burial practices 188, 192–3
'burials with dignity' 235
Burundi 237

Cambodia 3–4, 150
Caro, Juan 148–9
Catholicism 150–1, 164–5
Ceballos, Miguel Ángel 156
Chelmno 124
Chetniks 28–9
Chile 218
China 3–4
clandestine detention centres (CDCs) 152–7, 160–6
Coalition pour la Défense de la République (CDR) 228–9
collective burials 236
collective executions 187
Comisión Nacional sobre la Desaparición de Personas (CONADEP) 148–9, 153, 160
concealment of bodies 4, 8–9, 165–6
Confino, Alon 70
Congo, Democratic Republic of 237
'Cradock Four' 214
cremation, injunctions against 119–20
  see also destruction of bodies
crematorium procedures 51–5, 58–9, 80, 121–4, 137–8
Croatia see Nezavisna Država Hrvatska
Crossland, Z. 215
cruelty, definition and analysis of 230, 234–6
Cultural Revolution 4

Dara 92
Davis, Leslie 91
death marches 92–3, 109
Decker, Rolf 123–4
de Lame, Danielle 233
'demographic homogenization' 96

destruction of bodies 3–8, 47, 59, 93, 95, 108, 119, 147–52, 163–6, 235
  see also cremation, injunction against
Dilas, Petar 25–6
Dipsi camp 103
dismemberment 6, 22, 27, 32, 213, 232, 235
disposal of bodies 4, 7, 57–8, 78–80, 96, 121, 132, 158, 162, 204, 209–12
  typology for 162–4
  see also destruction of bodies
district surgeons in South Africa 210–11
Djemal, Ahmed 90, 94
Domanska, E. 215
Douglas, Mary 9, 80, 232
Durban 207

eastern Europe, German view of 70–2, 75, 78–81
Eichmann, Adolf 129
Endreß, Anton 52–3
entrapment 207–8, 212
Enver, Ismail 92
Equipo Argentino de Antropologia Forense (EAAF) 148–9, 166–7
Erfurter Mälzerei und Speicherbau 128
Esposito, Robert 8
ethnic cleansing 96
ethnicity, determination of 228–9
euphemisms for killing 74, 96, 231
exhibition of corpses 3, 6, 79, 209, 226, 235
  see also public executions
exhumation 25, 215
  see also return of corpses to families
extra-judicial killings 204–8, 212
Eyub, Selanikli 97

family relationships 231
Fátima massacre (1976) 148
fatwas 188
Faurisson, Robert 136
Ferziger, Adam S. 120
'Final Solution', the 124–5
The Final Solution (play) 132–4

firing squads 191
Florstedt, Hermann 53–4
Foucault, Michel 7–8
Frisch, Max 131
fuel supplies 121, 138
funerary rituals 9, 189–90, 193, 235
furnaces for incineration of corpses 121–4, 128, 135

gas chambers 117–21, 125
gas vans 124–5
Geneva Convention 74
Genosys database 234
German engineering and industrial production 119
Germanic traits 70
Gilbert, Gustave 121
Globke, Hans Maria 126, 128
Gooya News 183
Gordillo, Gaston 215
Grabner, Maximilian 52
Graif, M. 101
Graziano, Frank 156
Gregorowicz, Julian 52
Guatemala 3
gulags 157
Gumz, Jonathan 74
Gupta, P. 211

Habimana, Kantano 229
Hakim, Cemil 97
Hamitic myth 226–7
handbooks issued to German soldiers 73
handling of bodies 5
hangings 77, 190–1
Heine, Heinrich 117
hell, images of 118
Hertz, Robert 192–3
Hilberg, Raul 124
Himmler, Heinrich 46, 73, 122
Hinton, A.L. 150
hit squads 217
Hitler, Adolf 71, 74
Hobsbawn, Eric 1
Hochhuth, Rolf 131
Hoffmann, Hermann 99, 105–6
Holocaust, the 3, 6–8, 117–19, 124–7, 135, 157
  motivation for 131
Holocaust denial 135–8

Holstein, Walter 90
'homelands' in South Africa 215
Höss, Rudolf 52, 56, 121, 130, 139
Huseyin Bey 103
Hutu people 226–31, 236

Ibuka organization 234
ideology's role in mass killings 70, 165, 193, 226, 229–32, 236
imaginaire of destruction 149–52
immolation of victims 78–81, 117, 209
impaling 23
Indochina 8
indoctrination 149–51, 164–5
Inkatha 217
International Criminal Tribunal for Rwanda (ICTR) 233, 237
International People's Tribunal on the Abuse and Mass Killings of Political Prisoners in Iran 187
Iran 6–9, 183–97
  Human Rights Documentation Center 187
Irving, David 135–9
Iskân-ı Aşâyirîn ve Muhâcirîn Müdîriyeti (IAMM) 96
Islahiye camp 98

Jackson, Jesse B. 97, 103
Jewish communities 119–20

Kabuye, Rose 229
Kahta 93–4
Kalati 23
Kaltenbrunner, Ernst 121
Kalyvas, Stathis 22
Kamenetzky, Cecilio 161
Kanamugire, Laurent 230
Kangura magazine 230–1
Katma camp 99
Kertész, Imre 135
Khavaran cemetery 195–7
Khosrokhavar, F. 189
Kibeho 232–3
killing, methods of 234–5
Klettner, Martin 131
Koch, Karl-Otto 50
Koevoet police unit 208

Kori company 50, 55
Kranz, Tomasz 47–8
Kremer, Johann 130
Krnjeuša 22
Krntija, Marko Orešković 28
Krüger, Karen 228
Kulen Vakuf 16–33
Kut, Halil 92

Landau, Sonia 118, 127–30
  see also Zywulski, Krystyna
Lanzmann, Claude 124
Laqueur, T. 211
Lesotho 207, 217
Leuchter, Fred 136–7
Liebenberg, John 208
Lipstadt, Deborah 135–6
Liulevicius, Vejas 70
local factors in atrocities 32–3
Lüdtke, Alf 48, 59

McCuen, J. J. 214
Mahmud, Türki 107
Majdanek camp 7, 46–53, 56–60
Malatia 94–5
Mamura camp 98
Manukian, Sarkis 93
Marat camp 105
mass graves 18, 22, 25, 27, 50–2,
  77–80, 136, 162–3, 183, 192,
  216, 236
Matijević, Miroslav 17, 21–3
Mattogno, Carlo 138
Mbembe, A. 217–18
Meskene camp 102–3
Mihigo, Kizito 232
mixed marriages and mixed
  families 230–1
Moll, Otto 56
Montazeri, Ayatollah 191
mortuary records 210
motivation for mass killings 131,
  165, 212, 233
Mozambique 216–17
Muhsfeldt, Erich 48–60
Mujuwayo, Esther 228
Mulisch, Harry 128–30
Mulisch, Karl Victor 129
Musinga, King 229
Mutagwera, Frédéric 234
Mutwarasibo, Ernest 235

Nahoum-Grappe, Véronique 230
Namibia 206, 208, 216
Nandy, Ashis 218
Natal 209
necropolitics 212
Neumann, Robert 126–30
Nezavisna Država Hrvatska
  (NDH) 16–19, 22–4, 29
Niepage, Martin 101
Nyamata 235
Nyarubuye 233, 235

Oberländer, Theodor 126, 128
Odian, Yervant 97–8
Omanović, Halil 29
'Operation 1005' 7

Partisans: Bosnian 28–33
  in eastern Europe 71–81
Patent Pending (play) 132–4
patent protection 122–31, 134–5,
  138–40
Pena, Mario H. 159
Penguin Books 135–6
Perón, Isabel 146
Perón, Juan Domingo 152
Peronism 151–2
Piralian, Hélène 166
political violence 217
Polovina, Gojko 26, 31
Port Elizabeth 207
Posel, D. 211
Pretoria 207, 209
Prüfer, Kurt 138
public executions 77
punishment of killers 28

radicalization 27, 60
Radio Télévision Libre des Milles-
  collines (RTLM) 228–9
rape 23, 26, 101, 189, 237
Ras ul-Ayn camp 100–2
Red Army 73
Refif, Kerim 101
Reichspatentamt 119, 125, 134
religion see Catholicism
renaturalization of corpses 6
Reshid Bey 94
return of corpses to families
  155–6, 161, 195–6
  see also exhumation

reuse of bodies 3–4
revenge killings 23–9, 33, 217
revolutionary tribunals in Iran 188, 191
Robben, Antonius 193
Rössler, Walter 90, 97–106
Roualdés, Robert 159
Ruibal, Eduardo 158
Russia and the Russian Civil War 3, 72
Rutaremara, Tito 234
Rutayisire, Paul 235
Rutazibwa, Privat 235
Rutembesa, Faustin 235
Rwanda 3, 6–8, 165–6, 226–37

Sabić, Huso 29
Sabit Bey 94
Sacheri, Carlos 151
Sachs, Nelly 120
San Vicente cemetery 148–9
Sanders, Fritz 123–5, 135, 140
Santa Teresita 148
Sarrabayrouse, María José Oliveira 149, 158, 160
Schenkendorf, Max von 73
Schutzstaffel (SS) 47–9, 52, 57–60, 120–2, 127
Schwarz, Alice 129
'second life' of dead bodies 192
Seitz, Robert 48–53
Sémelin, Jacques 47, 59, 147
Semprun, Jorge 119
Sheddadiye 105
Shi'ism 189
shootings 47, 120, 190–1
Sidki, Mustafa 107
silence: culture of 30–3
    economy of 185–6, 193–7
Sipka, Ranko 26
Six Day War 134–5
Snyder, T. 59
Sobibor 120–1
social Darwinism 108
sorting of corpses 9
South Africa 6–9, 204–19
    State Security Council (SSC) 206
    Truth and Reconciliation Commission (TRC) 205–9, 216–17

sovereignty 218
spirits of the deceased 236
Stalin, Joseph 72–3
Steiner, George 118
stripping of victims 230
Suárez Mason, Guillermo 159
'subversion' in Argentina 146–7, 150–7, 165–6
Şükrü, Muftizâde 96–7
Swaziland 207, 217

taboos 80–1, 211
Tauber, Henryk 137–9
Taylor, Christopher 233
Tillim, Guy 208
tombs, erection of 195–6
Topf, Ernst Wolfgang 128
Topf, Ludwig 135
Topf & Söhne (company) 8, 50, 53, 120–32, 139
Torabpour, Majid 183
torture 20–3, 146, 153–61, 166–7, 183, 186–9, 196, 207, 235
Traverso, Enzo 7
Treblinka 4, 120–1
Tucumán 152–3
Tutsi people 226–32, 235–7
    characteristics of 228–32

Uganda 237
Uruguay 5
Ustašas 16–29, 32–3

van Leer, Wim 128–34
van Pelt, Robert Jan 49, 53, 136–9
Vidal, Claudine 231
Volkskrieg concept 72
Vrba, Rudi 135
Vrotče 21

'weaponization' of the dead body 214
weapons, choice of 231–5
Wehrmacht Directive No. 21 72
Weissruthenia 74–81
Wieviorka, Annette 135

Young Turk regime 89–90, 94, 102, 107–9

Zarei, Aziz 194
Zeki, Salih 105–7
'Zero Zero' operation (South Africa, 1985) 207–8, 213
Zeynel Bey 93
Zimbabwe 206, 217
Zor camp 104–8
Zündel, Ernst 136
Zurlinden, S. 92
Zywulski, Krystyna 118, 127–8
see also Landau, Sonia

EU authorised representative for GPSR:
Easy Access System Europe, Mustamäe tee 50,
10621 Tallinn, Estonia
gpsr.requests@easproject.com

www.ingramcontent.com/pod-product-compliance
Ingram Content Group UK Ltd.
Pitfield, Milton Keynes, MK11 3LW, UK
UKHW021840140426
5217IPUK00022B/1527